Punishment and Freedom

DIVINATIONS: REREADING LATE ANCIENT RELIGION

Series Editors: Daniel Boyarin, Virginia Burrus, Derek Krueger

A complete list of books in the series is available from the publisher.

Punishment and Freedom

The Rabbinic Construction of Criminal Law

DEVORA STEINMETZ

PENN

University of Pennsylvania Press

Philadelphia

Published by
University of Pennsylvania Press
Philadelphia, Pennsylvania 19104–4112

Printed in the United States of America on acid-free paper

10 9 8 7 6 5 4 3 2 1

Library of Congress Cataloging-in-Publication Data

Steinmetz, Devora.
Punishment and freedom : the rabbinic construction of criminal law / Devora Steinmetz.
p. cm.— (Divinations)
Heneq and the nature of law—Noachide law—Legal principles and prohibitions—Murder and the social response to wrongdoing—And live by them: Paul and the rabbis—Law, responsibility, and transformation.
Includes bibliographical references and index.
ISBN-13: 978-0-8122-4068-9 (alk. paper)
ISBN-10: 0-8122-4068-5
1. Criminal law (Jewish law)—Interpretation and construction. I. Title. II. Series.

KBM3800.S74 2008
296.1′8—dc22

2008007934

For the children—

And he said: "Let me go, for dawn is breaking."
And he said: "I will not let you go, unless you bless me."
. . . And he blessed him there.

—Gen. 32:27–30

May you wrest your blessings from the darkness.

Contents

Note on Transliteration

Transliteration of Hebrew and Aramaic follows the system outlined below. Names of rabbinic texts (such as Mekhilta) and commonly used words (such as *tzedaka*) do not follow this system, unless the word appears within a quotation.

Consonants	Vowels
ʾālef = ʾ	*pataḥ* = *a*
bēt = *b; v* (spirant)	*kāmeṣ* = *ā*
gimel = *g*	*pataḥ ḥāṭuf* = *ă*
dālet = *d*	*sĕgol*= *e*
hē = *h*	*sĕgol ḥāṭuf* = *ĕ*
wāw = *w*	*ṣērē* = *ē*
zayin = *z*	*ḥiriq*= *i* (short and long)
ḥēt = *ḥ*	*qibbuṣ* = *u* (short and long)
ṭēt = *ṭ*	*šuruq*= *u*
yod = *y*	*ḥolem* = *o*
kāf = *k; kh* (spirant)	full *ḥolem* = *o*
lāmed = *l*	*kāmeṣ ḥāṭuf* = *o*
mēm = *m*	vocal *šĕwaʾ* = *ĕ*
nun = *n*	
sāmekh = *s*	
ʿayin = ʿ	
pē = *p; f* (spirant)	
ṣādē = *ṣ*	
qof = *q*	
rēš = *r*	
šin = *š*	
śin = *ś*	
tāw = *t*	

- The letters *hē, wāw,* and *yod,* when used to indicate long vowels (*matres lectionis*), are not marked; *hē* with a *mappiq* at the end of a word is always written as *-h.*
- *Dāgēš forte* is always indicated by doubling the consonant.

Preface

This book offers an interpretation of selected rabbinic texts about criminal procedure and punishment. The premise of this book is that legal practices, like any cultural practice, have semiotic significance[1]—that is, that they can be read as expressing important cultural meanings. As Clifford Geertz argues, "The thing to ask" about cultural practices "is what their import is: what it is . . . that . . . is getting said."[2] But, it is important to note, this book is not an interpretation of legal practices; it is an interpretation of texts *about* legal practices. And texts about something are not simply windows onto that thing; reading a text about a practice is not the same as looking at the practice itself. Thus, interpreting texts about a practice is a kind of double interpretation: an interpretation of the practice that the texts set out to describe, and an interpretation of the way in which the texts construct the meaning of the practices that they describe.

It is important to note, as well, my assumption, discussed more fully at the beginning of Chapter 1, that the portrayals in rabbinic texts of criminal procedure and punishment are neither descriptions of actual practice that took place in the past nor prescriptions for actual practice that will take place in the future. This assumption has at least two implications for the way in which I read these texts. First, not only do we need to take into account that we are reading texts about a practice, rather than looking at the practice itself—as I have already noted—but we also need to take into account that the practices are themselves, to a large or small degree, constructed by the texts—that is, the text is not describing a practice out there; it is constructing the practice.[3] Second, the description of criminal procedure and punishment in rabbinic texts is not constrained by practical considerations; the legal world evoked by these texts is a world that is not bound by the exigencies of actual law enforcement. For both of these reasons, the legal world that is portrayed in rabbinic texts about criminal procedure and punishment is not only "an imaginative universe," as all cultures are;[4] it is an imagined universe. And so, ultimately, the reading that is offered here is a reading of a textual construct, of a world that is evoked in rabbinic discourse about criminal law.

Asking "what it is that is getting said," of course, can take one in a number of directions. Surely, rabbinic texts about criminal procedure and punishment can be read with a focus on the ideas that they express about a variety of topics: for example, about the proper way to treat people—even, or perhaps especially, the people whom we are most unlikely to think to treat well. My focus in this book is on a particular set of ideas: ideas about law. Reading rabbinic texts about criminal procedure and punishment, I ask the following questions about the legal world that they construct: What is law? What does it mean for certain acts to be forbidden? What is the nature of violation of law, and what are the consequences of a person doing what is forbidden? What is the nature of human responsibility and of human freedom?

The passages on which I focus in this book nearly all appear in the Bavli, including mishnayot on which the Bavli comments and *baraitot* that the Bavli cites.[5] I have chosen to focus on a particular rabbinic text on the assumption that we are more likely to find a coherent construction of a given topic within a single text than within the range of rabbinic texts. My turn to the Bavli in particular stems from the distinctive nature of this text. The Bavli is an especially rich text in its assemblage of a broad range of biblical, tannaitic, amoraic, and post-amoraic material, and it is an especially coherent text in the way that it organizes and synthesizes this material into complex *sugyot*. In reworking this material, the Bavli often sharpens, refocuses, or redirects the conceptual thrust of the traditional material, allowing the reader to focus on the ideas that are critical to this reworking.[6]

Nevertheless, while Bavli *sugyot* are highly redacted texts that allow for literary and conceptual analysis, the degree to which the Bavli as a whole may be seen as a coherently redacted text, and even the degree to which individual tractates may be seen in this way, is less clear. Recent scholarship has begun to suggest that individual tractates demonstrate coherent redaction,[7] but the question of overall Bavli consistency is much more difficult.

Furthermore, separate from the question of redaction, the reader must be attuned to the exegetical quality of many rabbinic statements as well as, especially when it comes to the Bavli, the rhetoric of the text. How can we tell whether what appears to be a semantic argument can arguably be taken to express a conceptual construct?[8] And when do we take an element of an argument in a Bavli *sugya* to express a central idea as opposed to seeing it as particular to the local literary context, driven by the rhetoric of the argument and peripheral to, if not sometimes inconsistent with, the larger ideational construct of the Bavli?[9] Analysis of such cases is, I think, more of an art than a science. But, while there is a measure of subjectivity in such an analysis, and no doubt some readers will err on the side of over-interpreting and others on the side of under-interpreting, judgment about individual cases can be strengthened by sensitivity to the rhetoric of the Bavli as well as by looking at the degree to which the statement in question expresses an idea that resonates with the broader conceptual construct.

In this study, I take a stance that lies somewhere between the extremes of skepticism about redactional and conceptual consistency and assumption of absolute coherence. I begin with the premise that Bavli passages express a fairly coherent conception of criminal procedure and punishment and of the nature of law. It should be noted that the passages on which I focus mostly appear in bSanhedrin and its partner tractate, bMakkot,[10] which makes the assumption of relative redactional coherence less bold. This assumption, like the others on which my analysis is based, is ultimately a working hypothesis that can only be justified, or not, by the degree to which it allows the reader to generate a compelling interpretation of the material.

I take a middle ground, too, with regard to the complicated relationship between the Bavli and the larger corpus of rabbinic material. As is well established, and as we will see throughout this study, Bavli *sugyot* often present a particular conceptualization of the issue at hand that is distinct, in small or large ways, from the way a topic is presented in other rabbinic texts. On the other hand, the Bavli is situated, to a large degree, in a conceptual universe shared with other rabbinic texts, and, it goes without saying, the Bavli is heir to a body of traditions within which it builds its own construct. In offering an interpretation of Bavli passages about criminal law, then, I am suggesting neither that this interpretation represents all rabbinic texts nor that this interpretation reflects a viewpoint that is entirely unique to the Bavli.[11] In many cases, I will suggest that the Bavli is expressing, perhaps in a particularly focused way, ideas that are common to a range of rabbinic texts. At times, I will demonstrate the ways in which a Bavli *sugya* reconfigures traditional material, reorganizing it, changing it, and introducing new elements that generate a significantly different construct from what we find in parallel texts.

Broadly speaking, while the particulars of the interpretation of a given passage should be understood as reflecting the construct that is crystallized in the Bavli, the overall interpretation that is offered here of rabbinic criminal law can be fairly said to represent a range of rabbinic texts. Thus, I will shift between talking about "the Bavli" and "rabbinic texts" or even "the Rabbis," depending on whether I am focusing on a construct that emerges from a Bavli passage or on an idea that seems to be shared by a wider range of rabbinic texts. The intention of this usage is to emphasize both the distinctiveness of the Bavli and the situatedness of the Bavli within rabbinic discourse; it is not, of course, meant to blur the distinctiveness of the varied rabbinic texts and traditions into a single amalgam of "rabbinic thought." Nevertheless, since the purpose of this book is to offer an interpretation of the rabbinic construction of criminal law, rather than to explore the relationship between the Bavli and other rabbinic texts, much of the material that relates to this relationship, as well as some discussion of the development of the ideas discussed here in later codes and commentaries, is included in the endnotes rather than in the body of the book.

The thesis that is developed in the first four chapters of this book is that the design of criminal execution and the description of the procedures that lead to the violator of law being condemned to punishment express a particular understanding of law and of violation of law. I characterize this as an extreme positivist conception of law—a conception of law as based exclusively in the command of the lawgiver. In the first chapter, I demonstrate how the conception of law as command is expressed in the rabbinic construction of criminal procedure and punishment, and, in the following three chapters, I show how rabbinic texts reflect an awareness of alternative conceptions of law, conceptions that I characterize as falling under the rubric of natural law. The end of the fourth chapter and the final two chapters look at the corollaries of a view of law as command. I argue that the Rabbis' insistence on the positive nature of sinaitic law, and their conception of sin and punishment in relation to this conception of law, is related to notions of human freedom and self-determination and of human action as redemptive of the world and the self.

It is important to recognize that, when I contrast the rabbinic conception of law with conceptions of law that I characterize as versions of natural law, I am talking about a classical construction of natural law. This view saw law as based in the natural order and as derivable from the world as it is. Observing law, in this view, means acting in a way that is congruent with the order of things as expressed in the natural world; violating law is a violation of the providential order that is expressed in the created world. Such a view is radically different from contemporary constructions of law that are considered to fall under the rubric of natural law. Contemporary versions of natural law, while many and varied, all emphasize the input of human reason and morality into law but do not retain the strong linking of law with the natural order that characterized classical versions of natural law.

This distinction is important to keep in mind while considering my argument about the ideational corollaries of the Rabbis' conception of law as based in command. The link that I draw between the notion of law-as-command and human self-determination might well seem counterintuitive. Indeed, a positivist conception of law, especially one that sees law as based in divine command, can well be seen to affirm the fixed nature of law—and to deny the input of human reason and morality—

while natural law, in its contemporary incarnations as an argument about the relationship between morality and law, seems to affirm the malleability of law in relation to changing circumstances and changing views about the world.

But, as noted, classical versions of natural law differ from these contemporary versions in seeing law as embedded in, and capable of being read off, nature. This classical view of nature as normative, the view that I will argue that the Rabbis self-consciously set their conception of sinaitic law up against, in fact suggests a static view of law, since, according to this view, the way the world is and has been is the way the world should be. In contrast, a conception of law as command can—and, in the case of the Rabbis, does—include within it the possibility of new law being made. In fact, rather than the notion of law-as-(divine-)command making human decision making impossible, the Rabbis developed the notion of the rabbinic power to make law as a direct corollary of their understanding of sinaitic law as based in command.[12] Thus, the rabbinic focus on law as statute and on sin as violation of command is consistent with the rabbinic belief in human autonomy and the freedom of rabbinic decision making; in fact, I think, it serves as the foundation for this core characteristic of rabbinic Judaism.

Nevertheless, it should be acknowledged that a conception of law as based in command—of the normativeness of law as deriving from the fact of legislation—might suggest that law is independent of morality. A view of law as based in command can lead to a stance of moral passivity, to a sense that law is self-sufficient and all-inclusive—that is, that law needs no input from anything outside of itself and that there is nothing outside of law that is normative.[13]

This possibility is, perhaps, particularly acute when we are talking not about a system of secular law but about a system of religious law, for two reasons. First, law here does not issue from a human sovereign or a human legislature; the laws have their source in divine command, and thus those who are bound by these laws have reason to presume that these laws are both right and good. Second, religious law is a component—for many Jews, the central component—of religious life. Thus religious law plays a role that goes well beyond the role that secular law plays, and there is an expectation of religious law that goes well beyond what one might expect from secular law. While secular law might be seen as the minimum set of demands that society places on its members in order to ensure civil order, to protect its citizens, and to promote basic moral values, religious law is seen as broader in scope and purpose—perhaps so broad that there is nothing outside of it. In short, if God expresses God's will in law, why should we look anywhere outside of law to discover God's will?

I do not wish to enter the massive debate within legal philosophy about the relationship between law and morality, nor to defend legal positivism in general against the charge of making law impervious to the dictates of morality.[14] But I do want to offer some reflections on the special case of Jewish law, which, I have argued, is radically based in command and yet which, I believe, should not be seen as asking those who are bound by it to relinquish their moral sensibilities as a guide to action. I want to suggest that the view of law as based in command renders law neither self-sufficient nor all-inclusive—that this view of Jewish law does not imply that law exists in a vacuum, isolated from the input and even the critique of morality, nor does it negate the notion that morality constitutes an additional religious imperative to aspire to things beyond what the law demands.

The second of these two points—that law is not all-inclusive and that rabbinic texts recognize what might be called a morality of aspiration[15]—is, I think, obvious from even a cursory familiarity with rabbinic texts.[16] One outstanding example of a rabbinic text that embraces moral aspiration—aspiration to ethical conduct that goes beyond the demands of law—can be found in the Appendix. I discuss this passage extensively in Chapter 5, but I would like to locate some brief reflections on the question of both the all-inclusivity and the self-sufficiency of law in rabbinic texts in relation to a crux in this passage that I will not be addressing later.

In this passage, David and various prophets are said to have "reduced" the 613 commandments from eleven to six to three to two and, finally, to one. That these progressively smaller lists of moral behaviors or qualities are presented as reductions of the body of *mitzvot* lends itself to different interpretations. One option, which I think it is impossible to see the Rabbis as proposing in a literal sense, is that these moral qualities are a replacement for the *mitzvot*—that the huge quantity of commandments is actually reduced to only these demands.[17] Another possibility, which is often proposed, is that the passage is asserting that these moral qualities are the principles that underlie the *mitzvot*—that the passage is maintaining the primacy of law as a way of life but is disclosing the moral principles on which the 613 *mitzvot* rest.[18] But there is yet another possibility, and I think that this third possibility is the interpretation that best fits the homily as it appears in the Bavli.

Note that, in the Bavli, there are two alternatives to the final element in the progression from 613 to one. The first is presented in a quotation from Amos: "Seek me and live." But Rav Nachman bar Yitzchaq challenges this: the verse could be construed, he points out, as meaning that one must seek God by means of all of the Torah; thus, it would be simply reaffirming the imperative of the 613 *mitzvot*. Instead, a verse from

Habakkuk is offered as articulating the single imperative by which one should live: *wĕṣaddiq beʾĕmunāto yiḥye,* "but the righteous shall live by his *ʾĕmunā*" (Hab. 2:4).[19]

ʾĔmunā here does not mean faith. Rather, the word connotes the attribute of faithfulness or trustworthiness.[20] But, if we take it to mean faithfulness in the sense of being faithful to the commandments, then this final verse lends itself to the same challenge that prompted its substitution for the Amos verse. Just as that verse, Rav Nachman bar Yitzchaq pointed out, could be construed as suggesting that one must seek God by means of fulfilling all of the commandments, this verse would mean that one lives by being faithful to all of the commandments. It is clear, then, that the meaning of *ʾĕmunā* here is not faithfulness to the commandments but faithfulness or trustworthiness as a moral quality, a quality that describes how one interacts with other human beings.

In including both alternatives for the final verse and Rav Nachman bar Yitzchaq's challenge to the first of these, the Bavli seems intent on making it clear that the homily is not focusing on doing the *mitzvot* and merely disclosing the underlying principles behind the *mitzvot.* Rather, as I will argue in Chapter 5, the homily is setting out two different modes of behavior: one guided by law and the other guided by moral qualities. As I said above, I do not think that we can construe the homily as suggesting that observing the law does not matter as long as our behavior is shaped by morality. But, then, what does the setting out of these two models suggest?

First, I think the homily is emphasizing that moral behavior has the quality of a religious imperative. This is suggested by the form of the homily: "Six hundred thirteen *mitzvot* were given to Moses. . . . David came and reduced them to eleven. . . . Habakkuk came and reduced them to one." While it is clear from reading these progressively smaller lists that we have moved from talking about laws to talking about moral qualities, the structure of the homily obscures this fact. In other words, the lists of eleven, six, three, two, and one moral qualities are presented, like the 613 *mitzvot,* as religious imperatives. The culmination of the homily with the Habakkuk verse makes this point even sharper. The verse talks about living "by" the moral quality of faithfulness or trustworthiness. But note that a different verse talks about living "by" the laws; this verse is Lev. 18:5, which is quoted in the mishna in relation to which this homily appears and which, I will argue in Chapter 5, echoes in the background of the entire passage. Thus, moral aspiration and law are two modes by which one lives. Law is not all-inclusive; moral imperatives exist side by side with the imperative of law.

Second, the passage seems to be claiming some sort of relationship between these two imperatives. It is not clear exactly what kind of relationship the passage is suggesting, but I propose that one could take the fact of a relationship to suggest that law, besides not being all-inclusive, is not self-sufficient. In other words, not only is there a moral imperative that exists separately from law, but there is a relationship between legal and moral imperatives. Thus, law and morality are neither absolute alternatives (if I am moral, I do not need law) nor absolutely reducible one to the other (if I keep the law, then I am moral—and thus I need not attend to dictates of morality that come to me from outside of the law).

If law and morality are non-independent but non-identical vectors to guide human life, then we have the possibility not only of morality filling in where law leaves off but of morality critiquing law.[21] In a sense, we have an aspirational view of law itself: law is not amoral—it is not entirely independent of morality—and it certainly then must not be immoral.[22] The idea of two distinct vectors that guide human behavior should not be taken as implying the idea of parallel and independent universes, in which law need not aspire to be shaped by morality, and in which I must be a moral person and I must follow the law, but I need not consider whether the law itself is moral. Rather, it should be the aspiration of law and of those who are committed to following the law to shape law in alignment with the voice of morality.

And here we come full circle, because I argued above that it is a corollary of the conception of law as command that law can be made, that law can deliberately be changed.[23] Just as the Rabbis' rejection of classical natural law is a rejection of the notion that we can read what *ought to be* off of what *is* in the world, the Rabbis' construction of law as command, generating the idea that human beings themselves can make law, is a rejection of the notion that what the law *is* is what the law *ought to be*.[24] Thus, the radical characterization by the Rabbis of law as command, along with the rabbinic belief in human autonomy and the freedom of rabbinic decision making that I suggest are the corollaries of this conception of law, sets out a vision of law as aspiring to be moral and of the doer of law as aspiring to the morality that law should, but may not yet perfectly, embody.

It goes without saying that the reflections that I have offered here are my personal attempt to consider what is at stake in the central argument of this book for those who, like me, see themselves as the spiritual heirs of the Rabbis. These reflections are an extension of the central argument of this book, but the validity of that argument should in no way be seen as hinging on the persuasiveness or value of these reflections. The argument of the book should be judged on its own merits, and different readers might come away with very different thoughts on the implications of the book's argument, whether for rabbinic thought, for rabbinic history, or for contemporary religious life.

Chapter 1

Ḥeneq and the Nature of Law

For cases involving the commission of a capital offense, rabbinic sources describe a precise criminal procedure that culminates, if the defendant is found guilty, in one of four modes of execution, *ʾarbaʿ mitot bēt din.* The power of Jewish courts to impose capital punishment and the precise nature of these modes of execution have long been the focus of intense scholarly discussion from a range of perspectives and within a range of academic disciplines—not least because of the execution of Jesus by crucifixion, a mode of execution not listed among the four methods that rabbinic texts specify for implementation by Jewish courts.[1]

One approach to examining these sources takes as its starting point the thesis that the talmudic descriptions of execution ought not be taken either as evidence of what, in fact, took place or as prescriptions for what courts should actually practice, were they to regain the power to impose capital punishment. Rabbinic sources that describe the system of criminal procedure and punishment date from well after Jewish courts ceased to try capital cases. And evidence both from non-rabbinic sources and from traditions preserved within rabbinic sources themselves suggest that the procedures and punishments that are mandated by rabbinic law do not reflect what actually took place during the time when rabbinic sources understand Jewish courts to have been mandated to try capital offenses.[2]

Just as it is unlikely that rabbinic sources about criminal procedure and punishment in capital cases describe what actually took place, it seems unlikely that these sources should be read as prescriptions for a legal system that their authors believe *should* be put into practice, were circumstances to allow. The stringent rules for testimony and for the examination of witnesses and, in particular, the requirement that a warning be delivered to and accepted by the would-be offender in order for the criminal to be executed render criminal procedure as described in rabbinic sources exceptionally impractical.[3] And not to be ignored is the Mishna's teaching that a court that executes even once in seven years is considered destructive, with R. Elazar ben Azaria remarking that this is true of a court that executes even once in seventy years.[4] These teachings are followed by a dispute between sages who say that, had they been on the Sanhedrin, no one would ever be executed, and R. Shimon ben Gamliel, who comments that such an approach would serve only to increase the number of murderers within the society. Apart from the ideological dispute about capital punishment, this mishna makes clear what is apparent in any event from the strict requirements of rabbinic criminal procedure: the rules of procedure make it extremely unlikely that a violator of law will be executed, and the strict application of such rules would lead to weak enforcement of social order. In fact, rabbinic sources recognize the need for courts to react to criminal behavior in ways that are not permitted under the basic rules of rabbinic criminal procedure and punishment.[5] And medieval authors elaborate on the need for political leaders to have the power to punish offenders of law, supplementing the judicial system portrayed in rabbinic texts, in order to maintain social order.[6]

We seem to have before us, then, a system of criminal justice that is entirely theoretical, not just in fact, in that it was never practiced as such, but also in design, in that it seems not to have been conceived in order to be functional. But how should we read rabbinic sources about criminal procedure and punishment if we can read them neither as descriptions of what took place nor as prescriptions for what ought to take place? The theoretical nature of the rabbinic texts on criminal justice, I propose, offers a distinctive opportunity to look at an ideal system of criminal law: ideal, that is, not in the sense of being perfect—for one of the critical points here is that such a system, in the real world, would be far from perfect, as R. Shimon ben Gamliel points out in his response to those who would apply the rules of criminal procedure to acquit all defendants in capital cases—but ideal in the sense of expressing fundamental ideas[7] rather than being bound to the realities of real criminals and the needs of real human societies.

It is important to note that, while the system of capital punishment described in rabbinic texts is not bound by the demands of social need—in particular, by the need for punishment to serve as a deterrent to violations of law[8]—it is bound by and takes shape in reference to biblical sources about the penalty of death.[9] Thus, while some elements of the rabbinic system of capital punishment seem to have been invented whole-cloth and others demonstrate a radical revision of the plain sense of the biblical material (as well as, no doubt, of actual practice in pre-rabbinic times[10]), we cannot see the rabbinic construct as a creation ex nihilo. Bound as it is to its biblical sources, rabbinic tradition is limited by the constraints of these texts; while there is ample room for innovation and interpretation, biblical material must still be accommodated.

For example, biblical texts mandate certain kinds of execution and assign certain violations of law to these modes of execution. As will be discussed below, rabbinic texts reenvision the biblical modes of execution, redesigning the biblical punishment of *sĕqilā* (stoning) as pushing the condemned person off a platform and the biblical punishment of *śĕrēfā* (burning) as an internal burning of the body. Similarly, as we will see, rabbinic texts add modes of execution that are not described as forms of judicial execution in biblical texts, resulting in a total of four modes of judicial execution. And rabbinic texts assign capital offenses whose mode of execution is not explicitly stipulated in biblical texts to one or the other of these four modes of execution. As we analyze rabbinic texts about criminal punishment, then, we must keep in mind the relationship between rabbinic texts and biblical tradition, noting both ways in which rabbinic texts reshape what comes before and ways in which rabbinic texts are constrained by the details of biblical texts and, indeed, may continue to be shaped by core ideas expressed in those texts.

"Death That Has No Mark"

In recent years, two Israeli scholars have written about capital punishment in rabbinic texts from an approach similar to the one adopted here: that the modes of execution that are described in rabbinic texts are shaped by a particular idea that was fundamental to rabbinic thought.[11] The idea that these scholars suggest shaped rabbinic sources about capital punishment, though, is different from the idea that I will suggest that these sources express. Before I turn to my own interpretation, I will present the basic thesis of these scholars and explain why I think that an alternative understanding of the ideational underpinnings of rabbinic sources about capital punishment is called for.

Moshe Halbertal, in a book about the place of values in shaping rabbinic interpretation, suggests that the goal of the rabbinic revision and redesign of capital punishment was to minimize damage to the body of the executed criminal—that is, to preserve his or her dignity as a person created in the divine image.[12] Yair Lorberbaum develops a similar idea but roots this concern in the mythic-theurgic, rather than in the ethical, domain—in a conception that sees the human being as an "iconic extension" of God.[13]

Both Halbertal and Lorberbaum take as their paradigm the punishment of *ḥeneq*—execution by strangulation—a mode of death that is described in rabbinic sources as *mitā šeʾēn bah rošem*, "death that has no mark."[14] *Ḥeneq*, as many have noted, is the one form of execution that has no precedent in biblical sources.[15] As such, its invention and design are unconstrained by biblical descriptions of execution, and thus it is here that one might turn to see what execution looks like when it takes shape solely as a reflection of rabbinic ideas.

But Halbertal and Lorberbaum go further. Once they have isolated what they understand to be the motive behind the design of *ḥeneq*—the goal of minimizing damage to the body of the person who is being executed—they take this same motive to explain the rabbinic revision of the modes of execution that are mentioned in the Torah, *sĕqilā* and *śĕrēfā*—stoning and burning. This approach has the attraction of offering a uniform motive, whether with mythic-theurgic or ethical foundations, to explain most of the details of the rabbinic design or redesign of modes of judicial execution.[16]

In what follows, though, I will question the primacy of the motive of minimizing damage to the body in the design of the modes of execution that are described in rabbinic texts. In fact, I will question the notion that minimizing damage to the body per se—that is, as distinct from a more general set of concerns about how human beings ought to be treated—is a goal of the rabbinic redesign of execution at all. Once I have argued against the explanatory power of Halbertal and Lorberbaum's thesis, I will suggest a different way of looking at *ḥeneq*, and I will analyze the place of this new mode of execution within the rubric of the four modes of judicial execution described in rabbinic texts. Finally, based on the understanding of *ḥeneq* that I will present, I will offer an interpretation of the assignment of *ḥeneq* as the default mode of judicial execution within the rabbinic construct of criminal law.

"Death by the Hand of Heaven"

In relation to the Mishna's description of the punishment of *ḥeneq* (mSan 7:3), the Bavli cites the following *baraita*:

Our Rabbis taught . . . "Die he shall be caused to die" (Lev. 20:10)—by strangulation. You say by strangulation—or perhaps it should be by one of the [forms of] death stated in the Torah?

Say—wherever it says "death" unspecified in the Torah you may not draw it to make it more severe, rather to make it more lenient—the words of Rabbi Yoshiya.[17]

Rabbi Yonatan says: Not because it is more lenient, rather—any "death" stated unspecified in the Torah is none other than strangulation.[18]

Rabbi says: "Death" by the hand of heaven is stated, and "death" by the hand of a human being is stated—just as "death" that is stated by the hand of heaven is death that has no mark [*mitā šeʾēn bah rošem*], so too "death" that is stated by the hand of a human being is death that has no mark.

(bSan 52b)[19]

Lorberbaum takes Rabbi's position to be emphasizing two interrelated points: "(a) Death by the hand of a human being may not leave a mark on the body of the defendant. (b) Judicial execution must imitate death by the hand of heaven: just as there is no mark in the latter, so too, in the former [plural]—it is forbidden that they leave a mark."[20] Lorberbaum's reading takes not leaving a mark on the body as desirable in and of itself. Thus, he sees point (a) as distinct from point (b), and he gives it pride of place in his analysis of Rabbi's position: the first point that Rabbi makes, according to Lorberbaum, is the independent assertion that judicial execution may not leave a mark on the body of the person who is being executed. Further, Lorberbaum reads Rabbi's statement as referring to judicial execution in general, not just to *ḥeneq*, and so Lorberbaum extends to all forms of execution his understanding of Rabbi's statement as articulating the goal of leaving no mark on the body.[21] And, beyond that, both Halbertal and Lorberbaum see the goal of leaving no mark on the body as the formative motive behind both the creation of *ḥeneq* and the rabbinic redesign of the biblical punishments of *sĕqilā* and *śĕrēfā*.

There are at least three significant problems with this argument: one relating to the claim that leaving no mark is a substantive goal for the design of judicial execution in general and even for the design of *ḥeneq* in particular; the second relating to the assumption that the idea of executing without leaving a mark on the body generates the requirement to minimize damage to the body; and the third having to do with the power of the supposed requirement to minimize damage to the body to account for the rabbinic redesign of the biblical modes of execution.

Looking again at Rabbi's exegesis, it is clear that the constraint of leaving no mark on the body is not stated as a general principle to be applied to all forms of judicial execution.[22] The idea that the person should be executed in a way that leaves no mark is stated specifically—and, without evidence to the contrary, we should assume exclusively—in relation to the punishment of *ḥeneq*. Further, even in relation to *ḥeneq*, it seems clear that leaving no mark on the body is not a substantive goal at all. That is, Rabbi is not asserting that, a priori, we want to find a mode of execution that leaves no mark. Rather, he is asserting that, when the Torah mandates simply "death," we ought to impose death. We ought to take the person's life, Rabbi is arguing, in a way that most closely approximates the way in which God takes life. This is a design principle that clearly is limited to *ḥeneq*—the mode of execution that Rabbi is trying to derive from the word *yumāt* ("he shall be caused to die")—and it does not have as a goal leaving no mark on the body. The objective, given the Torah's mandate to impose "death," is to approximate death by God's hand,[23] and we do this by imposing a form of execution that leaves no mark. I will return to this idea below, when we move on to an alternative understanding of the rabbinic innovation of *ḥeneq*.

A second problem with Halbertal and Lorberbaum's argument is the move from not leaving a mark on the body to minimizing damage to the body. This move may seem intuitive and justified, as, for example, we could well imagine an ideal such as inflicting no pain generating the requirement that, if it is impossible to kill without inflicting any pain at all, we should at least kill in a way that inflicts the most minimal amount of pain. But not leaving a mark on the body, in the context of Rabbi's argument, is not a spectrum characteristic. *ʾĒn bah rošem* is a characteristic of divinely imposed death, which *ḥeneq* is designed (or chosen) to approximate. According to Rabbi, we execute by *ḥeneq* in order to kill in a way that leaves no mark because that is how we approximate death by the hand of heaven. We cannot move from this argument to the idea that, when we execute in other ways—ways that are not designed to approximate death by the hand of heaven and that therefore do not need to kill without leaving a mark on the body—we must seek to minimize the mark left on the body. If the idea is to choose or design a form of humanly imposed death that simulates divinely imposed death by leaving no visible mark, then we either succeed—by depriving the condemned person of life in a way that leaves no physical trace of that process—or we do not. In *ḥeneq*, we do exactly that. But the requirement for *ḥeneq* that we execute without leaving a mark cannot be extrapolated to the other forms of judicial execution, nor can it be understood to generate the notion that there is a requirement to limit damage to the body.

Third, since Halbertal and Lorberbaum do take *ʾēn bah rošem* as a goal, construe it as the ideal realization of the goal of minimizing damage to the body, and understand it to apply to all forms of judicial execution, they attempt to explain many of the details of the rabbinic refashioning of the biblical modes of punishment—*sĕqilā* and *śĕrēfā*—as designed to minimize the mark left on the body of the condemned person. But, for most of these details, there are at least equally plausible alternate explanations. And, even when minimizing damage to the body does appear to be the goal, this can best be understood not as a distinct principle concerning the body, as Halbertal and Lorberbaum would have it, but rather as one particular application of a wider principle that requires one to treat people with respect and consideration.

"Choose for Him a Good Death": The Redesign of *Sĕqilā* and *Śĕrēfā*

For example, the Mishna's description of the punishment of *śĕrēfā*—burn ing—represents a radical refashioning of this biblical mode of execution from immolation of the body to an internal burning of the person (mSan 7:2).[24] Halbertal and Lorberbaum account for this shift as motivated by the desire to leave the body of the condemned person intact.[25] But one could offer several other explanations for the design of the kind of *śĕrēfā* that is described in the Mishna—the most obvious, of course, being the desire to minimize the suffering of the condemned by hastening death.[26] Indeed, this motive is explicitly mentioned in the Bavli in relation to both *śĕrēfā* and *sĕqilā*,[27] and it is given by the Bavli as the reason that internal burning is chosen over external burning as the way in which *śĕrēfā* is to be done.[28]

Another explanation that has been proposed for the redesign of *śĕrēfā* is that we have here, as we do in *ḥeneq*, an attempt to imitate divinely imposed death.[29] This possibility derives from the Bavli's attempt to derive the idea of internal burning by means of a *gezera shava*—an analogy based on the use of the same word in the context of the two cases that are being compared—between the penalty of *śĕrēfā* and the use of the word "burning" in reference to the miraculous death either of Aaron's sons (Lev. 10:2–6)[30] or of Qorach's congregation (Num. 16:35–17:4).[31] A closer look at the argument in the Bavli, though, makes it clear that this derivation is subordinate to the goal of minimizing suffering. The argument presents these *gezerot shavot* to demonstrate that internal burning qualifies as *śĕrēfā* within biblical discourse.[32] Once this has been established, according to the conclusion of the Bavli's argument, we can derive the manner in which we must fulfill the biblical requirement of *śĕrēfā* by applying the dictum of Rav Nachman: '*wĕʾāhavtā lĕrēʿăkhā kāmokhā*'—*bĕror lo mitā yāfā*, " 'you shall love your neighbor as yourself'—choose for him a good death." The good death that is chosen here is the manner of fulfilling the requirement of burning in a way that hastens death as much as possible and thus minimizes the person's suffering.[33]

Turning to *sĕqilā*, it is important to note that the Gemara itself offers as the explanation for one element of the description of the rabbinic version of this mode of execution the consideration of minimizing damage to the body. But this consideration alone is insufficient to explain even the detail that the Gemara offers it to explain—the height of the stoning platform—as we shall see in a moment. Rather, the Gemara presents the consideration of minimizing damage to the body as one of several considerations that need to be balanced in the implementation of *sĕqilā*. To demonstrate this point and to locate the consideration of minimizing damage to the body in its proper conceptual context, let me quote two brief passages in which the Bavli argues that details of the implementation of *sĕqilā* are shaped by the attempt to balance competing considerations.

The first passage addresses a tannaitic dispute about whether women who are condemned to die by *sĕqilā* are executed clothed or unclothed:

Our Rabbis taught: A man [who is about to be stoned] is covered a small part in front, and a woman two small parts both in front and in back . . . the words of R. Yehuda. And the Sages say: A man is stoned naked, and a woman is not stoned naked.

. . . Shall we say that [the teaching of] Rav Nachman is [disputed among] tannaim?

No—everyone has the teaching of Rav Nachman, and this is what they are disagreeing about here: one master thinks that the disgrace of a person is more important to him than the comfort of his body, and the other thinks that the comfort of a person's body is more important to him than disgrace.

(bSan 45a)

The Gemara raises the possibility that the tannaim in the *baraita* disagree about whether we are obligated to choose a good death, as Rav Nachman teaches. The Sages, who say that a woman is to be stoned while clothed, accord with Rav Nachman's teaching and thus require the court to preserve the woman's dignity while she is being executed. R. Yehuda, who has the woman stoned nearly naked, seems to be unconcerned about preserving the woman's dignity and so would appear not to agree with Rav Nachman's dictum. But the Gemara rejects this possibility and argues that both the Sages and R. Yehuda are in accord with Rav Nachman's requirement to choose a good death. The basis of their disagreement, rather, is what consideration takes priority for the average person. Would a woman prefer to endure the humiliation of being naked in order to die more quickly, or would she prefer to endure pain for a little longer in order to preserve her dignity by remaining clothed?

According to this passage, the imperative of *'wĕʾāhavtā lĕrēʿăkhā kāmokhā'—bĕror lo mitā yāfā* includes a range of possible considerations. In the dispute at hand, a good death means a death with the least violation of dignity and with the least physical suffering. The only point of disagreement, according to the Gemara, concerns what happens when these different considerations compete with one another. It is immediately after this that the Gemara once again introduces this pair of competing considerations, this time to explain the Mishna's teaching that the platform from which the condemned person is thrown must be two stories high:

And do we require all this [=so great a height]?! They cast [in contradiction to this the following mishna]: Just as a pit that has enough depth to cause death is ten *ṭĕfāḥim*, so all must have enough [depth] to cause death: ten *ṭĕfāḥim.*

Said Rav Nachman, said Rabba bar Avuha: Scripture said, "You shall love your neighbor as yourself"—choose for him a good death.

If so, let it be raised higher!

Because he would be disgraced.

(bSan 45a)

The Gemara wonders why the mishna requires a height of two stories to execute the person condemned to be punished by *sĕqilā.* After all, a teaching in a different context states that a fall from a height of only ten *ṭĕfāḥim* is potentially fatal. The reason for the greater height is provided by Rav Nachman's teaching: one must choose for the condemned criminal a good death. The greater height of the stoning platform is designed to ensure that the person die quickly, something that would hardly be certain were the height only ten *ṭĕfāḥim.* Nevertheless, the Gemara notes that even a height of two stories does not guarantee an immediate death. (Indeed, the Mishna itself discusses what happens if the person does not die immediately from the initial fall.) Why, then, if we are concerned to provide a good death, do we not raise the platform even higher? The answer is that a fall from a greater height would disgrace the person, by disfiguring his body.[34]

Much like in the preceding passage, then, the Gemara argues that we are obligated to choose a good death but that a good death includes a variety of elements. On the one hand, we want to execute in a way that is as painless as possible, and so we want to implement the punishment in a way that kills most immediately. On the other hand, we want to preserve the person's dignity. In the preceding passage, this meant that we might decide that a woman ought to be stoned while clothed. In this passage, it means that we do not raise the platform as high as we might like to because we want to preserve the condemned person's body from being made disgusting.

Taking these two passages together, I think it is clear that limiting the damage to the person's body is part of a broader conceptual rubric of preserving the person's dignity. And preserving the person's dignity, in turn, is part of the broader conceptual rubric of choosing a good death. In other words, there is no indication that there is an independent goal of minimizing damage to the body, as Halbertal and Lorberbaum argue.[35] The attempt to avoid damaging the stoning victim's body is one way of trying to avoid disgrace, not different in kind from stoning the woman while she is clothed. Just as we must try to minimize the person's physical suffering, we must try to avoid disgracing the person. But the Gemara does not suggest that there is anything absolute about the requirement to avoid mutilation of the body or that this requirement is different in kind from the other requirements that fall under the rubric of *bĕror lo mitā yāfā.*[36]

So far, we have focused on the explanations offered by the Bavli itself for elements of the rabbinic forms of the biblical modes of execution, *sĕqilā* and *śĕrēfā.* The motivation offered by the Bavli—*bĕror lo mitā yāfā*—accounts well for the radical shift of *śĕrēfā* from immolation of the body to internal burning. While the Bavli offers this principle as well to explain elements of the implementation of *sĕqilā*, it does not offer it for the main difference between the rabbinic form of *sĕqilā* and its biblical predecessor: the radical shift from stoning the condemned criminal to throwing the person off a platform. It is certainly possible, though, to understand this shift in the same way as the shift within *śĕrēfā*: as an attempt to minimize the person's suffering by implementing a more immediate form of the mode of execution.

But another approach to the rabbinic redesign of the biblical punishments of *sĕqilā* and *śĕrēfā* can be offered. In the redesign of these punishments, we have a radical institutionalizing of forms of destruction of the person that seem to have their roots in spontaneous expressions of communal outrage against those who violate central norms of the community.[37] Whereas the Torah mandates these acts as punishments[38] to be imposed within official contexts and following upon particular procedures of accusation, proof, and condemnation,[39] rabbinic sources go well beyond this in their systematization of criminal procedure and punishment. Many elements of the rabbinic design of the biblical punishments of *sĕqilā* and *śĕrēfā* can be understood as a function of their institutionalization as judicial execution with the attendant minimization of the participation of the larger community.[40]

First, the rabbinic forms of these punishments limit the number of people included in the process of execution. Gone, in practice, is the notion of the "entire community" stoning the condemned person, although that biblical requirement is still preserved in theory.[41] Second, the spectacular nature of these punishments is minimized. Along with immediate (or, at least, less prolonged) death, there is less attraction for spectators to come to watch the process of dying.[42]

Third, as Halbertal points out, the destruction and elimination of the criminal that is effected by biblical *sĕqilā* and *śĕrēfā* seems designed to eliminate the person as the embodiment of evil from the community that has been marred by the criminal act.[43] The conception of these forms of execution as judicial punishment situated within the institutional framework of the courts seems to focus, instead, on the person who has violated the law[44] and on what punishment the court must impose on that person according to the requirement of the law. Thus, while punishing the criminal might still be seen as having good effect on the nature and integrity of the community, the need to eliminate the person bodily, as the embodiment of sin, loses significance. The focus of execution, rather, shifts to doing justice to the person who has violated the law. It is noteworthy in this regard that *sĕqilā* and *śĕrēfā* as stoning and immolation of the body can be done from afar and may perhaps even incorporate the notion of distancing the criminal from the community.[45] As redesigned by the Rabbis, though, these forms of execution, like *hereg* and *ḥeneq*, require direct contact between the executioners, who function as agents of the court, and the condemned person.[46]

"He Shall Be Caused to Die"

I have reviewed a variety of explanations of elements of the rabbinic redesign of the biblical modes of execution in order to show that compelling alternatives exist to the argument that the redesign of *sĕqilā* and *śĕrēfā* is shaped by the requirement to minimize damage to the body. In fact, I have argued that there is no independent requirement to minimize damage to the body evidenced by rabbinic texts that discuss the shaping of these modes of execution. Further, I have challenged the assumption that the *baraita* about leaving no mark on the body in *ḥeneq* can be understood to imply the imperative of minimizing damage to the body or that it can be extrapolated to other forms of judicial execution. In sum, tannaitic texts that describe the modes of execution give no evidence that minimizing damage to the body is a motivating factor in the design of *mitot bēt din*, and, when this goal does appear in the much more extensive discussion in the Bavli, it appears as only one of a number of considerations having to do with choosing "a good death."[47]

If we want an explanation of the rabbinic innovation of *ḥeneq*, then, we must look elsewhere. What is the meaning of this particular form of judicial execution? And what is the meaning of the designation of *ḥeneq* as the default form of judicial execution, the mode of execution that is implemented in cases where the Torah does not designate a specific form of execution?[48]

It is possible, of course, that *ḥeneq* represents the adoption or adaptation of a form of execution that was common in the surrounding cultures during the rabbinic period.[49] And it is also possible that the idea of execution by *ḥeneq* was introduced simply because this mode of execution was seen as less painful or more immediate than the other, ancient options—the biblical sanctions of *sĕqilā* and *śĕrēfā*—even in their redesigned rabbinic forms.[50] Alternatively, as Aharon Shemesh has argued recently, *ḥeneq* might have been introduced as one of the forms of execution for exegetical reasons.[51] But even if the idea of *ḥeneq* has its historical source in surrounding practice, in a general reform (at least on a theoretical level) of criminal punishment, or in exegetical engagement with the biblical text, the question of how we might understand the meaning of *ḥeneq* within the system of criminal procedure and punishment that is described and discussed in rabbinic texts remains open. This is the question to which I wish to turn. In other words, I am not going to address the historical question of what led to the introduction of the punishment of *ḥeneq*. What I want to explain, rather, is what the punishment of *ḥeneq*, and the assignment of *ḥeneq* as the default mode of execution, expresses within the construct of criminal punishment in rabbinic texts.

I will begin by returning to look at how the punishment of *ḥeneq* is explained in these texts and then move on to look at the place of *ḥeneq* within the system of *ʾarbaʿ mitot bēt din*. I will take as my starting point the teaching of Rabbi, since it is this teaching that appears to describe the essence of *ḥeneq*.[52]

> Our Rabbis taught . . . "Die he shall be caused to die" (Lev. 20:10)—by strangulation. You say by strangulation—or perhaps it should be by one of the [forms of] death stated in the Torah?
>
> . . . Rabbi says: "Death" by the hand of heaven is stated, and "death" by the hand of a human being is stated—just as "death" that is stated by the hand of heaven is death that has no mark [*mitā šeʾēn bah rošem*], so too "death" that is stated by the hand of a human being is death that has no mark.

According to Rabbi, *ḥeneq* is indicated by the Torah's unqualified use of the word *yumāt*, "he shall be caused to die." Since forms of the word *mitā*—death—are used to connote "death by the hand of heaven," the Torah must be asking us to implement a form of judicial execution that is similar to divinely imposed death. What characterizes divinely imposed death is that it leaves no mark, and thus we must impose a form of death that, similarly, leaves no mark.

The simplest understanding of the notion that "death by the hand of heaven" is death that leaves no mark is this: "death by the hand of heaven" refers to the way people die, to what we might call a natural death.[53] The way people die, when there is no obvious cause of death such as an accident that harms the body,[54] is that they stop breathing.[55] Cessation of breathing is the reversal of how human beings come to life, both within the life cycle of each person and in the mythic creation of the human being. The breath of life with which God *in*spired the first human being, the *nišmat ḥayyim* that transformed the clay form into a *nefeš ḥayyā* (Gen. 2:7), is what now leaves the person. The person *ex*pires; the breath, or spirit of life, having been relinquished, a lifeless form remains.[56] And so dying by ceasing to breathe—just simply "dying"—is dying by the hand of heaven, relinquishing the breath of life to its divine source.

If, in *ḥeneq*, we are attempting to approximate natural expiration, then we are imposing death as God imposes death. And God imposes death by taking back the life force that God grants to human beings when they come to life. When a court imposes *ḥeneq*, then, it is acting as a human mediator in the drama of God reclaiming, imperceptibly, the life that God has given.

This understanding of *ḥeneq* is supported by a look at *ḥeneq* within the system of the four modes of judicial execution. It is important to note that these four modes of execution are not just a group of disparate ways in which the court implements capital punishment; rather, the four modes of execution constitute a system—the system of *ʾarbaʿ mitot bēt din*—in that each mode of execution has a place in relation to the other modes. The organization of these modes of execution as a system of *mitot* is evidenced, first, by the claim in the Bavli that the very existence of four modes of execution is a tradition: *ʾarbaʿ mitot gĕmārāʾ gĕmirē lĕho.*[57] Further, according to the Mishna, the four modes of execution come in pairs: victims of *sĕqilā* and *śĕrēfā* are buried in one cemetery, while victims of *hereg* and *ḥeneq* are buried in another.[58] The Bavli explains this grouping into two burial places as based on tradition, as well.[59]

Additionally, there is a dispute in the Mishna about the relative severity of the two modes of execution in each pair. While the standard (anonymous) opinion is that *sĕqilā* is more severe than *śĕrēfā* and that *hereg* is more severe than *ḥeneq*, R. Shimon reverses the order in each of the pairs.[60] From the perspective of either opinion, each mode of execution occupies a unique place within the total system. Each mode of execution is one of four *mitot*; it belongs to either the more or less severe pair of *mitot*; and it is either the more or the less severe mode of execution within that pair.

We can visualize the four modes of execution as occupying four quadrants of the system of *ʾarbaʿ mitot bēt din*, as in the following diagram:

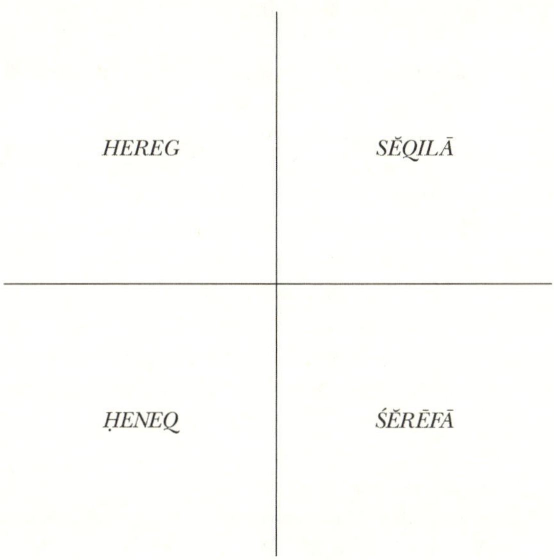

The vertical line separates the more severe pair, on the right, from the more lenient pair, on the left. This corresponds to the division that applies to the burial of the executed criminals, described by the Mishna. The horizontal line divides the more severe mode of execution in each pair, above the line, from the less severe mode, below the line, according to the standard opinion about the order of severity of the *mitot.* In order to reflect the view of R. Shimon, the chart would need to be flipped along the horizontal axis, putting *śĕrēfā* and *ḥeneq* above *sĕqilā* and *hereg,* respectively.

Once we arrange the four modes of execution in this schema, which reflects explicit rabbinic statements about the organization of these *mitot* in relation to one another, we can notice other things about the arrangement. First, moving back to the vertical axis, we can note that the *mitot* on the right are the ones that the Torah explicitly mandates for specific crimes,[61] while the ones on the left are innovations of the rabbinic system of criminal punishment.[62]

Focusing now on the left-hand column, we can note that the bottom of these two *mitot, ḥeneq,* is reserved as the default mode of execution for Jewish courts, while the top *mitā, hereg,* is said in rabbinic sources to be the way in which government officials and non-Jewish courts execute criminals.[63] Also, as will be discussed in detail in Chapter 2, the two left-hand *mitot* correspond to the two positions in the Bavli as to the form of punishment implemented for violations of noachide law.[64] Thus, the left side of the chart, the *mitot* that are introduced by the Rabbis, represents the primary ways in which rabbinic texts understand execution by judicial and governmental bodies as taking place.

Turning now to the actual forms of execution, we can note other things about this framework of *mitot.* On the right side, there are two modes of execution that kill by destroying: *sĕqilā* by crushing or breaking the body, and *śĕrēfā* by burning the insides of the body.[65] On the left side, in contrast, each mode of execution kills by removing a life substance from the body: *hereg* by removing the blood,[66] the vital force that human beings share with all creatures;[67] and *ḥeneq* by removing the breath,[68] the spirit of life with which God inspires human beings. Focusing on the horizontal axis, we can see that each of the forms of execution on top kills by imposing external, visible damage to the body. In contrast, in each of the bottom forms of execution, death comes internally and invisibly. Related to this contrast is the fact that *sĕqilā* and *hereg* are ways in which people kill.[69] *Śĕrēfā* and *ḥeneq,* though, are described in rabbinic texts in relation to ways in which God kills.

Looking at *ḥeneq* within the system of *ʾarbaʿ mitot bēt din* underscores the elements of *ḥeneq* that I have highlighted. *Ḥeneq* is the way in which God causes death when God removes the life force by which God brings people to life. This is Rabbi's understanding of the prescription *yumāt*, "he shall be caused to die": the person shall undergo "death" as mediated by a human court.[70]

We could, of course, see Rabbi as simply making a semantic argument.[71] Given a word whose connotation in a given context is undetermined—in this case, the word *yumāt*—rabbinic exegesis assigns or uncovers its meaning by analogy to other uses, or to the usual meaning, of the word. In analyzing all such exegetical arguments, we come up against an important methodological question: Do we treat the exegesis as simply a formal semantic argument, or do we give weight to the substantive content of the argument?[72] I will work with the assumption that Rabbi is making more than a formal argument—or, rather, that the formal argument hinges on, or generates, a substantive analogy. That is, even if we see Rabbi's exegesis as simply an attempt to disclose the meaning of the biblical verse, it discloses this meaning by making a substantive analogy. And the articulation of this analogy generates a critical point that, I will argue, is central to the rabbinic construction of criminal punishment. Rabbi's analogy construes *ḥeneq* as a human approximation of death by the hand of heaven: in the words of the Mishna, those performing the execution act *ʿad šennafšo yoṣēʾā*, until the person expires.

If we take Rabbi's exegesis as constructing a substantive analogy, and if we accept the understanding of *ḥeneq* that I have proposed based on an analysis of Rabbi's exegesis and supported by a look at the place of *ḥeneq* within the system of *ʾarbaʿ mitot bēt din*, we are left with the question of how to explain the meaning of the choice of this mode of execution as the default mode of judicial execution. What is the meaning of rabbinic sources' description of a criminal justice system in which the standard death penalty simulates "dying"—relinquishing one's life as in "death by the hand of heaven"?

The answer that I will propose to this question looks to a different domain from other explanations of *mitot bēt din* with which I am familiar. I will propose a jurisprudential answer, an explanation of the punishment of *ḥeneq* as expressing a particular understanding of a system of law and of the meaning, within that system, of violating law.

Rabbinic Jurisprudence

The rabbinic conception of sinaitic law[73] is rooted in the idea of command. To follow the law is to obey God's command; to violate the law is to disobey God's command.[74] God's law consists of those commands that are articulated in the Torah. According to the rabbinic conception of the system of criminal law, no violation of law is punishable unless it is a violation of a prohibition that is explicitly articulated in the Torah and for which the punishment is similarly explicitly articulated.[75] Rabbinic texts refer to the articulation of the prohibition as *ʾazhārā* and to the articulation of the punishment as *ʿoneš*, and much attention is paid in legal texts to locating the *ʾazhārā* and the *ʿoneš* for specific biblical prohibitions.

This conception of law as commanded and sanctionable is reflected, as well, in the requirement of *hatrāʾā*—warning—that is elaborated in rabbinic texts.[76] According to one opinion, the function of the warning that is issued to the person who is about to violate a prohibition is simply "to distinguish between *šogēg* [nondeliberate] and *mēzid* [deliberate]," and thus the *hatrāʾā* may be omitted in cases where the determination of the deliberateness of the act is unnecessary.[77] But the standard position sees *hatrāʾā* as an essential element without which the violator of law cannot be convicted in court of a criminal offense. The warning that is issued to the person who is about to violate a prohibition must consist of a statement of both the prohibition and the punishment; it must be issued immediately before the commission of the crime; and, moreover, the violator must verbally accept the *hatrāʾā*: "I know, and I do it on that condition."[78]

It is, of course, possible to explain the impossibly strict requirement of *hatrāʾā* as one of the ways in which the Rabbis seek to make sure that no one can be convicted of a capital offense.[79] But this leaves us with the important question of why the Rabbis chose precisely this way to limit the court's ability to bring a violator of a capital offense to punishment. In other words, even if we see the rules of *hatrāʾā* as a way to make capital punishment impossible to implement, we should recognize that there is a countless variety of means that the Rabbis could have designed to limit the law out of practical existence. And so, in all such cases,[80] we still must ask the interpretive question: What is the meaning of the particular requirements that the Rabbis construct?

It is important to notice that the *hatrāʾā* is a precise echo of the *ʾazhārā* and the *ʿoneš*. As we have seen, in order for a violation of law to be punishable, the commandedness and sanctionableness of the law must be articulated within the statutory formulation of the law in the Torah. The requirement of *hatrāʾā* says that this commandedness and sanctionableness must be rearticulated to the would-be violator of the law at the moment of violation.[81] And it is not enough for the person who is about to violate the law to hear the *hatrāʾā* and indicate that he has heard it. The violator must make it clear that he is about to violate the law in full acceptance of its prohibitedness and punishability. Without any one of these elements, the act is not a crime that is punishable in a court of law.

Thus, the procedural requirement of *hatrāʾā*, like the statutory requirements of *ʾazhārā* and *ʿoneš*, expresses a conception of sinaitic law as based on command and of violation of law as being sanctionable because it is a violation of God's command. The two parts of the acceptance of the *hatrāʾā* correspond to these same two elements. As noted above, the person who is about to commit the crime must respond to the warning with the words "I know, and I do it on that condition." "I know" indicates awareness of the prohibition (and, perhaps, of the punishment); "I do it on that condition" indicates acceptance of the sanction that attends violation of the command.

In the words of a *baraita* that the Bavli cites, the would-be violator of the Torah's command must both accept upon himself the *hatrāʾā* and give himself over to death.[82] The Gemara asks what the source is of this second requirement, that the criminal must give himself over to death in order to be subject to judicial execution for the crime that he is about to do. The source that is offered is the phrase *yumāt hammēt* (Deut. 17:6); translated literally, this means "the dead shall be caused to die."[83] While the Torah says: "By the mouth of two witnesses or three witnesses *yumāt hammēt*," the exegesis offered in the Gemara puts the responsibility for the death of the violator of law squarely on the violator himself. He is put to death because he has already condemned himself to die.[84] It is not, then, the court that imposes death on the criminal. The criminal comes to court already "dead" because by knowingly and willfully violating God's command he has relinquished his right to life. When the court executes this criminal, it is simply enacting that reality; "the dead person," the person who has given himself over to death, "shall be caused to die."[85]

From this perspective, intentional violation of God's command is tantamount to relinquishing life. The *hatrāʾā* and the acceptance of the *hatrāʾā* elevate the crime to nothing less than a violation of God's command and a handing oneself over to death. What is left for the court upon conviction of the criminal is a minimal role: essentially, the court makes real the process that has already transpired in theory. The court simply implements *yumāt*, effecting the death of the violator of God's command, who has already condemned himself to die through his willful violation of God's law.

If we bring this exegesis of *yumāt hammēt* together with Rabbi's exegesis of *yumāt* as the source of *ḥeneq*, we have the court mediating the already incurred death of the person by causing the breath of life to leave his body. Execution, then, is not the court killing a person; it is the court acting as a human agent in the relinquishing of life that the person has acceded to in choosing to violate God's command.

What I am suggesting is that the *mitā* of *ḥeneq*—Rabbi's derivation of this mode of execution from a comparison with divinely imposed death, the Mishna's description of the procedure of *ḥeneq* as culminating in the relinquishing of the person's breath, and the Rabbis' assignment of this form of execution as the default mode of execution for capital offenses—expresses a conception of law as God's command and of violation of law as a violation of God's command that results in a relinquishing of the life that God has given. *Ḥeneq*, as we saw, is the way in which a human court approximates divinely caused death. Execution by *ḥeneq* makes the court into an agent of the death merited and incurred by the person who has chosen to violate God's command.

Summary

This chapter began by examining a hypothesis that has been advanced in recent scholarship: that biblical forms of execution are redesigned by the Rabbis and that *ḥeneq* is introduced based on a single principle, the goal of limiting damage to the body of the executed criminal. I challenged this hypothesis on several counts. First, the goal of minimizing damage to the body does not offer a strong, much the less an exclusively plausible, explanation for the rabbinic redesign of the biblical forms of execution, *sĕqilā* and *śĕrēfā*. Second, the stated requirement to cause death without a visible mark on the body in the case of *ḥeneq* cannot be understood as the ideal realization of a general requirement to limit damage to the body. And, third, the requirement that is stated in relation to *ḥeneq* cannot be understood to apply to the other modes of judicial execution.

Instead, I offered a different understanding of the *baraita* that gives the source of *ḥeneq* as the default mode of judicial execution, an understanding that I suggested is supported by looking at the location of *ḥeneq* within the system of *ʾarbaʿ mitot bēt din*. *Ḥeneq*, I proposed, is the realization by a human court of the criminal's relinquishing of the life force that God has granted.

I went on to present a hypothesis about the meaning of *ḥeneq* as the default mode of judicial execution. I suggested that we can look at punishment as expressing a conception of law. The default *mitā* of *ḥeneq*, I argued, expresses the rabbinic conception of the nature of the legal system for violation of which the person is to be punished. I proposed a characterization of the rabbinic understanding of sinaitic law as based in divine command. Crime is a conscious, willful violation of a divine command. Punishment is knowingly accepted by the criminal, who "gives himself over to death" when he chooses to violate God's law.

The thesis that punishment within rabbinic sources can be seen as expressing rabbinic jurisprudence and the characterization that I have offered of the rabbinic conception of sinaitic law will be the subject of the next four chapters. In each of these chapters, we will see as well that rabbinic texts express alternative possible conceptions of the basis and nature of law. And it will become clear that the Rabbis see sinaitic law as they understand it—as a system of law that is grounded wholly in divine command—as a key marker of Jewish distinctiveness.

Before moving on, it is important to acknowledge that the idea that the assignment of a particular punishment within rabbinic sources reflects the nature of a given law or of a system of law is limited when one considers the whole system of *ʾarbaʿ mitot bēt din.* As noted at the beginning of this chapter, rabbinic sources are constrained by biblical sources that mandate specific forms of execution for particular crimes. These forms of execution—*sĕqilā* and *śĕrēfā*—are redesigned in rabbinic sources, and they are also limited in the scope of their application: *śĕrēfā* is not assigned to any crimes other than the two for which it is mandated in the Torah,[86] while *sĕqilā* is assigned to a few crimes in addition to the ones for which it is explicitly mandated in the Torah.[87] In the rabbinic redesign of these forms of execution, one can, in fact, discern important rabbinic ideas, such as the imperative to minimize suffering and to preserve human dignity, both of which fall under the rubric of *wĕʾāhavtā lĕrēʿăkhā kāmokhā.* And one can also see at work the motivation to institutionalize punishment within the framework of a judicial system. But it is to the nonbiblical modes of execution that one must turn in order to discover what rabbinic judicial execution might look like if it took shape without the constraints of the Torah's designation and description of modes of execution.[88] Hence, the focus in this chapter on *ḥeneq,* the mode of execution designed whole-cloth by the Rabbis and assigned as the default *mitā* for violations of law for which the Torah does not specify the form of death. It is to *ḥeneq* that we can look as an expression of the rabbinic conception of sinaitic law and its violation.

Chapter 2

Noachide Law

In the previous chapter, I proposed that the mode of execution that rabbinic sources assign to violations of sinaitic law can be seen as expressing the Rabbis' conception of the law that binds those who were commanded at Sinai. I focused on the rabbinic description of *ḥeneq*, the mode of execution that the Rabbis designed whole-cloth and that they assigned to violations of sinaitic law for which the Torah neither assigns nor suggests (according to rabbinic interpretation) a specific mode of execution. Since *ḥeneq* is the one mode of execution that is shaped by the Rabbis without any constraints of biblical sources, and since the Rabbis consider this mode of execution to be the default *mitā* for violations of sinaitic law, I argued that it is to this mode of execution that we should look if we want to find an expression of rabbinic jurisprudence in the Rabbis' construction of capital punishment.

Analyzing the passage in which the Rabbis present the source of the punishment of *ḥeneq* as well as the place of *ḥeneq* within the structure of the four modes of execution described in rabbinic sources, I suggested that *ḥeneq* is a simulation of *ex*piration, the human being's relinquishing of the life force with which God *in*spired the human being. The court-imposed punishment of *ḥeneq* is the court's realization of what, in essence, is simply death. *Ḥeneq* is not the way people are killed by other people; it is death in the way people naturally die, though this expiration is imposed and implemented by the court.

The nature of *ḥeneq* as court-imposed death, I argued, matches the rabbinic conception of sinaitic law as based wholly in divine command. Sanctionable violation of sinaitic law is a conscious and willful violation of God's command that results in the necessity of the violator giving up the God-given breath of life. Thus, *ḥeneq* is the judicial implementation of the process that is necessitated by the criminal's violation of God's command.

In this chapter, I want to test the core proposal of Chapter 1 that rabbinic sources on criminal punishment express a particular conception of law. If this is so, it stands to reason that systems of law that are envisioned in rabbinic sources as fundamentally different in kind from sinaitic law should be assigned punishments that reflect the different fundamental nature of those systems of law. In other words, if, as I have argued, the Rabbis' design of *ḥeneq* and assignment of this mode of execution as the default *mitā* for violations of sinaitic law expresses the Rabbis' conception of sinaitic law, and if the Rabbis' conception of sinaitic law is of a body of law that is entirely based on God's command, then a system of laws that are described in rabbinic sources as having their foundation in something other than command should have punishments that reflect those alternative conceptions of the foundation of law.[1]

My focus here will be on the Bavli's presentation of noachide law. Uniquely among rabbinic texts, the Bavli presents two different versions of noachide law, each of which is comprised of different laws, looks to different sources for derivations of the laws, and assigns a different punishment for violation of law. Each of these versions of noachide law, I will argue, reflects a conception of law that is different from the rabbinic conception of sinaitic law, and I will propose that the placement of the extended discussion of noachide law in the Bavli serves to highlight what the Rabbis see as the distinctive nature of sinaitic law.

Non-Sinaitic Law

The subject of noachide law—*ševaʿ miṣwot běnē noaḥ*—has captured the interest of scholars from a variety of disciplines throughout the ages.[2] What can be the meaning and purpose of rabbinic texts that, on the surface, talk about the obligations of non-Jews?

Some scholars have suggested that rabbinic texts about noachide law reflect particular historical circumstances. Thus, for example, Louis Finkelstein proposed that noachide law spells out the legal obligations of non-Jews living under Jewish political authority during the Hasmonean period,[3] while Saul Lieberman suggested that noachide law is a reflection of the various practices of semi-proselytes during the Second Temple period.[4]

Others have taken a philosophical approach to noachide law. Moses Mendelssohn, for example, saw in the notion of noachide law the idea that salvation is not dependent on revelation; rather, salvation is available to all human beings through the human capacity of moral reason.[5] Hermann Cohen, in an attempt to understand Judaism in Kantian terms, saw in the concept of noachide law the idea of autonomous ethics. "The Noachide," he wrote, "is not a believer but . . . a moral human being."[6]

Cohen also, like Hugo Grotius and John Selden before him, saw in noachide law a precedent for the creation of civil law by the secular state. Grotius understood noachide law to be a Jewish version of *jus gentium.* The noachide laws are seven universal legal imperatives inherent in human nature and discoverable through reason; thus, the idea of noachide law is the foundation for a theory of a civil state. Cohen and others focused in particular on the command of *dinin,* to be discussed below, seeing this as "the forerunner of natural law for the state." Nahum Rakover, a contemporary legal scholar, also focusing on *dinin,* sees noachide law as reflecting the idea that there is a universal obligation to establish a legal system.[7]

I do not want to conjecture about the historical setting in which the concept of noachide law came into being and the combination of historical and ideological factors that might have led to the development of the idea that those not commanded at Sinai are nevertheless bound by obligations. It bears noting, though, that the concept no doubt arose at least in part in relation to interpretation of the biblical text, as the linking of law to *noachides*—that is, to the sons of Noah, *bĕnē noaḥ*—suggests. The common reference to *noachide* laws (rather than, say, adamic laws)[8] and to *bĕnē noaḥ* (rather than *bĕnē ʾādām*) in reference to culpability under those laws most probably derives from the fact that, in the Torah, it is only after the flood that humankind is first given a set of rules. God's blessing as well as God's statement of the terms of existence in the postdiluvian world are addressed to Noah and his sons (Gen. 9:1–7),[9] and rabbinic reflection on the precise nature of what God is demanding from Noah's descendants is to be expected.

My focus here, in any event, is not on the general concept of noachide law but, rather, on a specific iteration of that concept in a specific rabbinic text. The Bavli includes an extended passage about noachide law in the middle of tractate Sanhedrin, and it is to the details of this passage that I want to turn my attention. Not surprisingly, the elaborate *sugya* in the Bavli develops the concept of noachide law in ways unparalleled in other rabbinic references to this concept. By adapting earlier sources, rearranging elements of these sources, and juxtaposing traditional material with wholly new material, the Bavli constructs a completely new and sophisticated conception of noachide law. I will begin by pointing out some of the features of the Bavli's presentation that are unique to this text, and I will offer an interpretation that takes into account the specifics of the Bavli's discussion of noachide law. Finally, I will suggest how we might understand the place of this extended *sugya* about noachide law within its literary context in tractate Sanhedrin.

The Bavli's Presentation of Noachide Law

The idea of a pre-sinaitic body of law appears often in rabbinic texts.[10] While generally the laws are linked to Noah and his sons, at times the *mitzvot* are said to have been commanded to Adam. Lists of commandments to Adam tend to limit the *mitzvot* to six, since one of the seven commandments is the prohibition to eat a limb from a living animal, a prohibition that could not have applied to Adam, since human beings are only permitted to eat meat at all after the flood.[11] In addition, some rabbinic texts include differing opinions about possible additional *mitzvot* that Noah might have been commanded along with the traditional seven.[12]

The Bavli systematizes the various traditions about this body of law by offering what it presents as two different traditions about a list of seven *mitzvot* that were commanded to the sons of Noah, along with various traditional opinions about possible additional commandments. In other words, while parallel sources, like the Bavli, include a variety of opinions about additional commandments that Noah and his sons might have been commanded, the Bavli alone suggests that, besides these opinions, there are two different traditions about which seven commandments were given to Noah's sons. These two different traditions about the content of noachide law, according to the Bavli, are linked to different biblical sources, and, further, the Bavli asserts that the two traditions assign different sanctions to violations of the law. I will argue that the two traditions about noachide law developed by the Bavli represent alternative conceptions of law and that these two conceptions are reflected in the different sanctions that are associated in the Bavli with each of these traditions. I will show how the conception of law that is expressed in each of these traditions is radically different from what I have described as the rabbinic conception of sinaitic law. Finally, I will suggest that the extended discussion of noachide law in the Bavli, by offering a vision of what law might look like absent the command at Sinai, is calling our attention to the nature of the system of law that binds those who are commanded at Sinai.

I will begin by presenting the core text that sets out the two different traditions and the biblical sources to which they are linked, returning to additional details of the *sugya* as the discussion progresses:

> Our Rabbis taught: Seven *mitzvot* were the sons of Noah commanded: ***dinin*, and blasphemy, idol worship, forbidden sexual relationships, murder, robbery, and a limb from a living animal**. . . .
>
>> Whence are these things derived? R. Yochanan said: Scripture says "The Lord God commanded the human being saying, of every tree of the garden you shall surely eat." (Gen. 2:16)—
>>
>>> "*commanded*"—these are the ***dinin***, and thus it says: "for I know him that he will *command* his children [and his household after him, and they will keep the way of the Lord to do justice and judgment]" (Gen. 18:19);

> "*the Lord*"—this is [the prohibition against] **blasphemy**, and thus it says: "And he who blasphemes the name of *the Lord* shall surely be put to death" (Lev. 24:16);
> "*God*"—this is [the prohibition against **idol worship**], and thus it says "You shall not have any other *gods*" (Exod. 20:3);
> "*the human being*"—this is [the prohibition against] **murder**, and thus it says "He who spills the blood of *the human being* [by a human being shall his blood be spilled]" (Gen. 9:6);
> "*saying*"—this is **forbidden sexual relationships**, and thus it says "*saying* if a man send away his wife and she goes from him and becomes another man's wife" (Jer. 3:1);
> "of every tree of the garden"—but not what is **stolen**;
> "you shall surely eat"—but not a **limb from a living animal**. . . .

[A] tanna from the school of Menashe taught: Seven *mitzvot* were the sons of Noah commanded: **idol worship, and forbidden sexual relationships, and murder, robbery, and a limb from a living animal, castration, and crossbreeding**. . . .

The tanna from the school of Menashe—if he interprets "commanded" [i.e., the verse that is interpreted as the basis for the first list of seven *mitzvot*], then those also [i.e., he should include also *dinin* and blasphemy]; if he doesn't interpret "commanded," then whence does he derive these [i.e., the commandments included in his own list of seven *mitzvot*]?

In fact, he does not interpret "commanded"; each one of these [*mitzvot*] is written by itself:

> **Idol worship** and **forbidden sexual relationships**—as it is written "The earth was *destroyed* before God" (Gen. 6:11), and a tanna from the school of R. Yishmael taught: whenever it says "destruction" it refers to nothing other than a matter of forbidden sexual relationships and idol worship: a matter of forbidden sexual relationships, as it is written "for all flesh had *destroyed* its way" (Gen. 6:12); idol worship, as it is written "lest you *destruct* and make [for yourselves an idol. . . .]" (Deut. 4:16) . . . ;
> **murder**—as it is written "He who spills the blood of *the human being* [by a human being shall his blood be spilled]" (Gen. 9:6) . . . ;
> **robbery**—as it is written "as the green herb have I given you all things" (Gen. 9:3), and Rabbi Levi said: as the green herb [i.e., something that grows in the wild], and not as the green of the garden . . . ;
> **a limb from a living animal**—as it is written "but flesh with its soul, which is its blood, you shall not eat" (Gen. 9:4) . . . ;
> **castration**—as it is written "bring forth abundantly in the earth and multiply in it" (Gen. 9:7) . . ."
> **crossbreeding**—as it is written "of birds according to their kinds" (Gen. 6:20).

(bSan 56a–57a)

The Bavli begins by presenting a *baraita* that lists seven noachide laws, followed by several opinions about possible additional laws (omitted from the excerpt above), to discussion of which the Bavli will return later. This first list presented in the Bavli consists of the same seven laws that are said in a variety of rabbinic texts to have been commanded to the sons of Noah.[13] It is noteworthy that, while the passage in the Bavli also says that these seven laws are commanded to the sons of Noah, it presents these laws as having their source in a command to Adam. Other rabbinic sources understand the command to Adam in Gen. 2:16 as the source of several laws,[14] but it is unique to the Bavli[15] that the entire set of seven noachide laws is linked to the verse about Adam, and it is striking that the laws that are presented here as derived from a verse in which God speaks to Adam are described as having been commanded to the sons of Noah: "Seven *mitzvot* were the sons of Noah commanded. . . . Whence are these things derived? R. Yochanan said: Scripture says 'The Lord God commanded the human being saying, of every tree of the garden you shall surely eat.' " Although the idea that a set of specific obligations first becomes binding on humankind after the flood is a reasonable conclusion from a reading of the Genesis narrative, an idea that takes shape in the general rabbinic notion of *noachide* law and in the frequent linking of these laws to verses from the flood story, the Bavli constructs a view of these seven laws as having existed from the very beginning of human history. Why this should be the case is a bit of a puzzle, and we will leave it until much later in my analysis of the Bavli's approach to noachide law.

After some discussion of the sources and details of some of these laws, the Bavli goes on to try to align this list of laws with another tradition that implies that *dinin* is not counted among the seven noachide laws. In order to solve this contradiction, a tradition attributed to a tanna from the school of Menashe, *tannā dĕvē mĕnaššе*, is introduced (the excerpt above resumes at this point). This tradition omits two of the laws included in the first tradition cited by the Gemara—a tradition that was introduced simply as a teaching of "our Rabbis" and to which I will henceforth refer as the opinion of the (anonymous) Sages—and includes two different laws. While the Sages' list includes *dinin* and blasphemy, Tanna deve Menashe's list includes instead the prohibitions against castration and crossbreeding. Castration and crossbreeding, in fact, occur in parallel sources as possible additions to the traditional list of seven noachide laws,[16] and they are two of the laws listed as possible additions to the traditional list in the Bavli passage as well. What is unique to the Bavli is the construction of an alternative list of seven noachide laws that includes these two prohibitions instead of two of the traditional members of the list of seven noachide laws.

The Bavli, then, presents two alternative bodies of noachide law, and, notably, it presents entirely different derivations of the laws for each of these two bodies of law. The Bavli presents all of the seven laws in the first list of noachide laws as deriving from a single verse, God's command to the first human being. Each of the laws is suggested by one or more of the words in the verse that are interpreted either independently or in reference to another verse. In contrast, the Bavli presents the second list of laws as deriving from a variety of sources. In fact, the Gemara denies the possibility that even the shared items in the two lists could be derived from the same source; Tanna deve Menashe, the Gemara insists, does not derive his laws from the verse in which God commands Adam at all. That the Gemara sees even the items that the two lists share as deriving from different sources underscores the fact that the Gemara is constructing two entirely different views of noachide law. The lists do not just differ in a couple of their members, the Gemara is emphasizing; rather, they are entirely different conceptions of what noachide law is and from where such law derives. To pinpoint what these conceptions are, then, we need to look closely at the sources that the Bavli assigns to each of the two traditions about noachide law that it has constructed.[17]

The Sources of Noachide Law and the Nature of Law

The first thing that we should notice is that the Sages' list is associated with a verse that describes a command: "The Lord God commanded the human being saying. . . ." And the very first item in the Sages' list is the commandment of *dinin*, understood by the Bavli as the requirement to set up a judicial system to implement law. In fact, according to the first of two opinions cited in the Bavli to show how the seven items are linked to the words of the verse, the requirement of *dinin* is derived from the word *wayyĕṣaw*, "commanded."[18] What is noteworthy about the Bavli's presentation of the Sages' list, then, is that we have here a conjunction of the content and source of law. The source of law is in command. These seven *mitzvot* are commandments in the literal sense of the word; they are not just obligations, but obligations that derive from legislation, from God's command—*wayyĕṣaw* (note that the roots of *wayyĕṣaw* and *mitzva* are the same). Noachide law, according to this conception, is grounded in legislation, and the very first law is the command to set up a legal system.[19]

Tanna deve Menashe's list, in contrast, is not associated with verses that describe commands. In fact, only one item on this second list, the prohibition against eating the limb of a living animal, is derived from a verse that can be read as taking the form of an injunction (Gen. 9:4).[20] The Bavli, as noted, emphasizes that Tanna deve Menashe does not derive his laws from the *wayyĕṣaw* verse, even though five of his laws are identical with the laws on the Sages' list that are derived from that verse. And Tanna deve Menashe's list does not include *dinin*.[21] In fact, what generates the introduction of this alternative list of laws in the Bavli passage is the introduction of a source that implies that *dinin* could not have been included in the noachide laws. While the Sages' list of noachide laws, then, is grounded in legislation and linked to the establishment of a judicial system, Tanna deve Menashe's list does not include the obligation to set up a judicial system, and the laws on his list do not have their source in commands.

What, then, does the Bavli see as the basis of noachide law according to the second tradition that it presents? Tanna deve Menashe, the Bavli says, omits from his list the laws of *dinin* and blasphemy and includes instead the prohibitions against castration and crossbreeding. Castration and crossbreeding are acts that are violations of the world as it was created and designed to be sustained. Castration negates the capacity of reproduction, and crossbreeding alters the categories of creation and, often, yields sterile progeny.[22] The creation account at the beginning of Genesis emphasizes over and over the categories of living things that God created and the capacity of each living thing to reproduce according to its kind.[23]

In fact, the Bavli derives these two items on Tanna deve Menashe's list from verses in the flood story that closely echo verses in the story of creation. The prohibition against castration is derived from God's charge to Noah and his sons after the flood: "bring forth abundantly in the earth and multiply in it" (Gen. 9:7). And crossbreeding is derived from God's instructions to Noah to bring specimens of each animal kind into the ark: "of birds according to their kinds" (Gen. 6:20).[24] Both of these verses recall the language of the creation story, in which living things are created according to their kinds and in which creatures are charged to reproduce, and thus these verses emphasize, along with many other verbal and thematic echoes, the reestablishment of the world after the flood as a re-creation of the world.[25] The Bavli, then, sees the source of the prohibitions added by Tanna deve Menashe not in verses that articulate commands but, rather, in verses that stress the good of procreation and of sustaining the kinds of creatures that God created—in fact, in verses that demonstrate how the world can be re-created and sustained after the un-creation of the flood.

The source that the Bavli offers for idolatry and sexual misconduct, two of the items that Tanna deve Menashe's list has in common with the Sages' list, is particularly striking in relation to the idea of creation and un-creation of the world. As already noted, the Bavli does not derive the shared items on Tanna deve Menashe's list from the *wayyĕṣaw* verse, and it does not associate these items with other verses that articulate *wayyĕṣaw.* But the verse from which the Bavli derives the prohibitions against idolatry and sexual misconduct for Tanna deve Menashe seems singularly unlikely as a source of law: "The earth was destroyed before God" (Gen. 6:11).[26] The Bavli goes on to cite a source that links the idea of destruction to sexual sins and idolatry by introducing two verses that refer to these misdeeds in relation to the word "destroy." The first of these verses is itself quite oblique: "for all flesh had *destroyed* its way" (Gen. 6:12). Not only is the reference to sexual misconduct unarticulated, but the verse is nothing more than the continuation of the verse that it is meant to explicate. Together, these two verses serve as the introduction to the story of the flood: "The earth was *destroyed* before God. . . . And God saw the earth and, behold, it was *destroyed*, for all flesh had *destroyed* its way on the earth."

The Bavli is well aware of the unlikeliness of these verses as a source of law. For each of the derivations of the *mitzvot* on Tanna deve Menashe's list, the Gemara asks how the opposing position would understand the biblical source. That is, since the Sages' laws are derived from the *wayyĕṣaw* verse, how would the Sages understand the biblical sources of Tanna deve Menashe's laws such that they do not generate these *mitzvot*? This series of questions in itself is unremarkable, since the Bavli often asks how the author of an opposing position might understand a verse that has just been presented as the source of the opponent's position. And so, of course, the Gemara suggests an alternative understanding of each of these sources such that none of them need be understood by the Sages as the source of any of the noachide laws. But there is a difference between the alternative reading that the Gemara offers for the sources of the first and last two laws and for the sources of the middle three laws. The middle three laws—murder, robbery, and eating the limb of a living animal—are derived from verses that are part of God's instructions to Noah and his sons after they leave the ark. While the Gemara denies that the Sages derive any of the seven *mitzvot* from these three verses, the Gemara does allow that the Sages could derive instructions from them. These instructions pertain in particular to the new rules of the postdiluvian world, in which human beings have new rights and new responsibilities. For example, "as the green herb have I given you all things" (Gen. 9:3) is understood simply as articulating the permissibility of eating meat.

But the first two laws on Tanna deve Menashe's list, idol worship and forbidden sexual relationships, and the last two laws, castration and crossbreeding, are not derived from God's instructions to Noah and his sons after they leave the ark. The source for castration—"bring forth abundantly in the earth and multiply in it" (Gen. 9:7)—while formulated in the imperative and appearing as part of God's speech to Noah and his sons after they leave the ark, seems more like a blessing than a command; it resumes, at the end of this passage, the blessing with which God begins: "God blessed Noah and his sons and he said to them: be fruitful and multiply and fill the earth" (Gen. 9:1).[27] The source for crossbreeding—"of birds according to their kinds" (Gen. 6:20)—does appear as part of God's instructions to Noah before the flood, but it refers specifically to what Noah is to do as the story unfolds in order to enable the animal species to survive the flood. The source of the first two laws is particularly un-lawlike, since the verse does not even appear as something that God says. "The earth was destroyed before God" (Gen. 6:11) cannot be construed as anything other than a narrative introduction to the story of the flood.

Indeed, the Gemara suggests exactly these objections on the Sages' part to the derivations of these four of Tanna deve Menashe's laws. "Bring forth abundantly and multiply in it," according to the Sages, is simply a blessing. "Of birds according to their kinds" enables each of the animals that Noah brings into the ark to have companionship with one of its kind. And "the earth was destroyed before God," the source for Tanna deve Menashe's prohibitions against idolatry and sexual misconduct, is merely the narrator of the biblical story telling us what people were doing in the period that led up to the flood. The Gemara does not need to suggest that the Sages derive alternative laws from these sources, because these sources, from the perspective of the Sages, are not legal sources. They are not formulated as commands, and the source of the first two laws is not even a verse in which God speaks to a human being. It is simply narrative, and law cannot be derived from narrative. Narrative, according to the Bavli's construction of what the Sages would reply to Tanna deve Menashe, simply tells us what happened. It cannot tell us what to do.

But then how does this narrative statement, "the earth was destroyed before God," generate laws for Tanna deve Menashe? What the Bavli seems to be saying is this: for Tanna deve Menashe, prohibited acts are those acts that run counter to the way the world was created. Such acts uncreate the world; they are destructive acts that bring destruction to the world, that undo the work of creation. It is noteworthy that the very next verse after the two verses cited by the Bavli as the source of the prohibition against sexual misconduct also includes the word "destroy": "God said to Noah: The end of all flesh has come before me . . . and, behold, I shall *destroy* them with the earth" (Gen. 6:13). God's words to Noah appear after the biblical narrator has already described the destruction of the world, in the verses that the Bavli brings as the source for Tanna deve Menashe's prohibition of sexual misconduct: "The earth was *destroyed* before God. . . . And God saw the earth and, behold, it was *destroyed*, for all flesh had *destroyed* its way on the earth" (Gen. 6:11–12). The implication of the repeated use of the word "destroy" in this passage is that God, in bringing the flood, is simply reifying the destruction that the world has already suffered through the destructive behavior of its inhabitants. By citing this passage as the source for the prohibition against sexual misconduct in Tanna deve Menashe's list, the Bavli is suggesting that the problem with sexual misconduct is that, like castration and crossbreeding, it runs counter to the way the world is created and to the way the world is sustained. It is world-destroying behavior and, because of this, it is prohibited.

While the *mitzvot* on Tanna deve Menashe's list are derived by the Bavli from the story of Noah, it is noteworthy that the Bavli does not present them as commands that are given to Noah, nor does the Bavli see them as rules that are given to Noah and his sons after the flood, rules through which human beings will govern the postdiluvian world. Presenting the noachide laws as commands that are given specifically to human beings after the flood, as noted above, would be a reasonable elaboration of the biblical narrative, in which human beings appear to be given more responsibilities after the flood and in which God instructs Noah and his sons about the terms of this postdiluvian existence after they leave the ark. In fact, I have suggested that such a reading might have generated the idea of noachide law in the first place. But the Bavli takes a different path, offering as the sources for Tanna deve Menashe's laws a mixture of verses from before and after the flood, verses that describe the destruction of the world as well as verses in which God instructs Noah how to re-create the world in the face of destruction and how to sustain the newly re-created world in the aftermath of destruction. What must go right after the flood is simply the opposite of what went wrong before the flood. The mixture of sources that the Bavli offers for Tanna deve Menashe's list suggests that the laws are not new to Noah; they are built in to the way the world was created and should have been sustained in the first place.

The Bavli's sources for Tanna deve Menashe's list of laws suggests that what brings the destruction of creation is the destructive acts of human beings, and thus what is required of human beings is to restrain themselves from those acts that are world-destroying. The prohibitions of this version of noachide law, then, are not based in command; rather, these acts are forbidden in that they are destructive of the world as God the creator meant it to be. Narrative, for Tanna deve Menashe, can generate law, because narrative tells us how the world is created, how it is designed to be sustained, and what kinds of acts cause the destruction of the world. It is the information that we glean from the narrative of destruction and re-creation that tells us how the world works and, thus, how we must align our behavior with the created world such that we do not bring destruction.

Two Versions of Natural Law

Thus, the two different views of noachide law that the Bavli constructs—the two lists of seven *mitzvot* along with the biblical passages from which the Bavli presents the laws in each of these lists as deriving—express different conceptions of the nature and source of law. The view that the Bavli attributes to Tanna deve Menashe is similar to natural law in its classical form.[28] According to the classical view of natural law, the world is created and operates according to certain principles. The principles according to which the world operates are normative. And the content of law is derivable from observation of the world as it is.[29] The Bavli's construction of Tanna deve Menashe's version of noachide law accords with these providential, ontological, normative, and epistemological elements of classical natural law. For Tanna deve Menashe, castration is unlawful because it violates the principle of reproduction inherent in the world as it was created and as it must operate. We can know that sexual offenses are unlawful because we observe that these acts cause destruction (un-creation) of the world. These acts are unlawful not because they are prohibited by a command but because they violate the world order. We know that they are unlawful not based on a statute that forbids them but because we can see how committing them brings destruction of the world as it is and ought to be.

The Sages' view of noachide law, in contrast, seems closer to contemporary "natural law" theories, which share little with the classical, ontological conception yet still are distinct from the positivist view that I have argued characterizes the rabbinic conception of sinaitic law.[30] The conception of law that underlies the Sages' view sees law as emerging with the beginnings of human society. God commands Adam at the moment that Adam is to be joined by a human partner; the *wayyĕṣaw* verse and its sequel immediately precede God's judgment that "it is not good for the human being to be alone" (Gen. 2:18). The content of law consists of basic prohibitions that are designed to ensure the functioning of human society. But these are not laws in the sense of normative principles within the natural order; they are commands within human society.

Though originating in command, this conception of noachide law is nevertheless different from a positivist conception of law. Positivism sees law as deriving exclusively from command; a law's legitimacy is dependent only on the generation of the law through a process of legislation. The content of the law is not what makes a law a law, nor is the content of a law a constraint on the legitimacy of the law.[31] In the case of the Sages' conception of noachide law, in contrast, while the laws are presented as legislated by God's command, the content of the laws is limited to that which is seen as necessary for social life (from a religious perspective, of course) to function.[32] It is human society that requires law, and human beings must work to implement the law.[33] Thus, the very first law, according to this conception, is the commandment of *dinin.*[34]

Since the element of commandedness in the Sages' version of noachide law and parallels has led some scholars to argue against the notion that noachide law can be seen as a form of natural law, I want to highlight the difference between the understanding of the Sages' version of noachide law offered here and the position of those scholars who see noachide law as deriving from command and thus not as a form of natural law.[35] My argument is that the commandedness of law, while a central component of the Sages'[36] position, does not negate the fact that the content of law is grounded in and limited by an understanding of what behavior is essential for the maintenance of human society. In fact, the commandedness of the seven noachide laws—based, as it is, on God's command to the first human being as he is about to become a member of human society—might be seen to express less the notion of law as deriving from the will of the commander and more the notion that law is based on constraints required by entry into a relationship with others outside the self. Thus, I have argued that the commandedness of law, for the Sages, is interrelated with the content of law, in that the very first command is *dinin.* The notion of law as a prerequisite of human interaction with others in society[37] is different from the notion of law as a truly "natural," ontological component of the world as it was created (as in Tanna deve Menashe's version), but it is also different from a notion of law as deriving exclusively from the will of the commander (as in sinaitic law). And so, commandedness as a feature of law within the Sages' version should not be seen as negating the importance of the content of law as grounded in essential principles. In fact, contemporary legal theories that are considered to fall under the broad category of natural law combine the notion of law as deriving from legislation and of the content of law as grounded in, justified by, or constrained by fundamental principles of justice or morality.

A detail in the extended *sugya* in the Bavli underscores the difference between the two conceptions of law that I am suggesting are expressed in the Bavli's two versions of noachide law. Crossbreeding, one of the laws in Tanna deve Menashe's list, is also suggested in this *sugya* as a possible addition to the Sages' list of seven noachide laws.[38] But the Bavli does not offer as the source of this law the passage that is cited as the source for the inclusion of crossbreeding in Tanna deve Menashe's list: "of birds according to their kinds" (Gen. 6:20). Instead, the Bavli offers as the source for this addition to the Sages' list the phrase with which the prohibition of crossbreeding is introduced in Leviticus: "you shall keep my statutes" (Lev. 19:19).[39] The Bavli explains this to mean "you shall keep the statutes that I have already legislated for you," suggesting that this law was legislated in pre-rabbinic times. So the Bavli, which has already explained this law in reference to Tanna deve Menashe's position as emerging from the way the world was re-created in the time of Noah, now explains this very same law, in reference to the Sages' position, as emerging from an act of legislation![40]

Punishment

The Bavli assigns to these two versions of noachide law, which I have argued express two different conceptions of the origin and nature of law, different forms of capital punishment. Tanna deve Menashe is said to hold violations of noachide laws to be punishable by *ḥeneq*,[41] while the Sages hold them to be punishable by *hereg*.[42] I will offer an interpretation of the assignment of these two forms of punishment to the two versions of noachide law, acknowledging at the start that my interpretation of the punishment of *ḥeneq* within noachide law appears to be in conflict with the interpretation that I have given of *ḥeneq* as the default mode of execution for violations of sinaitic law. I will return to this problem later; for now, I restrict my focus to noachide law in order to work out how the contrasting punishments of *ḥeneq* and *hereg* fit the contrasting versions of noachide law that are presented in the Bavli.

Tanna deve Menashe's prohibitions, I have suggested, are of acts that violate the principles of creation, that destroy the world as it is meant to be. Death by *ḥeneq* is indeed a fitting consequence of such acts. *Ḥeneq*, I argued in Chapter 1, is the undoing of the process by which the human being comes to life. In *ḥeneq*, the life breath with which the person is brought to life is taken away: the violator expires, reversing the inspiration with which the human being is created and each person is brought to life. If we see noachide crimes as acts that un-create the world, then it is natural that they result in the un-creation of human life.

In fact, *ḥeneq* is the cause of death of the human beings and other creatures who die in the flood.[43] The creatures who expire in the flood are described as "all which had the breath of the spirit of life in its nostrils" (Gen. 7:21–22), recalling the inspiration of the breath of life into the first human being as he comes to life (Gen. 2:7) and suggesting that it is that process of inspiration that is being reversed as God brings about the destruction of God's creation in the flood. As we have seen, the destruction of God's creation in the flood is attendant upon the destruction that the world has already endured through the actions of its inhabitants. It is from elements of this destruction and the re-creation of the world in its aftermath that the Bavli derives the noachide laws of Tanna deve Menashe. Thus, the sanction of *ḥeneq* for violation of noachide law is an un-creation of the person who has engaged in world-destroying acts similar to the un-creation of life effected by the flood.

In contrast, violation of noachide law according to the Sages incurs the penalty of *hereg*. I have suggested that the noachide laws of the Sages have their root in the establishment of human society; they are the fundamental laws that allow for a moral society that can govern itself. *Hereg* is "killing"; it is the way one human being kills another, not, like *ḥeneq*, an approximation of the way people die.[44] A conception of law that has as its basis legislation to human society and that incorporates as an essential element the establishment of a human system of justice fits well with the notion of execution by *hereg*.[45] The person who violates the legal underpinnings of human society deserves to be killed by fellow human beings.[46]

Noachide Law and Sinaitic Law

The two conceptions of noachide law that the Bavli develops, however different they are from each other, are both radically different from the rabbinic conception of sinaitic law. In sinaitic law, I argued in Chapter 1, commandedness is the essential characteristic; the prohibited act is criminal in that it is a violation of a command.[47] In noachide law, in contrast, commandedness is not the essential characteristic. For Tanna deve Menashe, as we have seen, the laws are not commands. For the Sages, the laws are commanded, and law is enforced within a judicial system that is itself legislated, but prohibited acts are criminal in that they violate essential norms of behavior within human society.[48] Thus, rabbinic sources make it clear that it is not necessary for a noachide to have a *hatrāʾā* in order for his violation of law to be punishable.[49] In contrast, a *hatrāʾā* is essential within the sinaitic system because a person is only to be punished if his intent in doing the act is to violate God's command. The lack of *hatrāʾā* as a component of noachide criminal procedure demonstrates that the criminality of behavior for a noachide has nothing to do with intent to violate a command; it has to do only with the nature of the act that the person has done. For a noachide, the act is criminal in itself, while for those commanded at Sinai, the act is only criminal to the extent that the person knowingly and willfully[50] violates the command.

It is this critical divide between sinaitic law and noachide law in both of the forms presented by the Bavli that accounts for other significant characteristics of the two kinds of law. Sinaitic law is an articulated legal system, different in kind from the basic list of prohibitions (plus, for the Sages, the imperative of *dinin*) that constitutes noachide law. Sinaitic law recognizes different punishments for different crimes; some crimes have penalties other than death, and capital offenses have different forms of capital punishment. In contrast, any violation of noachide law is punishable by death, and there is only one form of capital punishment for all crimes within each version of noachide law. In addition, sinaitic law includes minimum degrees of activity below which the prohibited act[51] is not punishable, while even the smallest violation of noachide law is punishable.[52] And, of course, sinaitic law is particular: only those commanded at Sinai are bound by sinaitic legislation, while all human beings are bound by noachide law.[53] The specificity and particularity of sinaitic law underscores the fact that sinaitic law, and sanctionability for its violation, derives from and is shaped by legislation. Noachide law has the character of simple forbidden acts; it lacks the specificity and particularity that can only derive from legislation.[54]

The Bavli's development of noachide law as forms of natural law, I think, accounts as well for the Bavli's presentation of both versions of noachide law as being in place from the beginning of human history. As noted above, in presenting the Sages' version of noachide law, the Bavli somewhat oddly juxtaposes the traditional list of seven laws "commanded to the sons of Noah" with a verse that describes a command to Adam. For Tanna deve Menashe's list of laws, the Bavli offers as sources verses from the flood story, but these verses are not limited to God's instructions to Noah and his sons after the flood. The particular mixture of verses from before and after the flood, I argued earlier, suggests that the laws are not new to the postdiluvian world. Rather, the laws that noachides must be sure to keep in the postdiluvian world are the very same laws that governed the world before the flood.

Now, a vision of law as based in command can easily see law as punctuating history. There is no reason that a law cannot come into existence at a particular moment in time. An act that becomes prohibited later is not criminal before the prohibition is established, but the very same act, once prohibited, is criminal and punishable. One cannot look to the current prohibitedness of an act to determine whether it was prohibited in the past, nor can one predict from the current permissibility of an act that the act will always be permissible.

In contrast, a vision of law as based in the nature of the act does not allow for law to change, short of, perhaps, a change in circumstances.[55] If the act is forbidden because it is a bad thing to do, because it is destructive of human society or because it runs counter to the way the world was created and is sustained, then it will always have been forbidden and it will always be forbidden. If, on the other hand, an act is permissible because it does not run counter to the natural world and does not threaten human society, then it will always have been permissible and will always be permissible. In the next chapter, we will see the Bavli make exactly such an argument about a particular noachide law. And, in Chapter 6, we will see the Rabbis acknowledge that the notion of a law that comes into being at a specific point in time is absurd from the perspective of natural law.

Thus, the Bavli's embedding of noachide law in sources that suggest that noachide law was in force from the beginning of human history is another element of the Bavli's development of noachide law as versions of natural law, in contrast with sinaitic law, which is based in command and which comes into being at the moment that the Israelites receive God's commands at Sinai.

The Bavli *Sugya* and Its Context

The Bavli works with traditional sources about noachide law, but, as I have demonstrated, it organizes, reshapes, and adds to these sources in order to construct two distinct versions of noachide law. By reshaping the material in this way, the Bavli is constructing conceptually coherent alternatives. That is, while other attestations of noachide law within the sources available to us offer a range of traditions and competing opinions about the content and sources of law, from which it is hard to argue with any certainty that noachide law represents one or another coherent conception of law,[56] the Bavli systematizes this material in a way that presents us with two clear and distinct visions of the nature, content, and sources of law.

What is particularly new in the Bavli is the construction of Tanna deve Menashe's view as an alternative version of noachide law. It is this version, I have argued, that corresponds to an extreme classical version of natural law, and thus it is the Bavli that offers us the most compelling vision of noachide law as natural law. Although the Sages' list of noachide laws is attested in parallel sources, it should be noted that the Bavli's construction of an alternative version of noachide law—the version of Tanna deve Menashe—gives new shape to the Sages' version as well. By sorting the laws and sources of law to create two versions of noachide law and by setting out these versions side by side as alternative constructions of noachide law, the Bavli lends new coherence to the traditional list of seven noachide laws. Thus, it is in the Bavli that the Sages' version of noachide law can be read, in parallel with Tanna deve Menashe's version, to express a coherent conception of law. The two alternative conceptions of law that appear in this extended passage in the Bavli—what I have argued are two different versions of natural law—in turn cast into sharp relief the rabbinic conception of sinaitic law.

The extended passage about noachide law seems at first glance to be a digression from the main focus of its broad context: judicial procedure and punishment for violations of sinaitic law. But my reading of the Bavli's presentation of noachide law suggests that the Bavli is envisioning alternative conceptions of law and portraying them as different traditions about the obligations of those who are not commanded at Sinai. By offering a vision of alternative possible systems of law, I propose, the Bavli is calling our attention to how it would like us to see the system of law to which those who *are* commanded at Sinai are bound.

The *sugya* about noachide law comes after the Bavli's discussion of capital procedure and punishment and at the beginning of its discussion of the lists of crimes punishable by different forms of judicial execution. At this crucial juncture, at the intersection of legal procedure with the content of law and punishment for the violation of law, the passage about noachide law underscores a central point about the broader discussion of crime and punishment in tractate Sanhedrin. It helps us read the Talmud's details about judicial procedure and punishment as expressing a particular conception of law and helps us characterize that conception by reference to the alternative jurisprudences that are expressed in the Bavli's two constructions of noachide law.

Ḥeneq Revisited

In the next chapter, I will focus on one particular sinaitic law in order further to sharpen the distinction between rabbinic conceptions of sinaitic law and noachide law and to demonstrate the interrelationship between the Rabbis' rules of criminal procedure and the Rabbis' conception of sinaitic law. But, before moving on, I want to address one problem with the interpretation that I have offered of the relationship between forms of punishment and conceptions of law.

I have argued that the two versions of noachide law in the Bavli represent two different conceptions of law, both of them different from the rabbinic conception of sinaitic law, and that the two conceptions of noachide law correspond to the modes of execution that are assigned in the Bavli to each version of noachide law. The problem is that the mode of execution that is assigned to Tanna deve Menashe's version is *ḥeneq*, which is the same mode of execution that is assigned by the Rabbis to capital offenses for which the Torah does not specify the mode of execution. It is the punishment of *ḥeneq* that, I argued in Chapter 1, expresses the rabbinic conception of sinaitic law and its violation. The assignment of *ḥeneq* both to violations of sinaitic law and to violations of noachide law in Tanna deve Menashe's version would seem to pose a challenge to my thesis that punishment is an expression of a conception of law. My analysis of the Rabbis' conception of sinaitic law and the Bavli's presentation of Tanna deve Menashe's version of noachide law demonstrates these two conceptions to lie on opposite ends of the jurisprudential spectrum, with the former representing an extreme version of legal positivism and the latter representing an extreme version of natural law. And so we should expect radically different, rather than identical, modes of execution for these two different conceptions of law.

In order to address this problem, it is important first to take into account the economy of *mitot bēt din* that was noted in Chapter 1. The Bavli is constrained by earlier sources to consideration of only four modes of execution, and *sĕqilā* and *sĕrēfā* have already been limited to a small range of crimes.[57] While this raises again the intriguing question of why the penalties of *sĕqilā* and *śĕrēfā* are so limited in application, it in any event leaves only *hereg* and *ḥeneq* as candidates for a penalty that is to be applied broadly. In fact, these two modes of execution are already applied broadly outside of the rubric of noachide law, as *ḥeneq* is the default *mitā* for violations of sinaitic law and *hereg* is the *mitā* that the Rabbis see as mandated to secular authorities.[58] Thus, short of reversing the tendency to limit *sĕqilā* and *śĕrēfā* to specific crimes or of introducing an additional mode of execution beyond the traditional four, the Bavli is limited in its construction of noachide law to the *mitot* of *hereg* and *ḥeneq*. Its only choice, if it is to distinguish between the two versions of noachide law that it has constructed, is to assign one of these two *mitot* to each version of noachide law, in order to achieve the best, if not a perfect, fit between the punishments and the respective conceptions of law.

Once we take as a given that the Bavli is constrained to *hereg* and *ḥeneq*, we can look again at *ḥeneq* as the mode of execution both for violations of sinaitic law and for violations of noachide law in Tanna deve Menashe's version and note that these opposite constructions of law and its violation share a common attribute. Violations of law, according to Tanna deve Menashe, are violations of God's will as incorporated in the created world, while violations of sinaitic law are violations of God's will as expressed in divine legislation. Both of these are different from the Sages' version of noachide law, which is situated within human society.

Thus, *ḥeneq* in each of these two systems represents the loss of the God-given breath of life as a result of disobedience against God: God as legislator, in sinaitic law, and God as creator, in Tanna deve Menashe's version of noachide law. In the sinaitic system, we might see *ḥeneq* as relinquishing the right to life by violating God's command as articulated in the Torah, while in the noachide system of Tanna deve Menashe, we might see *ḥeneq* as an un-creation of life resulting from violation of the laws of God's creation.

Looking again at the three conceptions of law that we have seen—

sinaitic law and the two versions of noachide law developed in the Bavli—it is clear now that these do not fall on a simple spectrum. Rather, based on different parameters, different pairs of these conceptions of law may have more in common than others. Tanna deve Menashe's version of noachide law shares with sinaitic law the idea of violating God's will, resulting in death by *ḥeneq*, while the Sages' version of noachide law is based in the idea of violating the requirements of human society, resulting in execution by *hereg*. The Sages' version of noachide law shares with sinaitic law the element of command, an element that is entirely absent from Tanna deve Menashe's version of noachide law. And both versions of noachide law share the understanding of prohibited acts as being criminal by their nature, since these acts are destructive of the world or of human society, while the obligations and prohibitions of sinaitic law are understood to derive exclusively from legislation.

It is this last contrast that highlights the distinctive nature of the rabbinic understanding of sinaitic law, an understanding that I have suggested is brought into focus by the Bavli through the inclusion of the extended *sugya* about noachide law. I want to further sharpen that focus in the coming chapter by analyzing a particular prohibition that is seen by the Rabbis as distinctively sinaitic, a prohibition that represents the disjunction between the natural law and positivist conceptions that, I have argued, underlie the Bavli's presentation of noachide and sinaitic law.

Chapter 3

Legal Principles and Prohibitions

Sinaitic law, I have argued, is understood by the Rabbis to be based in command. Violation of law is criminal because it is a violation of God's command, and it is punishable when the person has knowingly and willfully violated God's command. The Bavli's presentation of noachide law, I have also argued, offers contrasting conceptions of law that call into sharp focus the Rabbis' understanding of sinaitic law. As versions of natural law, the Bavli's two constructions of noachide law serve to highlight the distinctive features of sinaitic law as a legal system that is grounded entirely in command.

In this chapter, I will focus on one particular law—the biblical prohibition against brother-sister intercourse—in order to sharpen the distinction between the Rabbis' understanding of sinaitic and of noachide law. The Rabbis take brother-sister intercourse, although prohibited to Jews, to be permitted to noachides.[1] Notably, the biblical verses in which the prohibition against and punishment for brother-sister intercourse are articulated serve for the Rabbis as the source for a striking array of principles of criminal law. These principles, I will show, are rules that make sense only within the rubric of positive law—of law as based in command.

Why should the verses about brother-sister intercourse in particular be understood by the Rabbis as the source of this wide range of positivist legal principles? To answer this question, we will need to look at how the Rabbis understand the permissibility of brother-sister intercourse for noachides in the face of its clear inclusion in the list of forbidden sexual relationships for Israelites, several of which apply to noachides as well, since the prohibition against forbidden sexual relationships is one of the seven noachide laws. Once we understand why the Rabbis view brother-sister intercourse as a permitted act within their conception of noachide law, we can draw the connection between the substance of this law as a point of disjunction between the Rabbis' positivist and natural law conceptions and the Rabbis' view of this particular law as the basis of principles of sinaitic criminal law.

Biblical Verses about Brother-Sister Intercourse

The Torah includes the prohibition against a man sleeping with his sister in two passages. The first is the list of prohibited sexual relationships in Leviticus 18. Here, the Torah states: "The nakedness of your sister, the daughter of your father or the daughter of your mother, born at home or born abroad, you shall not uncover their nakedness" (Lev. 18:9).

In the second passage, the Torah offers a similar list of acts, this time in a casuistic formulation, in which the perpetrator of the forbidden act is said to be liable for punishment. About brother-sister intercourse, the Torah now says: "And a man who takes his sister, the daughter of his father or the daughter of his mother, and sees her nakedness, and she sees his nakedness, it is *ḥesed,* and they shall be cut off in the eyes of the members of their people; he has uncovered the nakedness of his sister—he shall bear his iniquity" (Lev. 20:17).

Like the other prohibited sexual relationships that are listed in both chapters 18 and 20 of Leviticus, the two formulations of the prohibition of brother-sister intercourse raise the question of why the Torah needed to state this law twice, once as a command prohibiting the act and once in a casuistic formulation stating the penalty if the act is committed. But, as we have seen, the Rabbis take as a given that, in order for an act to be punishable, the Torah needs to include both an *ʾazhārā*—a command not to do the act—and an *ʿoneš*—the provision of the sanction for violation of the command. These two requirements, I argued in Chapter 1, are essential components of the Rabbis' positivist approach to sinaitic law, with its fundamental assumption that law derives from command and that violation of law is only sanctionable if it is a willful violation of a command for the violation of which a punishment has been stipulated. In fact, I argued that the Rabbis' strict requirement of *hatrāʾā* and acceptance of the *hatrāʾā* is directly related to the requirements of *ʾazhārā* and *ʿoneš.* The *hatrāʾā* is a rearticulation, at the moment that the crime is about to be committed, of the *ʾazhārā* and *ʿoneš.* The witnesses call to the attention of the would-be violator of law that the intended act is a violation of God's command that is punishable by such-and-such sanction. And the person who is about to commit the act states his intention to violate God's command and to incur upon himself the attendant punishment.

And so the fact that the prohibition against brother-sister intercourse appears twice is not in itself noteworthy to the Rabbis, as it fits, along with the other laws in these two chapters of Leviticus, the Rabbis' core assumption about the way laws must be formulated in order for their violators to be held culpable.[2] But there are other things about the way that this particular law is formulated, especially the rather complex formulation of the second verse, that did raise questions for the Rabbis, among which are the following:

Why does the second verse need to repeat that the man has uncovered the nakedness of *his sister*, when it has already stated that he has taken *his sister who is his father's daughter or his mother's daughter*?

Why does this second verse mention the penalty of *kārēt*—excision—in contrast to the preceding verses that prescribe death as the consequence of committing each of the forbidden sexual acts? And how should we understand the mention of *kārēt* for this prohibition in particular when the passage in chapter 18 has suggested that violation of any of the prohibitions listed there results in excision (Lev. 18:29)?

Why is the act described in the second verse as the *seeing of nakedness* on the part of both the man and the woman, in addition to its description as the *uncovering of nakedness*, the term that is used to describe the prohibited acts in the neighboring verses and in the prohibitions of chapter 18?

And, most obviously, what does the Torah mean by saying of this particular act: "it is *ḥesed*"?

Principles of Sinaitic Criminal Law

The verses about brother-sister intercourse are taken by the Rabbis as the source of an additional pair of principles related to the requirements of *ʾazhārā* and *ʿoneš*. Not only does there need to be a prohibition and a statement of a punishment in order for violations of law to be sanctionable, but, the Rabbis maintain, the *ʾazhārā* and the *ʿoneš* must be stated explicitly[3] in the Torah; they cannot be derived by means of logical inference.[4]

Lev. 18:9, along with the additional mention of the word "your sister" in Lev. 18:11, is seen as establishing the principle *ʾēn mazhirin min haddin*: an *ʾazhārā* cannot be based on an inference from a different prohibition but must be stated explicitly.[5] Since the Torah has already stated the prohibition against a man sleeping with the daughter of his father or of his mother in Lev. 18:9, why does it need to say two verses later "she is your sister—you shall not uncover her nakedness"? Is it not obvious that, if you are forbidden to sleep with your half-sister, you are forbidden to sleep with your sister? The fact that the Torah goes out of its way to repeat the word "your sister" in the latter verse demonstrates, according to the Rabbis, that one is only culpable for violating a law if the prohibition is clearly articulated in the Torah, even though the prohibited nature of the act could easily have been inferred.

Similarly, Lev. 20:17 is seen as the source of the principle *ʾēn ʿoněšin min haddin*: a violation of law is not punishable unless the punishment is stated explicitly in the Torah; the violation's punishability cannot be inferred from that of a different prohibition.[6] The verse repeats the term "his sister" after having spoken of "his sister, the daughter of his father or the daughter of his mother." Since it goes out of its way to tell us that the punishment applies to a man who sleeps with his sister, and not only with his half-sister—an obvious point!—the verse must be instructing us that one cannot be held punishable for a violation of law unless the punishment is clearly articulated in reference to that particular violation.

This first pair of principles that are based by the Rabbis on the verses about brother-sister intercourse are clearly related to the Rabbis' view of sinaitic law as positive law, since they are an extension of the requirements of *ʾazhārā* and *ʿoneš*, requirements that are fundamental to a notion of law as based in command. The extension is an important one, it bears emphasizing, because these principles make it clear that there is no place for assumptions about what is reasonable when it comes to the legal quality of a prohibition. The prohibition and its sanctionability are based in statute, and they require a clear statutory formulation in order for the violator of the prohibition to be held punishable for his act.[7]

Lev. 20:17 is mustered within the Bavli as the source for a range of additional principles relating to punishability. At times, it is cited by a sage as the source of the principle that he introduces, and at other times it is brought by the Gemara as the source—or as a possible source—for a sage's position. The ubiquitous drawing on this verse as a source of legal principles gives the impression that this verse is marked in some way as particularly generative for the Rabbis of principles of legal procedure and punishment. I will briefly introduce the next four principles and their derivations from the verses about brother-sister intercourse, without going into the details of the complex talmudic discussions in which they appear.

The Bavli introduces a three-way tannaitic dispute about which violators of law are liable for the court-imposed punishment of flogging, *malqut*.[8] While two of the sages agree that those who violate prohibitions for which the Torah mandates *kārēt* nevertheless are liable to be punished in court, R. Yitzchaq disagrees. Looking to the verses about the forbidden sexual relationships in Leviticus 18, he points out that all these prohibitions would seem to result in excision: "For whoever does any of these abominations, these souls shall be cut off from the midst of their people" (Lev. 18:29). And yet, he notes, the Torah explicitly mentions *kārēt* in chapter 20 as the punishment for brother-sister intercourse; the preceding forbidden sexual acts in this chapter are described as incurring other punishments but do not mention *kārēt*. Thus, R. Yitzchaq argues, a crime for which *kārēt* is mandated—like the crime of brother-sister intercourse—results only in *kārēt*; it does not result in the court-imposed punishment of *malqut*.[9]

The Bavli also constructs a three-way disagreement about whether a person who violates a law for which there is a monetary penalty is liable for *malqut*.[10] While Ulla posits that such a person must pay the monetary penalty but is exempt from *malqut*, R. Yochanan is of the opposite opinion: such a person receives *malqut* and is exempt from paying the monetary penalty. The first source that the Gemara offers for R. Yochanan's position is Lev. 18:9: "The nakedness of your sister . . . you shall not uncover." If a man who sleeps with his sister would incur the standard monetary penalty that is incurred for sleeping with a young woman but would be exempt from *malqut*, the prohibition of Lev. 18:9 would be void.[11] The Gemara's assumption is that the purpose of a statement of a prohibition is to enable the act to be criminally punishable; if there were no criminal punishment to be imposed in this case, there would no purpose to the verse that articulates the *ʾazhārā* against brother-sister intercourse.

These two discussions are similar in that both raise the question of court-imposed criminal punishment in relation to acts that have other consequences. In the first case, the person who violates the law is to be cut off from his people, a punishment that is understood by the Rabbis to be divinely imposed.[12] Is the court mandated to impose a criminal sanction on this violator of law? In the second case, the act, in principle, demands financial compensation or a financial penalty. But is the criminal nature of the act to be expressed (instead, or in addition) in the court's imposition of a criminal punishment on the perpetrator of the act? In general, if the law prohibits a certain act, is it essential that a court of law impose a criminal punishment for violation of the law? These questions make sense within the rubric of positive law, in which crimes are defined by their statutory formulation in terms of prohibitions and punishments, and in which liability for criminal punishment results from the violation of a command.

The following two principles are even more embedded in a positivist approach to law, as both address the relationship between the formulation of a prohibition or the awareness of a prohibition and liability for violation of the law. The first principle, which the Gemara suggests is derived from Lev. 20:17 in different ways by different sages, has to do with a situation in which a person commits a single act that violates multiple prohibitions.[13] The Gemara offers as an example a man who sleeps with a woman who is both his sister and his father's sister and his mother's sister. The Torah forbids a man to sleep with a woman who is related to him in any of these ways (Lev. 18:9, 12–13; 20:17, 19). If a man performs a single act of sexual intercourse with one woman who is related to him in all these three ways, is this considered one crime or three? Lev. 20:17 is marshaled to teach that the person is liable for three crimes, even though he has done only a single act with one person. The Gemara refers to this kind of situation as *šēmot mĕḥullāqin,* distinct prohibitions. In such a case, we analyze what the person did wrong and evaluate his liability not based on his real-world act—which, after all, is not divisible—but based on the legal definition of what he did. If a single act falls under the rubric of multiple statutes, we consider the person to have done more than one crime, and he is liable for each of them.

The second principle is related, and the Gemara initially proposes that it, too, is derived from the verse about brother-sister intercourse, though it ultimately allows that it can be derived from a different verse, leaving Lev. 20:17 available for one or another of the principles discussed above.[14] This principle has to do with what the Gemara calls *heʿelēm ʾeḥād,* a single period of time in which a person acts in ignorance either of the law or of the circumstances that make his acts forbidden. The Rabbis take for granted that, if a person violates the same law multiple times during a single time span of ignorance, he is liable for only one sin-offering.[15] The question that the Gemara addresses is: What if a person violates multiple prohibitions during such a period of time—is he liable for multiple sin-offerings or only for a single sin-offering? R. Yochanan teaches that the person is liable for multiple unintentional violations of the law, and the Gemara suggests that the source of this principle is the verse about brother-sister intercourse. The fact that Lev. 20:17 goes out of its way to mention *kārēt*—despite the inclusion of all the sexual prohibitions under excision in Lev. 18:29—teaches that each violation of law, like the violation of this particular prohibition, is distinct and carries its own liability. The situation that the Gemara is addressing—violation of multiple prohibitions during a single time span of ignorance—pits against each other two issues that are central to a positivist conception of law: an analysis of the person's acts in relation to the statutory formulation of the law, and the relationship between liability and awareness of the prohibitedness of the act.

So far, we have seen an astonishing six principles of criminal law that the Rabbis propose can be derived from the verses about brother-sister intercourse. Each of these relates to questions of liability for violation of law, most of them address the issue of liability in relation to the Torah's statutory formulation of law, and the last one raises as well the relationship between awareness of the prohibitedness of an act and liability for violating the prohibition. The final principle that we will encounter is one that we have already discussed as central to the Rabbis' positivist view of sinaitic law: the requirement that, in order for a violation of law to be punishable, there must be a *hatrāʾā* before the crime is committed. As we look at the sources that derive this final principle from one of the verses about brother-sister intercourse, we will discover why this particular prohibition is seen by the Rabbis as the place to look when searching for the source of principles of sinaitic criminal law.

"Cain Married His Sister"

mSan 5:1 spells out the questions that the court must put to the witnesses in a capital case. One of these questions is whether the witnesses issued a warning before the commission of the act to which they are testifying. The Bavli introduces several opinions about the biblical source of the requirement of *hatrāʾā* in criminal cases. The first of these derives this requirement from Lev. 20:17: "Ulla said: From where in the Torah do we derive *hatrāʾā*?[16] As it says: 'And a man who takes his sister, the daughter of his father or the daughter of his mother, and sees her nakedness'—is the thing [i.e., liability for the act] dependent on seeing?! Rather, [the phrase comes to teach us that he is not punishable] until they show him the basis[17] of the matter."[18]

As noted earlier, the reference to seeing nakedness is redundant in this verse, as the verse goes on to use the term "to uncover nakedness." The expression "to see nakedness" is also different from the expression used throughout chapters 18 and 20, where "to uncover nakedness" is consistently used. And Lev. 20:17 uses the expression "to see nakedness" twice, to describe both the man's act and the woman's act: "and he sees her nakedness, and she sees his nakedness." Ulla takes this marked term to refer not to physical seeing but rather to awareness: the person is not culpable unless he is informed by the witnesses that the act is forbidden.

The parallel in ySan sheds light on why it is in reference to this particular act that the Rabbis think that the Torah chooses to make clear that the person must be made aware of the prohibitedness of the act that he is about to do in order to be held culpable for his act. Here, Lev. 20:17 is also cited as the first source for the requirement of *hatrāʾā*, but it is not entirely clear how the requirement is being derived from this verse: "From where do we derive *hatrāʾā*? R. Shmuel bar Nachman said in the name of R. Yonatan: 'And a man who takes his sister . . . it is *ḥesed*.' R. Bun said: Cain married his sister, Abel married his sister; I [says God] did an act of kindness [*ḥesed*] with the first ones so that the world would be built from them—'For I said: The world shall be built through *ḥesed*' (Ps. 89:3)."[19]

One way to understand the Yerushalmi is to see it as deriving the requirement of *hatrāʾā* in exactly the same way that the Bavli does.

According to this understanding, the requirement is derived from the words "and he sees," and the verse is simply being quoted in abridged form, with the critical words elided. The statement of R. Bun, on this reading, is unrelated to the derivation of *hatrāʾā*; it simply appears here as a tangential teaching on this same verse.[20]

But there is another possible reading of this passage. R. Yonatan may be deriving the requirement of *hatrāʾā* from the words "it is *ḥesed*" or from the juxtaposition of these words with the words "and he sees." R. Yonatan points out that the Torah needs to say, in connection with the law that a man who sleeps with his sister has committed a punishable offense, that this act is *ḥesed.* The passage goes on to explain why the Torah needs to say this by citing the teaching of R. Bun about the meaning of the word *ḥesed* in relation to Cain and Abel marrying their sisters. Taking R. Bun's teaching together with R. Yonatan's statement that the word *ḥesed* is the source for *hatrāʾā,* we have the following argument: the would-be committer of brother-sister intercourse is aware that humankind began with brothers sleeping with their sisters. This allowance was an act of *ḥesed* that God performed with the ancients in order to allow the world to be built. So the Torah needs to tell the would-be committer of this act that, although humankind did originate from brother-sister intercourse—although this act is indeed world-building—this act is now prohibited and the person who commits this act is to be punished.

According to this reading, the Yerushalmi's derivation of the requirement of *hatrāʾā* is similar to the Bavli's, but it makes clear why the Rabbis see the Torah as choosing this particular prohibition as the locus of the requirement that a person must have the prohibitedness of the act called to his attention in order to be held punishable. It is this verse that tells us that we need to make sure that the would-be violator of law knows that the act is prohibited, because this verse talks about an act that the person has good reason, in fact, to think is permissible. Thus, he needs to be made to "see" that the act is prohibited—not by its nature, but by God's command.

Whether or not this reading is technically correct, it discloses what I think is the import of the Rabbis' choice of the verse about this particular prohibition as the locus of the derivation of *hatrāʾā.* In other words, even if the Yerushalmi is deriving the requirement of *hatrāʾā* in exactly the same way as the Bavli, from the words "and he sees"—as the first reading would have it—the teaching of R. Bun that is juxtaposed in this passage with R. Yonatan's derivation of *hatrāʾā* shows us why the Rabbis thought that it is in connection with this particular prohibition that the Torah makes it clear that the person must be made to see that the act that he is about to perform is prohibited by God's command. In fact, the Sifra offers a derivation that appears to be exactly the same as the

Bavli's but that, like the Yerushalmi, includes the teaching about Cain: " 'and he sees her nakedness, and she sees his nakedness'—[they are not punishable] until they are both *mĕzidin* (=they deliberately violate the law). 'it is *ḥesed*'—and lest you say: Cain married his sister, Scripture teaches 'it is *ḥesed*'—and the world at its beginning was built only through *ḥesed*, as it says: 'For I said: The world shall be built through *ḥesed*' " (Ps. 89:3).[21]

The first exegesis seems to be the same as that offered by Ulla in the Bavli (which, according to the first reading of the Yerushalmi, is the same as the derivation offered there). From the mention of "seeing nakedness," the Sifra derives the rule that the man and the woman are not punishable unless they act deliberately. While the Sifra does not mention the requirement of *hatrāʾā*, it presumes a way to determine that the person is acting with deliberate intent to violate a command.[22]

Then the Sifra goes on to offer an exegesis of "it is *ḥesed*" that is almost identical to that in the Yerushalmi. Here, though, the exegesis is introduced by "and lest you say." The Sifra is making it clear that it sees the Torah in this verse as responding to something. What it is responding to is an assumption that one might make based on an observation about the world as it began and as it might be presumed to continue. You might well argue, the Sifra says, that Cain married his sister—and hence, presumably, that it is acceptable for you to do the same. So the Torah acknowledges that, yes, brother-sister marriage was an act of *ḥesed* at the world's beginning. It was, indeed, a world-building act, says the Sifra, but you cannot use the argument from the world's beginning to reason that this behavior is allowed now.

While in the Sifra, as in the Yerushalmi, it is not clear that we should take the two parts of the passage that I have cited as forming a single explanation of the derivation of *hatrāʾā*, the Sifra makes it clear that the exegesis of "it is *ḥesed*" is not irrelevant to our understanding of the awareness of the committer of this forbidden act. While it is possible to read the second part of the Yerushalmi passage as an unrelated teaching explaining the word *ḥesed* by referring to the practice of the ancients, the second part of the Sifra passage offers an exegesis that tells us why the Torah bothers to make reference to this ancient practice. It bothers because we are no doubt aware of this practice, and the Torah wants to tell us that the fact that it was permitted to the ancients has no bearing on us; the practice is forbidden to us because the Torah includes a statute prohibiting it. This piece of information is crucial because, without it, there is really no such thing as a deliberate act; a person can only be punished for the act if he is aware that it is prohibited. Thus, the two exegeses in the Sifra are integrally related because the second shows us why it is in the context of this particular act that the Torah chooses to teach us the principle that a person is only punished for an act that is demonstrably deliberate.

What I am suggesting is that all three sources that derive *hatrāʾā* from Lev. 20:17 choose this verse because of a particular view of the act of brother-sister intercourse. According to this view, it is not at all obvious that this act is wrong; in fact, from a certain perspective, this act is not only permissible but, possibly, laudatory. It is, after all, world-building behavior: "the world shall be built through *ḥesed.*" It is here, then, that the Torah needs to tell us that the would-be committer of the act needs to be informed that the act that he is about to perform is prohibited by the Torah. And, by extension, we learn that every would-be committer of a prohibited act must be aware that the act is a violation of God's command. Without that warning, the person cannot be held culpable, because it is only by willfully violating God's command that he incurs punishment. There is no other way, within the sinaitic system as understood by the Rabbis, that an act can be construed as forbidden. Lev. 20:17 tells us this because it gives us an example of an act that, from a natural law perspective, would not be forbidden. The act is forbidden simply because of God's command, and it is only awareness of that command that makes a person culpable for performing this—or any—act.

"The World Shall Be Built through *Ḥesed*"

Although the Bavli does not include the exegesis of "it is *ḥesed*" in the context of its derivation of *hatrāʾā* from Lev. 20:17, it does include a similar teaching about humankind beginning with brother-sister intercourse in the context of its discussion of noachide law. As part of a long discussion about which sexual relationships are forbidden to a noachide, the Bavli discusses the permissibility of brother-sister intercourse (or intercourse between a man and a woman who is related to him through a sibling relationship, such as his aunt). Through an analysis of a variety of tannaitic statements, the Gemara establishes that, according to one opinion, a noachide is permitted to sleep with his paternal sister (or a woman who is related to him through a paternal sibling relationship, such as his father's paternal sister) but not with his maternal sister (or a woman who is related to him through a maternal sibling relationship, such as his father's maternal sister), while, according to another opinion, even a maternal sister is permitted to a noachide.[23] In other words, according to the second opinion, there is no prohibition of brother-sister intercourse for a noachide, while, according to the first opinion, there is a limited prohibition.

The Gemara then raises a series of challenges to one or the other of these positions. The final challenge is raised against the position that denies that there is any prohibition of brother-sister intercourse for noachides. Here is the challenge and the response that the Gemara offers to this challenge: "Come and hear: Why didn't Adam marry his daughter? In order that Cain would marry his sister, as it says: 'For I said: The world shall be built through *ḥesed*' (Ps. 89:3). This implies that otherwise it would have been prohibited! Once it was permitted, it was permitted."[24]

The Gemara introduces a source that says that Adam kept from marrying his daughter in order that his son would be able to marry her, thus allowing humankind to emerge. The challenge is generated by the inference that, had it not been necessary for Cain to sleep with his sister, the act would not have been permitted. The Gemara understands the source to be suggesting that this is a one-time dispensation that allowed the world to be built at its inception, implying that, in general, a noachide cannot sleep with his maternal (or full) sister. But the Gemara then rejects this argument. "Once it was permitted," the Gemara says, "it was permitted." Behavior that is permissible at the beginning of time—behavior that, indeed, allowed the world to be built—remains legitimate for all time.[25]

This argument is exactly the opposite of the argument that I suggested is made by the sources that derive the requirement of *hatrāʾā* from the verses about brother-sister intercourse. Those sources made the point that culpability derives from awareness that an act is prohibited by God's command as articulated in the Torah. The act of brother-sister intercourse is the locus of the requirement of *hatrāʾā*, because this act could well be thought to be permissible since it was permitted—in fact, necessary—at the beginning of time. The point is that one cannot derive permissibility from the fact that something was once permitted; one cannot reason that an act must be permitted because the world could not have come to be without that act. The only thing that tells us whether an act is permissible or prohibited under sinaitic law is the command of the Torah, and thus it is the Torah's command that must be brought to the attention of the would-be committer of the act if he is to be held culpable for the act that he is about to commit.

For noachides, though, the Bavli suggests precisely the inference that rabbinic sources reject for those who are commanded at Sinai. It is as if the Sifra's "lest you say" becomes, for noachides, "Say!"—"Say: Cain married his sister, and thus we are permitted to do the same." For noachides, the Bavli argues, one can indeed reason that an act is permissible from the fact that it was once permitted; one can look at behavior that one knows was necessary for the world to be built and be assured that such behavior cannot be prohibited now.

The act of brother-sister intercourse, then, represents a critical divide between sinaitic and noachide law. From a natural law perspective, according to the Rabbis, there is nothing wrong with brother-sister intercourse.[26] On the contrary, at a certain point in time—the beginning of human history—brother-sister intercourse was a necessary act. Far from being world-destroying behavior, like the forbidden acts in Tanna deve Menashe's list of noachide laws, or behavior that is antithetical to the construction of human society,[27] like the Sages' list of prohibited acts, brother-sister intercourse was a world-building act: "The world shall be built through *ḥesed*."[28] Thus, within noachide law, there is no absolute prohibition of brother-sister intercourse.

Yet for those who are commanded at Sinai, this act is prohibited. The fact that this act cannot be prohibited from the natural law perspective that underlies the Rabbis' conception of noachide law highlights the fact that the prohibition of brother-sister intercourse for Jews derives exclusively from command. The derivation of the requirement of *hatrāʾā* from the verse about brother-sister intercourse emphasizes that culpability for *any* violation of law derives from the fact that the committer of the act has violated God's command.

The prohibition of brother-sister intercourse represents a disjunction between the Rabbis' views of sinaitic and of noachide laws in a second way as well, because the verses in which this prohibition is formulated serve as the source for the variety of principles of sinaitic criminal law that we have seen. The requirement of *hatrāʾā* is derived from the formulation of this law in a way that is integrally related to the fact that the substance of the law is evaluated in opposite ways from a positivist and natural law perspective. And, as we have seen, a range of other principles of sinaitic criminal law are derived from these verses, from the requirements of explicit statutory formulations of *ʿoneš* and *ʾazhārā*—the prohibition and punishment that are to be rearticulated before the would-be violator of law in the form of the *hatrāʾā*—to the assortment of other principles about culpability for violations of law that we surveyed.

Thus, the prohibition of brother-sister intercourse represents a convergence of critical substantive and procedural elements of the rabbinic conception of sinaitic law, for in this law we have an act that is a violation of positive law but not of natural law, and it is from the formulation of this law that we derive principles central to the jurisprudence of sinaitic positive law: an act is forbidden because a command prohibits it, it is sanctionable because the law states the sanction, and a violator can be punished only if he is aware that he is violating a command that is punishable by the stipulated sanction.[29]

The Convergence of Substance and Procedure

The main purpose of this chapter was to underscore the difference between the rabbinic conceptions of sinaitic and noachide law by looking at how the Rabbis understand one particular act that is prohibited under sinaitic law but that the Rabbis see as permitted to noachides.[30] In the course of analyzing the law prohibiting brother-sister intercourse, I noted as well that principles of sinaitic criminal law in general and of criminal procedure in particular are related to the Rabbis' conception of sinaitic law. In addition, I disclosed a striking relationship between the substantive and procedural elements of the rabbinic conception of sinaitic law, elements that converge in the Rabbis' interpretation of the biblical prohibition against brother-sister intercourse. As a paradigmatic sinaitic law—a law that, according to the Rabbis, can only derive from command—the biblical prohibition against brother-sister intercourse serves for the Rabbis as the locus for principles of sinaitic criminal law, principles that themselves reflect the Rabbis' conception of sinaitic law as based in command.

The convergence of substantive and procedural elements of sinaitic law in the prohibition against brother-sister intercourse leads us back to the claim with which I began: that the Rabbis' rules of criminal procedure and punishment express the Rabbis' understanding of the nature of law. In the next chapter, I will turn from my focus on this paradigmatic sinaitic law to analyze an exceptional sinaitic law: the prohibition against murder. This law, I will argue, is seen by the Rabbis as different in nature from other sinaitic prohibitions. And this difference in the rabbinic understanding of the substance of this law is reflected in the particular punishment that the Rabbis assign to the crime of murder as well as in some differences in criminal procedure for cases of murder.

Chapter 4
Murder and the Social Response to Wrongdoing

Punishment in rabbinic sources, I have proposed, expresses the Rabbis' conception of law. *Ḥeneq*, the default mode of execution for violations of sinaitic law, reflects the Rabbis' understanding of the nature of sinaitic law. Noachide law represents the Rabbis' vision of an alternative conception of law; in particular, I have argued that the two versions of noachide law constructed by the Bavli represent two different conceptions of law that is not based in sinaitic command. Each of these versions, in turn, is assigned a mode of execution that reflects the conception of law that underlies the version of noachide law to which it is assigned.

In this chapter, I turn away from a focus on the Rabbis' conception of a body of law to look at one particular law within the sinaitic legal system that, I will argue, is understood by the Rabbis as different in kind from other sinaitic laws. While in the preceding chapter I analyzed the prohibition against brother-sister intercourse as a *paradigmatic* sinaitic law, in this chapter I will focus on the prohibition against murder as an *exceptional* sinaitic law. If the prohibition against brother-sister intercourse stands at the point of *disjunction* between sinaitic and noachide law, the prohibition against murder, I will argue, stands at the *intersection* between sinaitic and noachide law.

The exceptional nature of murder within sinaitic law is reflected in the distinctive punishment assigned by the Rabbis to the murderer, a punishment that expresses the Rabbis' view of murder as a violation of natural law. Further, subtle differences in criminal procedure in the case of murder reflect the Rabbis' understanding of murder as a crime that is different in kind from all other acts that are prohibited to those commanded at Sinai: different not only in the severity of the act and the threat that it poses to society but in the conception of the criminal nature of this act as deriving from something other than command. Thus, the analysis of rabbinic sources about murder constitutes a further test of the thesis that the Rabbis' rules of criminal procedure and punishment express a conception of law, at the same time extending the thesis from applying to entire systems of law to apply as well to a particular law within a system of law.

The Punishment for Murder

Murder is the one crime to which the Rabbis assign the execution of *hereg*. The Mishna's listing of those violators of law who are executed by each of the four modes of execution includes also the residents of *ʿir hanniddaḥat* as executed by *hereg*,[1] but this derives explicitly from the Torah's description of what should be done to the residents of such a city (Deut. 13:16).[2] Other than murder, all crimes for which the Torah does not state a mode of execution are either assimilated by the Rabbis to the category of crimes punishable by *sĕqilā* or assigned to the default mode of execution, *ḥeneq*. Thus, from the perspective of its punishment, murder stands out as unique within sinaitic criminal law.

In contrast, within each of the constructions of noachide law presented by the Bavli, murder shares the same punishment as every other violation of law. In fact, as the one noachide criminal act for which the Torah describes the consequences,[3] murder can be seen as paradigmatic for the punishment of crimes within each system of noachide law. If murder results in *ḥeneq*, as in Tanna deve Menashe's version, then all violations of noachide law—acts that violate the natural order—result in *ḥeneq*. If murder is punishable by *hereg*, as the dominant position holds it to be, then all noachide crimes—acts that violate the social order—are punishable by *hereg*.[4]

While the punishment for murder locates murder within, and perhaps at the center of, both constructions of noachide law, the assignment by the Rabbis of the punishment of *hereg* to murder within sinaitic law marks the crime of murder as unique within the Rabbis' construction of sinaitic law. My task, then, is twofold. First, I must look at the crime of murder to see why and in what way it is understood by the Rabbis as different in kind from other prohibited acts within sinaitic law. Second, I need to show how the sanction of *hereg* reflects the Rabbis' particular understanding of the nature of this act and how it links murder to the dominant rabbinic conception of noachide law. I will begin by looking briefly at the biblical antecedents of the Rabbis' understanding of the crime of murder.

The Biblical Background

Within biblical law, murder is unique among crimes in that the act has an essential reality distinct from the legal responsibility of the perpetrator and the possibility of bringing the murderer to justice. Murder is a wrong that has been done, and the wrong needs to be addressed. Thus, for example, the Torah includes the ritual of the *ʿeglā ʿărufā*, a ritual that is designed to atone for the spilling of a murder victim's blood when the murderer cannot be identified (Deut. 21:1–9). It should be noted that rabbinic sources insist that, if the murderer is later identified, he must be killed even though the atoning ritual has already been performed.[5] If, however, the murderer is known at first, there is no need for a separate atoning ritual, as the killing of the murderer serves also to atone for the spilling of blood. Thus, for the Rabbis, the requirement to bring the criminal to justice goes beyond the need to atone for the spilling of the victim's blood, but it includes the element of atonement as well.

The need for atonement is explicit in the Torah in another context as well. The Torah includes an extended passage about the *ʿārē miqlāṭ*—the cities of refuge to which unintentional murderers flee for protection from the blood redeemers—which details the rules of both intentional and unintentional murder. The passage concludes with the following exhortation: "And you shall not pollute the land in which you are, for blood pollutes the land, and the land cannot be atoned for, for the blood that is spilled in it, but by the blood of its spiller. And you shall not make the land in which you live—in which I dwell—impure, for I, the Lord, dwell among the children of Israel" (Num. 35:33–34). Murder, according to this passage, pollutes the land, the land in which the people of Israel live and in which God dwells.[6] The requirement to kill the intentional murderer, then, cannot be seen simply as imposing a sanction for violating a command. The murderer, rather, has violated the world in which he lives—the land, the people, and God—and that violation requires the spilling of the murderer's blood.[7]

It should be noted that even the law of the unintentional murderer includes the idea of atonement and emphasizes the distinction between legal responsibility and the need for atonement. While the cities of refuge are designed to protect the unintentional murderer from being killed by the *goʾēl haddām*—the blood redeemer—the law that the unintentional murderer must flee to one of these cities includes as well the element of atonement and the element of exile.[8] The fact that the unintentional murderer is required to flee to the *ʿir miqlāṭ*—that this is not just a benefit that is offered to him—is clear from the verses that immediately precede the verses that I just quoted: "And you shall not take a ransom for the life of a murderer who is guilty of death; rather he shall surely be put to death. And you shall not take a ransom [for one who is] to flee to his city of refuge, to return to live in the land, until the death of the priest" (Num. 35:31–32). The verses juxtapose the prohibition to take a ransom for the life of the intentional murderer with the prohibition to take a ransom that allows the unintentional murderer to remain in the land instead of going to the city of refuge. And these two verses immediately precede the verses that explain how murder pollutes the land and requires atonement. The implication of the four verses that conclude the passage about cities of refuge is that even unintentional murder requires atonement:[9] atonement that is accomplished by the exile of the unintentional murderer from his land.[10] Murder, we see once again, creates a reality that must be addressed even when the act is unintentional. Murder demands a response—it must be atoned for—separate from the legal responsibility of the committer of the act.[11]

The Torah's explanation that "the land cannot be atoned for, for the blood that is spilled in it, but by the blood of its spiller" (Num. 35:33) clearly echoes God's words to Noah and his sons after the flood: "He who spills the blood of a human being, by[12] a human being shall his blood be spilled" (Gen. 9:6).[13] The notion of murder as a violation of the world that ought to require the killing of the murderer comes up even earlier in the Torah, though, in the story of the first homicide, Cain's killing of Abel. While God describes the effect of this murder as a violation of the land that results in an alienation of the human being from the land (Gen. 4:10–12), Cain elaborates further on the consequences of his deed: he has been banished from the face of the earth, he will be hidden from God's face, and, finally, "anyone who finds me will kill me" (Gen. 4:14).[14] As in the Numbers passage, homicide is portrayed here as an act that has an effect on the human being's relationship with the land, with God, and with fellow human beings. The result that Cain anticipates, but from which God protects him (Gen. 4:15), is that he will be killed for killing his brother. This protection is denied to the murderer in God's words to Noah and his sons after the flood in Gen. 9:6,[15] a verse that is echoed, as noted, in the Torah's injunction in Num. 35:33–34 to restore the land in which the people live and in which God dwells by spilling the blood of the murderer.

It is noteworthy in this regard that the Torah does not portray the blood redeemer as an individual who functions wholly outside of the system of justice, as someone who attempts privately to redress a private wrong done to his kinsman whether purposely or inadvertently. While the *gōʾēl haddām* does seek the death of the killer and might, in fact, kill him without the mandate of the communal authorities, the Torah additionally portrays the *gōʾēl haddām* as someone who has a legal claim against the murderer[16] (Num. 35:24) and as the person into whose hands the murderer is delivered if determined to be guilty[17] (Deut. 19:11–12). The notion of a human being spilling the blood of the spiller of blood, then, forms the backdrop of and constitutes a component of the community's formal response to this act that has violated the life of the community.[18]

My goal here is not to attempt a full analysis of the biblical understanding of the nature of the act of murder, of the consequences of this act, and of how killing the murderer restores the disruption effected by the act of murder.[19] Rather, I offer this brief survey of some biblical passages about murder in order to establish two points about how murder is seen in the Torah. First, murder is an act the commission of which leaves a real mark on the world. Second, murder is an act that of necessity ought to result in the killing of a killer by a fellow human being.

"He Shall Surely Be Avenged"

Both these elements are retained in rabbinic sources about murder and the punishment of a murderer. Addressing the Mishna's teaching that a murderer is executed by *hereg*, the Bavli cites two *baraitot* that offer possible sources for the assignment of this form of execution to the act of murder.[20] The first *baraita* derives the form of execution from a verse that talks about a person who kills a slave: " 'He shall surely be avenged' (Exod. 21:20)—this vengeance I don't know what it is. When it says, 'I will bring upon you a sword avenging the vengeance of the covenant' (Lev. 26:25), say: vengeance is [killing with a] sword." That "vengeance" is the source of the judicial execution of *hereg* for a murderer suggests that, at its core, murder is an act that demands a human response.[21] The killer has killed a human being, and a human being will kill the killer.[22]

The second *baraita* derives the punishment for a murderer from the ritual of the *ʿeglā ʿărufā*: " 'And you shall rid the innocent blood from your midst' (Deut. 21.9)—all spillers of blood have been compared to the *ʿeglā ʿărufā*: just as there it is with a sword and from the neck, so too here it is with a sword and from the neck." Deriving the punishment of a murderer from the way in which the *ʿeglā ʿărufā* is killed suggests that the execution of a murderer, like the ritual of the *ʿeglā ʿărufā*, has the function of atoning for the blood that has been spilled.

The two *baraitot* that the Bavli cites as offering sources for *hereg* as the punishment for a murderer correspond to the two points that I have pointed to as emerging from biblical passages about murder. The comparison to the *ʿeglā ʿărufā* suggests that murder is a crime whose commission results in an essential reality that requires atonement. And the linking of death by sword to vengeance suggests that the act of murder demands this social response, the killing of the killer by a fellow human being.[23]

The link between *hereg* and vengeance, in particular, suggests that judicial execution of the murderer is seen in rabbinic sources as the institutionalization of society's natural response to the effects of a crime against society, rather than as a purely judicial sanction for violating a sinaitic command. A striking indication that this is so appears in a number of rabbinic texts that, in the course of describing commissions or would-be commissions of murder, mention the *hatrāʾā*, the warning that the witnesses give to the person who is poised to commit this act. As we have seen, the requirement of a *hatrāʾā* underscores a fundamental premise of sinaitic jurisprudence: that a criminal is punished for intentional violation of a sanctionable command. We would expect, then, that the *hatrāʾā* for murder would include reference to a statute addressed to Israelites forbidding murder and to the punishment that the law stipulates for violation of this statute. But, instead, the *hatrāʾā* that appears in these texts is this: "See—he is an Israelite and a member of the covenant, and the Torah has said: 'He who spills the blood of a human being, by a human being shall his blood be spilled.' "[24]

The verse that is quoted in this *hatrāʾā* describes, or perhaps prescribes, the consequence of murder, but it does not have a legal formulation as the statement of a prohibition—such as "thou shalt not commit murder" (Exod. 20:13)—with the attendant punishment—such as "the murderer shall surely be put to death" (Num. 35:16). In fact, this verse is not even addressed to those who are commanded at Sinai; it is a passage with universal application.[25] Further, it is a text that highlights the reciprocal consequences of murder; the chiastic structure of the passage suggests that the killer, of necessity, is to be killed by a fellow human being. The consequence of murder is something that must happen; it is not described, in this verse, as a formal punishment that an authoritative body is mandated to impose. Finally, this is the paradigmatic noachide verse: spoken by God to Noah and his sons and addressing the consequences of a criminal act, this verse is the paradigm for punishment within noachide law.[26]

The extraordinary choice of this verse as the way in which the witnesses articulate the *hatrāʾā* supports the idea that the Rabbis do not see the prohibition against murder as fundamentally based in command and that they do not see the punishment for murder as punishment for violation of a command. Rather, murder is a violation of human society that is punished within human society. The court, of course, manages this process, but criminal procedure and punishment for this crime do not supplant the role of society in responding to a crime that is a fundamental violation of society. The *hatrāʾā* embodies these contradictory poles of the response to murder within sinaitic law, for, on the one hand, the requirement of *hatrāʾā*[27] places murder within the sinaitic system of criminal law, and, on the other hand, the particular form of this *hatrāʾā* shows murder and its consequences to be different in kind from other criminal acts and their punishments.

The nature of the execution of a murderer as a punishment imposed within human society rather than as a purely judicial sanction is also suggested by several specific laws about how a murderer may be killed. For example, while the mandated form of execution for a murderer is *hereg*, if the court is unable to implement this form of execution, it is mandated to execute the murderer in any way it can.[28] If a murderer cannot be convicted because there are no witnesses, he is nevertheless punished by placement in *kippā*.[29] If there is no *goʾēl haddām* to kill the murderer, another person kills him in the *goʾēl haddām*'s stead.[30] These irregular allowances suggest that murder is not a crime whose place is solely within the sinaitic system of law, a crime that is to be addressed solely within the constraints of the sinaitic system of judicial procedure. Murder is a crime against society, and, while the court is mandated to punish the murderer, judicial punishment does not replace civil society's sanctions against the murderer. Rather, it is the court's role to implement those sanctions, and there is ample room to dispose of the murderer in other ways if the court cannot do it within its regular procedures.[31]

The Court-Appointed *Goʾēl*

The incomplete assimilation of the punishment for murder into the judicial system is suggested also by a difficult passage in the Bavli. One of the irregular allowances noted above is the rule that if the murderer is not killed by the *goʾēl haddām*, he may be killed by someone else. According to a *baraita* in the Bavli, the court actually appoints a *goʾēl haddām* if the murder victim has no redeemer: "As it is taught in a *baraita*: 'The *goʾēl haddām* will put the murderer to death' (Num. 35:19[32])—it is a *mitzva* [for the murderer to be killed] by the *goʾēl haddām*. And whence do we know that, if he has no *goʾēl*, the court sets up a *goʾēl* for him? As it says: 'when he encounters him' [these words follow the words quoted earlier]—in any case."[33] The difficulty in this source lies in trying to figure out for what purpose this *goʾēl haddām* is appointed: What function of the *goʾēl haddām* does this source have in mind when it asserts the need for the court to appoint someone to serve this function?

One possibility is that the source is referring to the role played by the *goʾēl haddām* in the case of unintentional murder. As we have seen, the Torah mandates that the unintentional murderer flee to a city of refuge, where he must stay until the high priest dies. If the unintentional murderer leaves the city of refuge, the *goʾēl haddām* is permitted—or perhaps expected—to kill him.[34] If there is no *goʾēl haddām*, this source could be read as saying, the court appoints a *goʾēl haddām* whose job it would be to monitor the unintentional murderer and to take action should he leave the city of refuge prematurely.

While such an interpretation is, in fact, offered by Rashi,[35] other commentators point out that this reading of the passage in the Bavli is difficult, not least because the *baraita* cites a verse that talks about the case of intentional, not unintentional, murder.[36] If we take the passage to be addressing the case of intentional murder, though, then what is the role of the *goʾēl haddām*?

The Torah does talk of the role of the *goʾēl haddām* in relation to the case of intentional murder in the verse quoted in the *baraita* itself: "The *goʾēl haddām* will put the murderer to death; when he encounters him, he will put him to death" (Num. 35:19; cf. 35:21). But this verse is not much help in clarifying why the court might need to appoint a *goʾēl haddām*, since the verse does not seem to be talking about any kind of institutional procedure; it seems, rather, to be describing what happens if the *goʾēl haddām* should encounter the person who has intentionally murdered his kinsman, just as the passage later describes what the *goʾēl haddām* might do if he encounters the unintentional murderer outside of the city of refuge (Num. 35:27).[37] What the communal body's role is in the case of intentional murder is left unclear in the Numbers passage. The passage describes the role of the community in saving the person whom it has deemed to be an unintentional murderer from the *goʾēl haddām* by returning him to the city of refuge (Num. 35:25), but it says nothing about its role in relation to the person whom it has deemed to have murdered intentionally.

In other words, it is clear in this passage that the *goʾēl haddām* is poised to kill the person who has murdered his kinsman, either in the case where he has murdered intentionally or in the case where he has murdered unintentionally but he has failed to take advantage of the protection of the city of refuge. And it is also clear that it is the communal body's job to determine whether the person killed intentionally or unintentionally and to offer the unintentional murderer the protection of the city of refuge. But the passage does not describe any interaction between the communal body and the *goʾēl haddām*. In particular, what happens if the communal body determines that the person killed intentionally? Whose job is it to kill the intentional murderer after this formal determination has been made?

While the Numbers passage does not address this procedural issue, a brief passage in Deuteronomy does. Here, the Torah talks of a person who has killed intentionally and has gone on to escape to one of the cities of refuge: "And the elders of his city shall send and take him from there and give him into the hand of the *goʾēl haddām*, and he shall die"

(Deut. 19:11–12).[38] While the Numbers passage describes the separate roles of the communal body and the *go'ēl haddām* as, in essence, parallel activities that do not intersect, the Deuteronomy passage prescribes a specific interaction between the communal body and the *go'ēl haddām*. And this interaction takes place in the event that the communal body has judged the person to have murdered with intent.

While clearly these biblical passages are not working with the same kind of judicial model as we find in rabbinic sources, it is important to consider how these passages can be read to speak to the judicial context that the Rabbis envision. Transposed into such a context, the Deuteronomy passage suggests an important interaction between the court and the *go'ēl haddām*. The *go'ēl haddām* does not act solely outside of the rubric of the judicial system. Rather, it is the *go'ēl haddām* who kills the intentional murderer—not only if he encounters him outside of the rubric of the communal institutions, as is made clear in the Numbers passage, but even if the killer has been judged in court.

This understanding of the role of the *go'ēl haddām* offers one possible reading of the difficult *baraita* about the need for the court to appoint a *go'ēl haddām* if the murder victim has no redeemer. While no rabbinic source is explicit about who kills the person whom a court has judged to have murdered intentionally, this reading of the *baraita*, which takes Deut. 19:11–12 as its point of departure, fills in this gap. According to this reading of the *baraita*, it is essential for the court to appoint a *go'ēl haddām* if the murder victim has no redeemer, because it is the job of the *go'ēl haddām* to execute the person who has been convicted of murder in court.[39]

This, I think, is the most plausible reading of the difficult passage about the surrogate *go'ēl haddām*. But the notion that the *go'ēl haddām* retains a role within formal judicial criminal procedure—a role so essential that the court needs to appoint a person to fulfill this role if no such person already exists—is remarkable and marks murder yet again as utterly unique within the system of sinaitic criminal law. For murder, the social dimension of the crime and what is seen as a natural, spontaneous response to that crime is foregrounded even when the crime is brought under the purview of the judicial system. The Rabbis' portrait of the consequences of murder may tame the element of vengeance—among other ways, by circumscribing the sphere of activity of the blood redeemer—but it does not erase it. The *go'ēl haddām* is given his place as the implementer of the execution for which the court has judged the murderer to be liable. Thus, the judicial punishment of a murderer is an institutionalization of the natural, social response to this crime, but it does not replace that response.[40]

Hereg

Moving back to the form of execution assigned in rabbinic sources to the crime of murder, we can now note a correlation between the form of execution and the person to whom the role of executioner is assigned. First, we should recall the derivation of the punishment of *hereg* from the words "He shall surely be avenged" (Exod. 21:20). The punishment of *hereg* is presented, by means of this derivation, as an institutionalized form of vengeance, much as the implementation of this punishment by the *goʾēl haddām* is an institutionalization of the act of vengeance.

Further, the assignment of *hereg* to the crime of murder marks the judicial punishment of the murderer as an irregular procedure.[41] *Hereg*, as already pointed out, is uniquely assigned by the Rabbis to the act of murder. Moreover, as discussed in Chapter 2, this particular form of execution, death by sword, is the way people kill. Killing by sword is a social act; the assignment of this form of execution to the crime of murder both underscores the reciprocal nature of the punishment for a murderer and emphasizes that that punishment is in the hands of human society. Execution by sword, like the assignment of the role of executioner to the *goʾēl haddām*, suggests that the court incorporates rather than supersedes the social response to murder. While it is the court's job to regulate this response, to acquit the inadvertent homicide and to convict the intentional murderer, the judicial response to murder, at the end of the process, reverts back to the primordial notion that "he who spills the blood of a human being, by a human being shall his blood be spilled" (Gen. 9:6).

While *hereg* is an irregular procedure for the court, rabbinic sources see *hereg* as the standard way in which communal bodies other than *bēt din* perform executions. The non-Jewish government executes by sword,[42] and so does the Jewish king.[43] And, of course, execution by sword is the punishment mandated for violations of noachide law within rabbinic sources. Within the Bavli's construction of two different versions of noachide law, *hereg* is the punishment associated with the position of the Sages, whose approach I have characterized as a system of law basic to the functioning of human society.[44] Thus, *hereg* is an expression of the mandate to society, both to individuals and to social institutions, to establish order by killing those who threaten the basic order of human society.

The assignment of *hereg* as the punishment for murder within sinaitic law mirrors the irregularities in criminal procedure in the case of a murderer. And both criminal procedure and punishment reflect the nature of murder as different from other crimes within sinaitic law. The Rabbis see murder uniquely as a crime grounded in the foundations of human society—a violation of a kind of natural law[45]—rather than as a crime grounded in divine command.

Once again, we see the rabbinic construction of punishment and criminal procedure expressing the Rabbis' understanding of the nature and basis of law. But our look at the punishment for murder extends the notion of punishment as a reflection of jurisprudence, for here we have a particular punishment within a system of law reflecting the distinctive nature of a particular law. The Rabbis, then, not only recognize different possible conceptions of law—as articulated in versions of noachide law in contrast with sinaitic law—but recognize that, within a single system of law, different laws can have different foundations. Sinaitic law, though conceived of by the Rabbis as radically based in command, can include laws that have their basis in something other than command. We can read what the Rabbis understand to be the basis of these laws by analyzing rabbinic texts about punishment and criminal procedure.

"I Know, and I Do It on That Condition"

In this chapter and the chapters that preceded it, I have argued that we can read rabbinic texts about criminal procedure and punishment as expressing the rabbinic conception of law. I argued that the punishment of *ḥeneq* reflects a conception of sinaitic law as based in command and that certain general principles of criminal law in rabbinic texts highlight this conception of law and violation of law. In particular, the requirement that a prohibition and its punishment be articulated explicitly in the Torah in order for a violation of the prohibition to be punishable—the requirements of *ʿoneš* and *ʾazhārā*—underscores the notion of law as based in command. Similarly, the procedural constraints surrounding the *hatrāʾā*—the requirement that a warning be issued before the crime is committed, the necessity of including in the warning both a statement of the prohibition and a statement of the punishment, and the requirement that the would-be committer of the crime accept the warning—cohere with a view of law as based in command, for the violator of law is liable for punishment only if he acts in full awareness of the prohibition and of the consequences of disobedience.

Focusing on the Bavli passage about noachide law, I proposed that the two versions of noachide law detailed in the Bavli can be seen as forms of natural law and that both of these versions contrast with the extreme positivist view of sinaitic law suggested by rabbinic texts about criminal punishment and procedure. I suggested as well that the contrast between these versions of natural law, on the one hand, and sinaitic law, on the other, is expressed in a crucial procedural difference between these kinds of law: the absence of the requirement of *hatrāʾā* in noachide law. This absence suggests that the consequences of violating noachide law are unrelated to the existence of or the person's awareness of a prohibition and its punishment. A noachide is punished for doing the act that he did; a person who was commanded at Sinai is punished for knowingly and willfully violating God's command.

The connection between the content of law and principles of legal procedure as well as the contrast between sinaitic and noachide law was developed further in the analysis of rabbinic texts about the sinaitic prohibition against brother-sister intercourse. I demonstrated that the biblical verses about this prohibition are seen in rabbinic texts as the source for an astonishing array of principles of sinaitic criminal law, many of which relate to elements that are central to a positivist view of law. Of special note, the verses about this prohibition are seen as the source of the requirement for the Torah to explicitly articulate a prohibition and punishment in order for an act to be punishable as well as of the requirement that a person be made aware of the prohibitedness of an act and of the punishment for violation of the prohibition. Brother-sister intercourse is forbidden only under sinaitic law, not under noachide law, and I suggested that rabbinic texts see this particular act as a paradigmatic example of a behavior that is not criminal in and of itself but rather is criminal because it is prohibited by God's command. That this paradigmatic positive law is seen as the locus of principles of sinaitic law such as the requirements of *ʿoneš* and *ʾazhārā* and of *hatrāʾā* underscores the centrality of these requirements to the rabbinic conception of sinaitic law.

This chapter extends the arguments of the preceding chapters by focusing on what I have portrayed as a distinctive sinaitic law, one that straddles the boundaries that I have drawn between sinaitic and noachide law. The act of murder is seen by the Rabbis as criminal in and of itself; the murderer violates the world in which he lives, and that violation must inevitably result in the killing of the murderer by a member of the human society that he has violated.

While murder is prohibited under sinaitic law and while the crime of murder is subject to most of the same principles of criminal procedure as other violations of sinaitic law, I pointed out that subtle differences appear in rabbinic texts about criminal procedure and punishment for the murderer that suggest the retention, even within the sinaitic system, of elements of natural law in relation to this act. Thus, for example, the *hatrāʾā* in the case of murder makes reference to the consequences of murder within human society, articulated in a pre-sinaitic verse, rather than to a sinaitic statute prohibiting murder and a statement of the legal punishment for violation of that statute. And, it would appear, the judicial execution of the murderer is performed by a blood redeemer rather than by the witnesses or by court officials. The punishment for murder itself—*hereg*—points to murder as different in kind from other violations of sinaitic law and expresses the conception of murder as a violation of human society that is punished within human society. Thus, the case of murder demonstrates once again that the punishment that rabbinic texts assign to violations of law (at least the nonbiblical punishments, *hereg* and *ḥeneq*) expresses the Rabbis' understanding of the nature of law, though in this case it emerges that the claim is true not only for systems of law but even, at times, for an individual law within a system of law. And the case of murder demonstrates once again that criminal procedure reflects the Rabbis' understanding of law; and this claim too turns out to be true for an individual law as well as for a system of law.

While the case of murder, then, serves as a confirmation of the theses of the preceding chapters—that the Rabbis have a particular conception of sinaitic law, that they are aware of alternative conceptions of law, and that punishment and criminal procedure express the Rabbis' conception of the nature of law—it also leads to an important observation. In the case of murder, we have a law that the Rabbis see as fundamentally a violation of natural law, a view that is expressed in the punishment that the Rabbis assign to murder as well as in subtle procedural differences for the case of murder. Yet murder is still situated squarely within the rabbinic system of criminal punishment and procedure. Thus, for example, execution of a murderer still requires issuance and acceptance of a *hatrāʾā* before the act was committed,[46] a requirement that, as we have seen, is absent within the rabbinic construction of noachide law. The case of murder, then, shows that, even when the Rabbis acknowledge the essential wrongness of an act, they retain a fundamentally positivist view of law.

This observation highlights a question that begs to be asked in any event, but that rises to the surface most clearly now: What is the significance of the rabbinic construction of sinaitic law as positive law? Clearly, the Rabbis are not denying the possibility that an act can be wrong absent a prohibiting command. So much is clear from our analysis of the case of murder within sinaitic law itself as well as from our analysis of the Rabbis' construction of noachide law. So why do the Rabbis construct a system of criminal punishment and criminal procedure that expresses a conception of law as based in command? And what are the corollaries for the Rabbis of this conception of law?

In the coming chapters, I will return to this question. But a few thoughts are in order before moving on. I want to take as a focal point the words of the would-be committer of a crime in response to the warning that is issued at the moment that he is about to act: "I know, and I do it on that condition." In Chapter 1, I discussed the words of the acceptance of the *hatrāʾā* in relation to the *hatrāʾā* itself and in relation to the requirements of the *ʾazhārā* and *ʿoneš*. Each of these relates directly to the Rabbis' conception of law as based in command. The *ʾazhārā* and *ʿoneš* are statutory articulations of the prohibitedness of the act and of the punishment attendant on violation of the prohibition. The *hatrāʾā* is a restatement of the *ʾazhārā* and the *ʿoneš* as the law is about to be violated, calling both the prohibition and the punishment to the attention of the person who is about to violate the law. And the acceptance of the *hatrāʾā* indicates both awareness of the prohibition and acceptance of the punishment that attends violation of the prohibition.

The rules of *hatrāʾā* and the acceptance of the *hatrāʾā* are perhaps the most unrealistic element of rabbinic criminal law. These rules, along with the strict requirements of testimony, are what suggest most clearly that the rabbinic system of criminal law should not be taken as prescriptions for real-world implementation. I argued in Chapter 1, though, that the unrealistic requirements surrounding the *hatrāʾā* should not be explained exclusively as a way in which the Rabbis seek to eliminate the possibility of convicting people of capital offenses. Rather, like the punishments themselves, elements of criminal procedure described in rabbinic texts can be read as expressing fundamental ideas. The requirements of *hatrāʾā* and the acceptance of the *hatrāʾā*, I suggested, along with the construction of *ḥeneq* as the default mode of execution, express the Rabbis' view of law as based in command and of violation of law as violation of a command that results in one's handing oneself over to death.

Returning now to the words of the would-be violator of law as he is about to violate God's command, I want to look at what these words express and suggest that what these words express discloses the core ideational framework within which the Rabbis' understanding of law is situated. It is difficult for us to imagine a person stating "I know, and I do it on that condition" at the moment that the person is about to commit a crime. On the most practical level, we find it hard to imagine that anyone would be so foolish as to make a statement that will result in his conviction of a capital offense, when simply remaining silent will make it impossible to bring him to trial. But there is another reason that we might find it difficult to imagine a person stating these words, a reason that has to do with the conception of human action that these words express.

The words of the acceptance of the *hatrāʾā*—"I know, and I do it on that condition"—suggest knowledge, choice, and responsibility. The person not only knows that there is a prohibition; he understands the circumstances of what he is about to do, and he knows that those circumstances fit the parameters of the prohibition. The person chooses to do the act in full awareness of the circumstances and of the prohibition; his act is deliberate in the strongest sense of the word. And the person takes responsibility for his action; he is fully aware of the consequences of his behavior and he accepts those consequences at the moment that he engages in his act.

These words express a view of the person as a deliberate, aware, and free actor.[47] The acceptance of the *hatrā'ā*, then, in reflecting a view of law, also expresses a view of the person in relation to that view of law. This view of the person coheres well within the constructed universe of rabbinic criminal procedure and punishment and the conception of law that it reflects. Rabbinic texts ask us to imagine, say, a person about to pluck a radish from the ground on Shabbat. The person is standing in the presence of two people, and the bystanders make sure that the person is aware that the radish is, indeed, rooted in the ground, that it is Shabbat, that plucking a plant from the ground is forbidden on Shabbat, and that this act is punishable by death. The person acknowledges that he is fully aware that this act is forbidden and that he is fully aware of the consequences of his act and that he is doing it nonetheless. Immediately thereafter, he plucks the radish from the ground, thus incurring the death penalty.

But the notion of the person as a fully knowing and free actor who chooses to act in clear awareness of the consequences of his choice fits less well with our intuitions about human beings and human behavior once we move outside of the kind of legal universe that is constructed by rabbinic texts.[48] Outside of the legal domain, we often do not know clearly what to do or not to do, we rarely are fully aware of all the circumstances that would make our choice a good or a bad one, and we almost never can envision the precise consequences of our actions.

The radical portrait of purposeful human behavior that is expressed in the construction of *hatrā'ā* and acceptance of the *hatrā'ā*, I suggest, achieves two moves simultaneously. On the one hand, the requirements of *hatrā'ā* and acceptance of the *hatrā'ā* leave a wide-open arena of behaving in the world in ways that are less than fully deliberate and aware and, hence, less than fully responsible. It creates a space in which people are not fully responsible for their actions and thus not fully deserving of the possible consequences of their actions because, to some degree, they were not fully aware of what they should and should not do and of the consequences that would attend their actions.[49] Thus, the extreme requirements of *hatrā'ā* and acceptance of the *hatrā'ā* leave space for the real world in which most action takes place and suggest a partial excuse for actions that one ought not to have taken. A misdeed is, to some degree, a mistake, and, recognizing that we have done wrong, we can seek to excuse ourselves and try again.[50]

But, on the other hand, this portrait of purposeful human behavior sets out a radical vision of the human being as, at least potentially, a fully responsible, knowing, and free agent. It creates a world in which people can imagine taking full responsibility as actors and as determiners of their fate. It is the creation of this world that is the subject of the next chapter, in which we will look at another rabbinic text about punishment: the extended *sugya* at the end of bMakkot that comments on the Mishna's discussion of the punishment of *malqut.* I will analyze this text from a number of perspectives, finally suggesting that here, too, the Rabbis' conception of the nature of law is intertwined with their conception of the nature of the human being.

Chapter 5

"And Live by Them": Paul and the Rabbis

Rabbinic texts about criminal punishment and criminal procedure, I have argued, set out a vision of purposeful human behavior and a portrait of the human being as a fully responsible, knowing, and free agent. Yet the notion that a system of punishment reflects a vision of human beings as people who act freely and who determine their own fate may strike us as oddly contradictory. After all, punishment is inherently coercive; a system of punishment seeks, among other possible goals, to control people's choice of how they will act, and it forces its power against those who do not comply.

In this chapter, I will focus on a text that interweaves reflections on punishment, on law, and on the human being as a self-determining actor. I will offer an extended, multitiered analysis of this text, a famous passage in the final *sugya* of bMakkot. The end of Makkot is the end of the Talmud's discussion of criminal punishment and procedure, a topic that begins partway into tractate Sanhedrin and continues through the discussion of the punishment of flagellation in the final chapter of Makkot. Thus, the final *sugya* of bMakkot can be seen as the culmination of the Bavli's discussion of punishment.

In addressing teachings in the Mishna about the punishment of flagellation and about the consequences of violating and fulfilling the law, the passage on which I will focus addresses the nature of law and discloses core ideas that emerge from a consideration of the possible consequences of a person's violation of law. The passage as well as the *sugya* in which it is embedded, I will argue, expresses the Rabbis' view of the nature of the human being and of the potential for human creativity and human action. Thus, consideration of this passage within its literary context offers an opportunity to reflect on the relationship within rabbinic texts between punishment, the nature of law, and the nature of human freedom.

The passage on which I will focus is the statement by Rabbi Simlai that there are 613 *mitzvot,* followed by an extended homily about the progressive reduction of this great number of *mitzvot* to eleven, six, three, two, and, finally, one: *wĕṣaddiq bĕʾĕmunāto yiḥye,* "but the righteous shall live by his faith[fulness]"[1] (Hab. 2:4). This passage is famous as the source of the idea that there are 613 *mitzvot* and also because of the intriguing statement about reducing the number of *mitzvot* to a small number of behaviors or of qualities that shape behavior. The passage has drawn attention not only because of its inherent interest but also because of elements that can be seen as parallels to two different ideas that occur in the New Testament: the notion of fulfilling the law through a single commandment, in the case of the New Testament through the commandment to love your neighbor as yourself (Gal. 5:14 and Rom. 13:8–10;[2] see also James 2:8–11), and the idea that Hab. 2:4 encapsulates the path to life (Gal. 3:11 and Rom. 1:17).

In discussing this passage, I will revisit it from a variety of perspectives and within a variety of contexts. I will begin by looking at the passage as a literary unit within its literary context. It should be noted that the passage includes a brief aggadah about Rabban Gamliel and Rabbi Akiva, and I will consider this aggada as central to the passage as it appears in the Bavli. I will consider the entire passage—the homily as well as the aggada that appears within it—in relation to multiple, concentric literary contexts: the mishna in relation to which the passage appears, the *sugya* of which the passage is a part, and the chapter and tractate-pair[3] of which the *sugya* in which this passage is embedded forms the conclusion. I will also look at the passage in comparison with passages from the Pauline letters which, it turns out, not only bear the parallels noted above but have striking similarities to what I will argue is the central problem that this passage addresses as well as to verses cited in this passage and to interpretations offered and rejected in this passage. And, finally, I will look at this passage within these two contexts from the perspective of legal philosophy and psychology, especially using the lens of the writings of Herbert Morris on "shame morality" and "guilt morality."

The passage occurs in the middle of a *sugya* on the last mishna[4] of Makkot:

> All those who are liable for *kārēt* (excision) who have been flogged become exempt from their *kārēt*, as it says: "and your brother shall be dishonored [*niqle*] before your eyes"—once he receives *malqut* (flogging), he is like "your brother"—the words of Rabbi Chanania ben Gamliel.
>
> Rabbi Chanania ben Gamliel said: If one who transgresses a single transgression loses his life on account of it, one who does a single commandment—how much more so that his life will be given to him.
>
> Rabbi Shimon says: It can be learned from its place, as it says "[For whoever does any of these abominations], the souls who do shall be cut off [from the midst of their people]" (Lev. 18:29) and it says "[And you shall keep my statutes and my judgments] which a person shall do and live by them" (Lev. 18:5)—thus

anyone who sits and does not commit a transgression is given reward as one who does a *mitzva.*

Rabbi Shimon ben Rabbi says: Behold it says "Only be strong not to eat the blood, because the blood is the soul . . . [in order that it be good for you and for your children after you when you do what is straight in the eyes of God]" (Deut. 12:23–25)—If blood, by which a person's soul is repulsed, one who separates from it receives a reward, robbery and forbidden sexual relationships, which a person's soul desires and covets, one who separates from them—how much more so will he gain merit for him and for his generations and for the generations of his generations until the end of all the generations.

Rabbi Chanania ben Aqashia says: The Holy Blessed one wanted to give merit to Israel, therefore he multiplied for them Torah and *mitzvot,* as it says "God desires for the sake of his righteousness to make the Torah great and to glorify it." (Isa. 42:21)[5]

Here is an abridged version of the Bavli passage (the complete passage appears in the Appendix), which, as noted, includes a brief aggada embedded in the extended homily on the reduction of the number of *mitzvot:*[6]

Rabbi Simlai expounded: Six hundred thirteen *mitzvot* were given to Moses: three hundred sixty-five negative commandments, corresponding to the number of days in a solar year, and two hundred forty-eight positive commandments, corresponding to the number of limbs of a person. . . .

David came and reduced them to eleven, as it is written: "A psalm of David: God, who will dwell in your tent? Who will dwell in your holy mountain? One that walks in perfectness and works righteousness and speaks truth in his heart; has no slander on his tongue, has not done evil to his fellow, and has not borne disgrace against one who is close to him; in whose eyes a contemptible person is repulsive and who honors those who fear God; who swears to his detriment without retracting; his money he did not give with interest, and a bribe against the innocent he did not take. One who does these will never be moved" (Ps. 15). . . .

> When Rabban Gamliel would reach this scriptural passage he would cry. He said: "It is only the person who does *all* of these who will not be moved, thus [the person who does] *one* of them will be moved!"
>
> They [ms. Munich—Rabbi Akiva][7] said to him: "Is it written 'one who does *all* of them'?! 'One who does them' is written—even by means of *one* of them.
>
> "For if you do not say this, another scriptural verse is written: 'Do not become defiled by means of any [*kol*—which can mean 'any' or 'all'] of these' (Lev. 18:24)—there too, is it the one who touches *all* of these who is defiled, but [one who touches] *one* of them not?! Rather, no, [a person is defiled] by means of *one* of all of these—here, too, by means of *one* of all of these."

Isaiah came and reduced them to six, as it is written: "One who walks in righteousness and speaks in straightness, despises the gain of oppressions, shakes his hands from grasping bribery, closes his ear from hearing bloodshed, and shuts his eyes from seeing evil" (Isa. 33:15). . . . And it is written: "He will dwell on high" (Isa. 33:16).

Micah came and reduced them to three, as it is written: "He has told you, oh human being, what is good and what God seeks of you: only doing justice and loving kindness and walking humbly with your God" (Mic. 6:8). . . .

Isaiah came again and reduced them to two, as it says: "Thus said God: Keep justice and do righteousness" (Isa. 56:1).

Amos came and reduced them to one, as it says: "Thus said God to the house of Israel: Seek me and live" (Amos 5:4).

> Rav Nachman son of Yitzchaq challenged: I could say "seek me" by means of all of the Torah! Rather—
>
> Habakkuk came and reduced them to one, as it says: "but the righteous shall live by his faith[fulness]" (Hab. 2:4).

(bMak 23b–24a)

Before we can consider the meaning of this passage and its place within the final *sugya* of bMakkot, we must look at the final mishna of Makkot and the subject of the third chapter of mMakkot, the punishment known as *malqut,* flogging.

ʾĒlu hēn halloqin, "These Are the Ones Who Are Flogged"

The final mishna of Makkot resumes a topic that was introduced implicitly at the beginning of the chapter: the idea that those who the Torah says get *kārēt*[8] (excision) are subject to *malqut.* The first mishna of the third chapter of Makkot lists violators of law who are subject to *malqut.* The first group of laws in this list are those for which the Torah says that the violator is cut off: *k-r-t.*[9] The Gemara on that mishna (bMak 13a–b) introduces a three-way tannaitic dispute about which violators of law are subject to *malqut.* Rabbi Akiva holds the position that those who are liable for *kārēt* are subject to *malqut,* while one of the opposing positions includes even those who are liable for criminal execution as subject to *malqut,* and the other excludes those who are liable for *kārēt* from being subject to *malqut.* The Gemara points out that the mishna's list of violators of law who are subject to *malqut* corresponds to the view of Rabbi Akiva that those who are liable for *kārēt* are subject to *malqut.*

The final mishna of the tractate returns to focus on the violator of law who is subject to *malqut.* The mishna begins with the astonishing teaching of Rabbi Chanania ben Gamliel that anyone who is liable for *kārēt* becomes exempt from this punishment by means of suffering the punishment of *malqut.* This teaching goes well beyond the implication of the first mishna of the chapter, which includes those subject to *kārēt* under the rubric of those who suffer the sanction of *malqut,* but which does not make the claim that this sanction exempts them from suffering *kārēt.*

The teaching of Rabbi Chanania ben Gamliel in this final mishna invites comparison with the position of Rabbi Akiva introduced in the Gemara's discussion of the first mishna in the chapter: "Rabbi Akiva says: Those who are liable for *kārēt* are included in the category of those subject to forty lashes, for if they repent the heavenly court forgives them."[10] Rabbi Akiva's teaching can be read in two very different ways. The first has to do with a legal technicality: the principle that one cannot be liable for two punishments for one violation of law. Rabbi Akiva can be understood to be explaining that, even though one is generally not subject to two punishments, one can receive *malqut* for a sin that the Torah says results in *kārēt* because it may well happen that the person will ultimately not be subject to *kārēt*. If the person repents, then the heavenly court forgives him, and he will not suffer *kārēt*; thus, imposing *malqut* does not violate the principle of not inflicting two punishments for a single violation of law.[11]

An alternative, though not mutually exclusive,[12] reading understands Rabbi Akiva not to be explaining why the court *may* impose *malqut* in a case where one is subject to *kārēt* but, rather, why the court *should* impose *malqut* in such a case. Rabbi Akiva can be understood to be saying that the court should impose *malqut* because the person who is subject to *kārēt* has an opportunity to be absolved from that dire consequence of his actions. If the person repents, he will be exempt from *kārēt*. According to this reading, Rabbi Akiva is taking the court's imposition of *malqut* as creating an opportunity for the person to repent and thus to avoid the penalty of *kārēt*—a penalty that, without this opportunity, would be the inevitable consequence of his violation of law.[13]

Such a position might be seen as differing from the teaching of Rabbi Chanania ben Gamliel in the final mishna of Makkot, in that Rabbi Akiva seems to be focusing on the need for repentance,[14] while Rabbi Chanania ben Gamliel's teaching might suggest that *malqut* itself, even without repentance, exempts the person from *kārēt*. It is also possible that the two teachings are consistent with each other, with both sages understanding *malqut* as an opportunity for repentance, even though Rabbi Chanania ben Gamliel does not say this.[15] In fact, the idea of repentance, and even of atonement, is completely absent from the mishna's discussion of *malqut*, which focuses on legal categories of liability and exemption.[16] It is certainly possible that Rabbi Chanania ben Gamliel's position presupposes that repentance accompanies *malqut* and is essential for atonement and for exemption from *kārēt*, even though his teaching in the mishna is silent on this point.[17]

Whether or not we see Rabbi Akiva's and Rabbi Chanania ben Gamliel's teachings as reflecting identical positions, their teachings are certainly aligned in two ways. First, both sages see *kārēt* as not inevitable; the cutting off from the people that the Torah describes as the inevitable consequence of certain actions is, in the eyes of these two sages, avoidable. Second, the teachings of these two sages both mandate *malqut* for those who are subject to *kārēt*, a position that is reflected as well in the opening mishna of the third chapter of Makkot.

But, as noted, Rabbi Chanania ben Gamliel's teaching at the end of mMakkot goes beyond the implication of the mishna with which the chapter begins. If the court imposes *malqut* on those who the Torah says are subject to *kārēt*, as the first mishna suggests, and if the imposition of *malqut* exempts the sinner from *kārēt*, as Rabbi Chanania ben Gamliel teaches in the final mishna, then the Torah's mandate of *kārēt* for violations of law is effectively nullified. As Aharon Shemesh points out in his analysis of *kārēt* in rabbinic texts, the court's action in inflicting *malqut* trumps God's ability to act in response to violation of God's law, and the Rabbis' teaching about *malqut* overturns the rule of the Torah.[18]

Kārēt

What the Torah means by the sanction of *kārēt*—which appears in the Torah in verbal forms: the soul or person is cut off—is disputed both in classical sources and in modern scholarship. Interpretations range from premature death (the person's life is cut off) to death of the soul (the person is permanently cut off, even after life is over) to excommunication (the person is cut off from his people in the sense of permanent expulsion from the community), among others.[19] The passive form of the verb[20] also leaves unclear whether *kārēt* is a penalty that is imposed on the person—and, if so, whether it is a punishment imposed by God or by human beings—or whether it is the natural and inevitable consequence of the person doing a deed that removes him from inclusion in the community (in life or, perhaps, even after death).[21]

It is also not fully clear for what sins people are subject to *kārēt* in the Torah. While we tend to think of *kārēt* as a sanction for specific sins, it is possible to read the Torah as suggesting that a person is subject to *kārēt* for any purposeful violation of a prohibition.[22] A general statement about *kārēt* appears in the context of the atoning sacrifices that people bring if they violated God's law inadvertently. Following the rules for inadvertent violations of law, the Torah says this about intentional violations of law: "But the soul that does with a high hand . . . he has blasphemed the Lord, and that soul shall be cut off from the midst of its people. Because he has despised the word of the Lord and broken his command—that soul shall be surely cut off; its iniquity is in it" (Num. 15:30–31). Shemesh has argued that this passage refers to the purposeful violation of any commandment.[23] While for an inadvertent violation the person can achieve forgiveness by means of an atoning sacrifice, for a purposeful violation the person is cut off. The purposeful violation of law, in the view of the Torah, constitutes dishonor to God and the despising of God's word; the person bears his sin and is cut off from his people.

Classical rabbinic interpretation limits the scope of this passage in Numbers to the sin of idolatry, partly to address the exegetical problem posed by an apparent inconsistency between the sacrifice mandated for unintentional sin here and the sacrifice mandated for unintentional sins in Leviticus 4,[24] though perhaps also in an attempt to limit the category of those who fall under the rubric of this harsh penalty. Once this passage is read as referring only to the sin of idolatry, we are left with a conception of *kārēt* as applicable only to the sin of idolatry and to other specific sins in relation to which the Torah explicitly says that the violator will be cut off.[25] These sinners, and these only, according to rabbinic interpretation, are subject to *kārēt.*[26]

The limitation of *kārēt* to specific sins goes hand in hand with the conception of *kārēt* as a sanction that is imposed, rather than as a consequence of sin. *Kārēt,* in rabbinic texts, appears as a specific penalty that is imposed by God, parallel to but different from other penalties that are imposed by human courts in response to violations of specific laws, such as judicial execution.[27] Thus, rabbinic texts can talk of one who is liable for (or exempt from) *kārēt*—which now appears as a noun, not as a (passive) verb—just as they talk of those who are liable for or exempt from judicial punishments and penalties.

Nevertheless, the possible (and perhaps most likely) meaning of this biblical passage raises an important problem that, indeed, can be raised even without the support of any biblical passage. If the Torah requires adherence to laws, is it not the case that any violation of law puts into question the person's ability to live as a member of God's people?[28]

There is, after all, an inherent asymmetry between good and bad behavior in *any* system—whether a system of formal rules, such as a legal system, or a system of largely unarticulated norms of behavior—with a single violation of norms often weighing more heavily than a person's general adherence to the norms;[29] how much more so within a religious system in which norms are clearly articulated and in which law is an expression of God's will. A single intentional violation of law could well call into question the person's continuing to live as a member of the community. Whether one looks to the model of the biblical passage concerning *kārēt,* to other biblical passages concerning communal acceptance of norms and the consequences of breach of the commandments,[30] or to biblical passages that stress the life-giving nature of the *mitzvot*—"which a person shall do and live by them" (Lev. 18:5)[31]—one could well worry that sin will lead to the sinner's being cut off from life within God's community.[32]

Yet we all recognize that there is no one who never sins: *ki ʾēn ʾādām*

ʾăšer lōʾ yeḥĕṭāʾ (1 Kings 8:46). If sin leads to being cut off, and if everyone sins, then how can we live?

This problem is the cause of Rabban Gamliel's despair in our passage: "It is only the person who does *all of these* who will not be moved!"[33] Rabban Gamliel's despair is inevitable from within a worldview that sees living before God as predicated on fulfilling God's law and that sees every person as necessarily failing to fulfill God's law. In fact, as we will see, Paul addresses exactly this problem in his discussion of law, concluding that law simply cannot offer a way to live before God. It is important to emphasize the seriousness of this problem because, from where we stand within the history of Judaism, the cause for the despair expressed by Rabban Gamliel is not obvious. We are so familiar with the emphasis within Judaism on repentance, forgiveness, and atonement that it is hard for us to imagine crying along with Rabban Gamliel. But the point is that the emphasis on repentance and methods to achieve atonement are responses to a problem. We take the responses so much for granted that it is hard for us to see the seriousness of the problem. But the problem is there, and bMakkot gives voice to it by inserting the Rabban Gamliel anecdote into the final *sugya* of this tractate-pair that focuses so extensively on law and on the consequences of violating law.

We begin our look at the final *sugya* of bMakkot, then, by noting a link between the Rabban Gamliel anecdote and the opening of our mishna. If sin cuts one off and everyone sins, how can we hope to live before God? The mishna offers one response to that problem: "All those liable for *kārēt* who receive *malqut* are exempt from their *kārēt,* as it says: 'and your brother shall be dishonored [*niqle*] before your eyes'—"once he receives *malqut,* he is like 'your brother'—the words of Rabbi Chanania ben Gamliel."

Of course, the mishna is speaking specifically of those who are liable for *kārēt* within the rabbinic understanding of the limited scope of that sanction.[34] My focus above on the idea that *kārēt* can be seen as a cutting off that is the consequence of *any* intentional violation of God's law suggests, though, that this teaching about *kārēt* can be read as responding to more than the limited situations in which one has violated a law that the Rabbis understand to be punishable by *kārēt.* Similarly, while the Rabbis see *kārēt* as a particular punishment that is imposed by God, the range of possible significations of the Torah's passages about being cut off that I reviewed above suggests that a teaching about *kārēt* and its revocation relates to more than just the person becoming legally exempt from this divinely imposed punishment. The issue of the revocation of *kārēt* raises the question of whether the consequences of sin are inevitable or whether the person who has sinned can somehow alter the consequences of his action: Can he ever be fully reincorporated into the community from which he has been cut off? That is, the situation of *kārēt* can be seen as paradigmatic for the distancing of the sinner from God and from God's people, the inability to live before God when one violates God's life-giving commandments. And, thus, a teaching that stresses the revocable nature of *kārēt* can be read as responding not only to the problem of those who have violated one of a particular group of laws that have *kārēt* as a sanction, but to the problem of anyone who tries to live as a member of God's community, bound by God's law, but who inevitably fails to follow that law perfectly. And so, what I am suggesting is that the appearance of the anecdote about Rabban Gamliel in this *sugya* extends (or restores) the field of significance of *kārēt*. The anecdote raises (or discloses), in the context of the mishna's legal teaching about the punishment of *kārēt* and exemption from that punishment, the universal problem of the inevitability of sin and its consequences.

Revoking *Kārēt*

This mishna's teaching—"once he receives *malqut*, he is like 'your brother' "—resonates with an insight of Herbert Morris, to whose philosophy of punishment we will return below. Distinguishing between what he calls a "shame morality" and a "guilt morality"[35] (more on what he means by these terms later), Morris says: "A shame morality leads to casting outside the community, exile; a guilt morality, to suffering in order to be accepted back within. We only trouble to punish those we still care about and respect."[36] The mishna, in Morris's terms, mandates suffering in order to enable the violator of law to be accepted back within.[37]

It is important to recall, though, that the idea that everyone who is subject to *kārēt* receives *malqut* and the idea that *malqut* exempts the sinner from *kārēt* have no support from the Torah, where *kārēt* is portrayed as the inevitable consequence of sin (or at least of certain sins). This teaching is a prime example of rabbinic *derasha* overriding the clear rule of the Torah and, in parallel, of human activity (court-imposed *malqut*) subverting divine activity (*kārēt*).[38]

Indeed, consideration of this teaching propels the Gemara into a series of passages about the power of human beings to determine things through their own power of exegesis or judgment. In fact, this can be seen as the core idea knitting together all the passages in the final *sugya* of Makkot. The *sugya* begins with a discussion about R. Chanania ben Gamliel's teaching in relation to alternative positions. About a comment that the halakha is in accordance with R. Chanania ben Gamliel, Rav Yosef says: "Who went up and came and said?!" Abaye responds that there is no need for someone to have gone up to heaven to find out, because we determine the law by means of *derasha*. Note that this is not just a question of how halakha is determined in general—that is, about how human beings should act. The issue at hand goes well beyond that, because the question of whether a person becomes exempt from *kārēt* is a question about what *God* does; once we, the human court, impose *malqut*, does God still impose *kārēt* or does God not impose *kārēt*? How can we know, says Rav Yosef, since we cannot go up and ask God? Abaye insists, though, that human beings have a way of finding such things out; we do so by means of *derasha*. *Derasha* here, then, is not merely a way of finding out what the law is; it is a way of finding out what would seem to be exclusive to God's domain—or even, as Shemesh points out, of establishing, by means of law-generating exegesis, what it is that God will or will not do.[39]

The connection between the ability of human beings to find out God's position and the power of human beings to establish that position comes to the fore in the source to which Abaye refers in his response to Rav Yosef. Abaye refers to a teaching by Rabbi Yehoshua ben Levi about three things that were established by human courts and endorsed by the heavenly court. Ostensibly, Abaye cites this source to demonstrate that we are able to find out about decisions made on high. But, of course, the teaching to which Abaye refers makes a very different point: that decisions made by human beings can shape divine positions, that God, at times, confirms the decisions that human beings make or the actions that human beings take. Thus, the passage concludes with a discussion of a teaching of Rabbi Elazar about times when a heavenly voice supported the determinations of human courts.[40]

Following this passage appears the extended homily of Rabbi Simlai, in which human beings progressively reduce the number of God-given commandments. Within this passage is inserted Rabbi Akiva's rereading of a biblical passage in order to comfort the despairing Rabban Gamliel. The next passage presents the teaching of Rabbi Yose bar Chanina about harsh decrees of Moses that were overturned by later prophets. And, finally, the tractate concludes with two stories in which Rabbi Akiva employs hermeneutical rules to reinterpret not a biblical text but rather the devastating reality that confronts him and his colleagues.[41]

This brief scan of the final *sugya* of Makkot from Abaye's statement about *derasha* through the Rabbi Akiva stories discloses a critical point about this *sugya*. The issue of sin and its consequences is not just a legal issue; it is a question of whether human beings—the sinner and/or the community—can shape their destiny, can alter the course of their lives, or whether, once an action is taken, the future is determined and is out of human hands. The *sugya* conflates the ability of the Rabbis to reread Torah and the ability of human beings to shape reality. It does this in its discussion of the mishna's teaching about *malqut*, where *derasha* overrides Torah law just as the action of the court subverts God's actions. And it does this in the range of passages in the final *sugya* that I just inventoried—where exegesis and destiny go hand in hand, where prophets overturn fateful Torah teachings, where the actions and decisions of human beings gain God's assent, and where Rabbi Akiva, the master of exegesis, applies his skill to offer an interpretation of reality in which what *is*, rather than signifying the fateful judgment of what *will be*, is instead read to yield a radically hopeful vision of the future.

What I am arguing is that this final *sugya* in Makkot offers an understanding of the person: human beings and human communities determine who they are and what their future will be; they are not only creative readers of Torah but creative shapers of self and of the community's future. This is a particular view of the person, a view that is antithetical to the idea that, once a critical juncture is taken, there is no turning back. It is, in essence, a rejection of the view of human behavior and its consequences of which the irrevocable sanction of *kārēt* is paradigmatic. In making *kārēt* revocable, in suggesting that human action trumps *kārēt*, the passage rejects the notion that what the future seems to hold is ever inevitable, sealed by the past.

Transgressions and *Mitzvot*

I want to leave aside for a while the teaching about *malqut* and *kārēt* and its relation to the larger *sugya* and return to the core problem: the asymmetry between good and bad deeds, between following the law and violating the law. Rabbi Chanania ben Gamliel, the author of the teaching in the mishna about *malqut* superseding *kārēt*, goes on in the mishna to teach a teaching that is very similar to Rabbi Akiva's teaching in response to Rabban Gamliel's despair: "If one who transgresses a single transgression loses his life on account of it, one who does a single commandment—how much more so that his life will be given to him." Now, this teaching actually makes no sense. If you lose your life for transgressing a single commandment, you cannot gain your life by fulfilling a single commandment. This teaching tries to restore the symmetry between good and bad deeds, but it leads to a paradox when applied to the real lives of ordinary mortals. Since we all do some good and some bad, even perhaps mostly good and a little bad, do we merit life?

The same paradox characterizes Rabbi Akiva's teaching in response to Rabban Gamliel's expression of despair: "Is it written 'one who does *all* of them'?! 'One who does them' is written—even by means of *one* of them. For if you do not say this, another scriptural verse is written: 'Do not become defiled by means of any [*wĕkhol*] of these' (Lev. 18:24)—

there too is it the one who touches *all* of these who is defiled, but [one who touches] *one* of them not?! Rather, no, [a person is defiled] by means of *one* of these—here, too, by means of *one* of these."

A verse that appears a bit later in the same Leviticus passage that Rabbi Akiva cites makes the point even more clearly: "For whoever does *any* [*mikkol*] of these abominations, the souls who do shall be cut off from the midst of their people" (Lev. 18:29). Here, the Torah is clearly saying that even one of the sins mentioned in the passage causes the sinner to be cut off from his people. This verse, in fact, is cited in the mishna in relation to yet another verse from the same passage: "You shall keep my statutes and my judgments, which a person shall do and live by them" (Lev. 18:5). In the mishna, Rabbi Shimon cites these two verses to support the second teaching of Rabbi Chanania ben Gamliel, which, as noted, is very similar to Rabbi Akiva's argument.

The clear message of the Leviticus passage to which Rabbi Akiva refers in his response to Rabban Gamliel, and to which Rabbi Shimon refers in his argument in support of Rabbi Chanania ben Gamliel's teaching, is that violating *any* law leads one to be cut off. Rabbi Akiva's argument, then, seems to make sense as exegesis: he argues from the clear implication of the Torah about the consequences of negative actions to demonstrate that the Torah's promises, like the Torah's warnings, are contingent on a single act. But, as applied to real life, the argument makes no sense at all. If the Torah says that violating even a single law cuts one off, then it is quite impossible to say, as Rabbi Akiva does here and as Rabbi Chanania ben Gamliel does in the mishna, that doing even one good deed grants life! [42]

The problem of symmetry is even clearer in the biblical passage quoted in a parallel to the Rabban Gamliel/Rabbi Akiva anecdote in bSanhedrin:

Rav Acha son of Rabbi Chanina expounded: What is it that is written "upon the mountains he did not eat" (Ezek. 18:6)?—that he did not eat through the merit of his ancestors;
"and to the idols of the house of Israel he did not lift up his eyes"—that he did not walk with an upright (=haughty) posture;
"and his neighbor's wife he did not defile"—that he did not enter his neighbor's trade;
"and to a menstrous woman he did not come near"—that he did not benefit from the charity fund;
and it is written: "He is righteous; he shall surely live" (Ezek. 18:9).

> When Rabban Gamliel would reach this scriptural passage he would cry, and he said: "It is only one who does all of them who will live, thus by means of one of them not!"
>
> Rabbi Akiva said to him: If so, "Do not become defiled by means of any of them (Lev. 18:24)—so, too, by means of all of them, yes [he is defiled], by

means of one of them not?! Rather, by means of one of all of these, so too here, by means of one of all of these."

(bSan 81a)

Here, Rabban Gamliel cries in response to a passage from Ezekiel 18: "He walks in my statutes and keeps my judgments to do the truth; he is righteous—he shall surely live" (Ezek. 18:9). This chapter clearly is commenting on Lev. 18:5: "You shall keep my statutes and my judgments, which a person shall do and live by them," the verse that is cited by Rabbi Shimon in our mishna. Ezekiel 18 sets out opposing visions of the good and the bad person. The bad person is guilty of a variety of sins, while the righteous person commits none of them. The bad person is subject to death; the righteous person gains life.

It is noteworthy that Ezekiel 18 is cited further on in the Makkot *sugya* as one of the examples of a prophet overturning Moses' decree. While the Torah teaches that the sons are implicated in the sins of the fathers (Exod. 34:7), Ezekiel declares that each person lives or dies based only on his own actions: "the soul that sins—it shall die; the son shall not bear the iniquity of the father, and the father shall not bear the iniquity of the son; the righteousness of the righteous shall be upon him, and the wickedness of the wicked shall be upon him" (Ezek. 18:20). The juxtaposition of the Exodus and Ezekiel verses in this passage highlights the idea that I argued above links together all parts of the final *sugya* of Makkot. As in Rabbi Chanania ben Gamliel's teaching about *malqut,* the ability of the prophet to overturn the words of the Torah corresponds to a declaration of the freedom of each person to shape his own future irrespective of the past deeds of his father or even of his own past deeds.[43]

But Ezekiel 18 raises a problem as well. The chapter talks in extremes; it talks of the evil person who will die based on his own actions and the righteous person who will live based on his own actions.[44] The chapter does not describe the standard person, the person who mostly does good and desists from evil but who sometimes sins. It does describe wholly good people who become wholly evil and wholly evil people who become wholly good, thus emphasizing the possibility and power of *teshuva,* but it does not offer a vision of the ordinary person, the person whose actions combine some bad with the good.

It is this problem that animates the mishna in Makkot and the Rabban Gamliel anecdote (as it appears both in the final *sugya* of Makkot and in the parallel in bSanhedrin). Both the second teaching of Rabbi Chanania ben Gamliel in the mishna and Rabbi Akiva's response to Rabban Gamliel in the anecdote in the Gemara make an outrageous and, I have argued, paradoxical claim. The fact that a single violation causes a forfeiting of life, rather than being a cause for despair, leads to the conclusion that a single positive act (indeed, according to Rabbi Shimon's explication of Leviticus 18 in the mishna, even desisting from negative acts) merits life.

But how can one live through the performance of *mitzvot* if one forfeits life by violating even a single one of God's commands? The claim becomes sensible only if it is accompanied by a mechanism to erase or atone for violations in this life, since there is no person, no matter how righteous, who never sins. Hence, the teaching of Rabbi Chanania ben Gamliel with which the mishna begins[45] asserts that the system has within it a way to undo the effects of sin, to trump the cutting off that sin brings in its wake. The suffering caused by the human-imposed punishment of *malqut* (possibly along with the opportunity for forgiveness and atonement that it offers, as discussed above) undoes the forfeiting of life that sin brings, allowing life to be gained through the performance of *mitzvot.*

I want to return now to the classic essay by Herbert Morris that was quoted above and that will be discussed at greater length below. In "Persons and Punishments,"[46] Morris makes the claim that people have a *right* to punishment—that punishment is a *benefit* in that, among other things that Morris spells out, it enables people to be restored to their place in the community. Morris lays out what he presents as two contrasting visions of morality: what he calls a "shame morality" and a "guilt morality." In the former, misdeeds are construed as evidence of something fundamentally wrong with the person. In the latter, misdeeds are conceived of as deviations from a rule, deviations that require some sort of penalty or punishment in order to set things right.

Morris lays out a number of striking contrasts between the two models; for the moment, I will quote just two short passages:

> [S]hame links essentially to worth concepts and guilt does not. We may react to the shameful person with contempt; to the guilty we react with condemnation. With shame there is an inevitable derogation in one's status as a person; with guilt one's status is intact but one's relationship to others is affected. The shameful is not worthy of association; the guilty is still worthy but a price must be paid. Abandonment by others is the spontaneous result that follows upon knowledge of a contemptible nature; punishment is not a spontaneous response but a price paid for restoration. A shame morality leads to casting outside the community, exile; a guilt morality, to suffering in order to be accepted back within. We only trouble to punish those we still care about and respect.[47]
>
> [I]t may well be that, everything considered, we should prefer the pain and suffering of a system of punishment to a world in which we only experience shame on the doing of wrong acts, for with guilt there are relatively simply ways of ridding ourselves of the feeling we have, that is gaining forgiveness or taking the punishment, but with shame we have to bear it until we no longer are the person who has behaved in the shameful way.[48]

Earlier, I suggested that the imposition of *malqut* in place of *kārēt* is parallel to the substitution, in Morris's terms, of a guilt morality for a shame morality. Rather than being cast out of the community, as *kārēt* mandates, the person is punished and, by means of this punishment, reinstated within the community—he is, once again, "your brother." Thus, rather than violation of God's law being seen as evidence of a person's fundamental unworthiness, sin is seen as a deviation that requires imposition of a penalty in order to set things straight again.

But what happens if we take the alternative point of view? That is, what happens if we retain the notion that sin renders one fundamentally unworthy? And what if we then acknowledge that there is no person who does not sin—that sin is part of the human condition? In that case, we are thrown back into the core asymmetry between good and bad deeds. *Any* bad deed makes a person fundamentally unworthy to live before God—or demonstrates the person's fundamental unworthiness. And thus, since we all sin, we are all unworthy to live before God.

This problem is the starting point of Paul's argument about law in the two letters in which he addresses this subject most comprehensively, Galatians and Romans. I want to make it clear at the outset—though I will return to this point later on, when I locate this discussion in the context of the contemporary debate about Paul—that by "starting point" I do not mean what motivates Paul's position or what the core problem is for Paul. I am not taking a stand here about what led Paul to his views about law or about whether a problem with law was the core problem for Paul. Rather, by "starting point" I mean that Paul takes the following as a premise of much of his argument: if a person gains life ("is justified")[49] by means of obeying the law, all people will inevitably fail to gain life, since no person can avoid sinning.

I cannot analyze here all of the passages in which Paul articulates this problem and works out his solution, but I want to look at a few passages that strike me as particularly interesting in light of the Makkot passage and the verses that are interpreted there. I will begin by looking briefly at two famous passages in Galatians and move on to discuss the broad contours of the argument in Romans.

Galatians: "By the Works of the Law No Flesh Shall Be Justified"

In chapter 3 of Galatians, Paul has been arguing that justification is by faith and that Gentiles are included in God's promise to Abraham. Having supported the notion of justification by faith by quoting Gen. 15:6—"Abraham believed [*wĕhe ʾĕmin bā-*] God, and it was reckoned to him as justice [*ṣĕdāqā*]"[50] (Gal. 3:6)—Paul argues that blessing comes through faith (Gal. 3:9), while law bring a curse:

[**10**] For as many as are of the works of the law are under a curse. For it is written: Cursed is every one who does not abide in *all* things that are written in the book of the law to do them.

[**11**] But that in the law no man is justified with God is manifest, because the just man will live by faith.

[**12**] But the law is not of faith, rather he that does those things shall live by them.

[**13**] Christ redeemed us from the curse of the law, becoming a curse for us, for it is written: Cursed is every one that hangs on a tree.

* * *

[**21**] Is the law then against the promises of God? May it not be! For if a law had been given that could give life, indeed justice would have been by the law.

[**22**] But the Scripture has shut up all under sin, that the promise by the faith of Jesus Christ might be given to those who believe.

[**23**] But before the faith came, we were kept under the law, shut up to the faith that was to be revealed.

[**24**] Therefore the law was our pedagogue in Christ, that we might be justified by faith.

This passage juxtaposes Lev. 18:5—*ʾăšer yaʿăśe ʾotām hāʾādām wāḥay bāhem*—with Hab. 2:4—*wĕṣaddiq beʾĕmunāto yiḥye.* These two verses are quoted in 3:11 and 3:12 and are referred to again in 3:21 and 3:24[51] (the verses and the references to them are underlined in the passage above). These two verses, for Paul, contrast the notions of gaining life through adherence to law and of living (or being justified) by faith.

The Habakkuk verse, for Paul, offers a clear, concise statement of the point that he wants to make.[52] As we will see below, Paul uses this same verse to launch his extended argument about faith and law in Romans. The three components of the Habakkuk quotation (expressed in the three words of the clause in the Hebrew) link together the main elements that Paul uses in his extended argument: justification, faith, and life. Paul shapes his argument by linking this verse with other verses that contain some of these key elements: the Genesis verse, which includes the elements of faith and justice, and the Leviticus verse, which talks of how a person gains life.

In the section quoted above, as noted, Paul introduces the Habakkuk and Leviticus verses as offering two contrasting pathways to life. Paul must argue that the model of Lev. 18:5 cannot work; for him, the idea that one can gain life through doing the law (3:12) is incompatible with the idea that it is faith that justifies/grants life (3:11). And so, to mediate between these two verses, Paul introduces another verse, Deut. 27:26

(3:10) and offers an argument based on this verse (3:21–22). The following outlines the structure of the passage in relation to the verses that Paul cites and to the argument that he makes based on these verses (3:13–20 and 3:23 are omitted in this outline; these verses relate to the argument about the promise to and blessing of Abraham and to an argument about why the law was given if it cannot bring blessing):

3:10 Deut. 27:26 (the mediating verse)
3:11 Hab. 2:4 (the verse that expresses Paul's point)
3:12 Lev. 18:5 (the verse that offers what Paul presents as contradicting the point of Habakkuk)

3:21 argument in relation to Lev. 18:5
3:22 argument in relation to Deut. 27:26, which shows why the model of Lev. 18:5 cannot work
3:24 conclusion in relation to Hab. 2:4

In order to dismiss the possibility that one can gain life through the law, as Lev. 18:5 says, Paul states simply that all people sin (Gal. 3:22). Thus, even though doing the law could, in *theory*, grant life, in *fact*—given that all people sin—there can be no law that gives life, and thus justification cannot be by law (Gal. 3:21).

Paul introduces this point by quoting Deut. 27:26, a verse that talks of the curse that comes from disobedience to law, in stark contrast to the blessing that Paul had argued comes to Abraham and to his descendants through faith.[53] Paul quotes Deut. 27:26 in a way that differs slightly from the Masoretic text, although it conforms to the LXX. While the Masoretic text reads: *ʾārur ʾăšer loʾ yāqim ʾet divrē hattorā hazzoʾt laʿăśot ʾotām,* Paul renders: "Cursed is every one who does not abide in *all* things that are written in the book of the law to do them" (3:10). Paul's inclusion of the word "all" suggests that everyone is under a curse *because* no one fulfils all of the law.[54] The life promised in Lev. 18:5[55] depends on doing the law (*ʾăšer yaʿăśe ʾotām*), but curse devolves upon those who do not fully do the law (*laʿăśot ʾotām,* Deut. 27:26).[56] Since all people sin, law cannot bring life, and there must be an alternative to justification by law—living by faith (3:11).

This passage offers a striking parallel to the Makkot passage, both in the juxtaposition of the verses and in the exegesis offered. The Rabbi Simlai passage about the number of *mitzvot* appears in this *sugya* as a commentary on the mishna's emphasis on the power of *mitzvot* (and even of desisting from sin) to grant life. This is first articulated in Rabbi Chanania ben Gamliel's second teaching in the mishna: "If one who transgresses a single transgression loses his life on account of it, one who does a single commandment—how much more so that his life will be given to him." It is further worked out in Rabbi Shimon's exegesis of Lev. 18:5—"which a person shall do and live by them"—in relation to Lev. 18:29—"the souls who do shall be cut off from the midst of their people" (which returns to the issue of *kārēt* with which the mishna begins). And, finally, it is emphasized in Rabbi Chanania ben Aqashia's statement about God giving so many *mitzvot* in order to give merit to Israel[57] (note the use of *ṣ-d-q* in the verse cited in this final teaching, to be discussed below).

The capstone of the Rabbi Simlai passage is the citation of Hab. 2:4: *wĕṣaddiq bĕʾĕmunāto yiḥye.* What the homilist intends by saying that Habakkuk came and reduced the *mitzvot* to one is not entirely clear; some possible understandings of this statement were discussed briefly in the Preface. But it should be remembered that the homily appears in the Bavli as a reflection on the mishna about *mitzvot* granting life, and it has interpolated within it Rabbi Akiva's assurance to Rabban Gamliel that it is within a person's ability to achieve life through *mitzvot.* Thus, the homily in bMakkot, however exactly we might understand it, is surely different from the teaching of Paul, who presents Habakkuk as offering a paradigm that supersedes the notion of gaining life through obedience to law.[58] Yet, like Paul, the *sugya* juxtaposes the Habakkuk verse with Lev. 18:5, which is introduced by Rabbi Shimon in the mishna[59] and which, I have argued, encapsulates the problem that the mishna is addressing: How can we live, rather than be cut off, if we will inevitably fail to follow the law by which we are told we gain life?[60]

In the middle of the Rabbi Simlai passage, as I discussed above, Rabban Gamliel gives expression to the hopelessness of meriting life by means of good behavior. Earlier, I discussed Rabbi Akiva's difficult response which, I noted, is similar to Rabbi Shimon's argument in the mishna in that both bring a verse from Leviticus 18 about sinning in order to make a point about the ease of gaining life by doing good or by not sinning. But here I want to call attention to Rabban Gamliel's argument: "It is only the person who does *all* of these who will not be moved, thus [the person who does] *one* of them will be moved!" (In the bSan parallel, the verse in question is Ezekiel's restatement of Lev. 18:5: "He is righteous; he shall surely live," and Rabban Gamliel worries: "It is only one who does all of them *who will live,* thus by means of one of them not!")[61] Rabban Gamliel worries that the verse is saying that, in order to attain life, one has to keep *all* of the law, and that requirement is simply impossible to fulfill. Rabbi Akiva responds: "Is it written 'one who does *all* of them'?! 'One who does them' is written!" Rabban Gamliel's understanding corresponds precisely to Paul's rendering of Deut. 27:26: "Cursed is every one who does not abide in *all* things that are written in the book of the law to do them." Rabbi Akiva's response is a sharp rejection of such an interpretation: he points out that the verse does not say "all," precisely the word that Paul includes in Deuteronomy's curse of the person who does not fulfill the law.[62] Rather, Rabbi Akiva argues, much like Rabbi Chanania ben Gamliel in the mishna, doing even a single *mitzva* grants life.

And so, the Makkot passage and the Galatians passage bear striking similarities. Both address the problem of Leviticus 18: Does law grant us life, or do we inevitably fail to fulfill the law and thus are cut off from God? Both introduce Hab. 2:4 as the passage that holds the key to the extended argument. And both attempt to resolve the conflict between the promise that law grants life and the reality that no one is perfectly obedient to the law by citing a verse that relates to the question of whether one can gain life only if one obeys *all* of the law.

The arguments of the two passages, though, could not be more different. The Makkot passage (that is, the mishna along with the extended Rabbi Simlai passage) emphasizes that even partial obedience to the law grants life and that disobedience does not inevitably cut one off, since human beings have a way to bring the sinner back in. Paul, in contrast, uses the fact of imperfect obedience to dismiss the possibility that obedience to law can grant life. For him, the faith of Hab. 2:4 offers a necessary alternative to achieving life through law.

In the preceding chapter of Galatians, Paul cites another biblical passage that includes the elements of faith, justice, and life, the same elements that appear in the Habakkuk, Genesis, and Leviticus verses on which Paul builds his argument in Galatians 3. Paul works out the implication of this passage in relation to the fact of Christ's death in order to present the notion of justification by faith and to address the question of how one might live. The passage on which he builds his argument is Ps. 143:1–2 (LXX 142:1–2): "in your faithfulness [*be'ĕmunātĕkhā*] answer me in your justice [*bĕṣidqātekhā*]. And do not enter into judgment with your servant, for none living [*ḥay*] will be just [*yiṣdaq*] before you."

Here is Paul's argument in Galatians 2 (again, omitting verses that make a point not germane to the central argument):

> [**16**] But knowing that man is not justified by the works of the law, but by the faith of Jesus Christ, we too believe in Christ Jesus, that we may be justified by the faith of Christ, and not by the works of the law, because by the works of the law no flesh shall be justified.
>
> * * *
>
> [**19**] For I, through the law, died to the law, that I may live to God: with Christ I have been crucified.
>
> [**20**] And no longer do I live, but Christ lives in me. And that which I

now live in the flesh, I live in the faith of the Son of God, who loved me, and gave himself up for me.

[**21**] I do not set aside the grace of God. For if justice be by the law, then Christ died in vain.

Since the law brings a curse, as Paul will demonstrate later by quoting Deut. 27:26 (Gal. 3:10), Christ was made a curse for us and died on a tree as one accursed (Gal. 3:13). Not only did Christ die for us, but, Paul now argues, we die *in* Christ, by means of faith in him. Thus, we both achieve atonement through the death of Christ and enter, through his death, into a new life in faith, freed from the law (Gal. 2:19–21).

For Paul, then, there is no way to live in the flesh under the law. Law brings death; thus, we die in Christ. And we can achieve life only in a new existence, freed from the law; thus, we are dead to the law and reborn into a life lived by faith.

Note that in Gal. 2:16 Paul doubly recasts Ps. 143:2. First, he emphasizes that it is *by law* that no person can be justified. Second, he renders "one living" as "flesh."[63] Paul is suggesting that it is one's incarnation in flesh that makes it impossible not to do evil. He makes this claim explicitly and graphically in a variety of passages, such as Gal. 5:16–24 as well as Rom. 3:10–18, Rom. 6:13 and 6:19, and Rom. 7:23–25. His argument here is continuous with the argument that he goes on to make in Galatians 3. One *can* be justified, Paul argues, but not through law, since our fleshly existence makes it impossible not to sin (2:16). Since we cannot obey the law, law brings death (2:19; rather than the life of Lev. 18:5—see Gal. 3:21), but our death with Christ (2:19) brings us new life in faith (2:20).

Justification by the faith of Christ (2:16) is Paul's understanding of Ps. 143:1: *beʾĕmunātĕkhā ʿănēni bĕṣidqātekhā.*[64] As Paul construes this phrase, it fits perfectly with his understanding of Hab. 2:4—*wĕṣaddiq beʾĕmunāto yiḥye*—the verse around which he builds his argument in the passage from chapter 3 discussed above. The third element of the Habakkuk passage—life—appears in the following verse in Psalms, a verse that, as noted, Paul renders as saying that no one ("no flesh") can be justified through the works of the law. But, although Paul renders "living" as "flesh," he does not ignore the occurrence of the element of life in the Psalms passage. Rather, Gal. 2:19–20 is a reflection on the question of life, as Paul argues that law brings death and that one must die and come to life again in faith. This, then, is how Paul is reading the verses in Psalms: no one who lives/no flesh can achieve life through the law, since law brings death ("for none living will be just before you"); thus, it is only through faith that one can be justified ("in your faithfulness answer me in your justice")—one lives in the flesh only by dying to the law through the crucifixion of Christ.

Romans: "The Just Man Lives by Faith"

The broad contours of Paul's argument about faith and law in Romans are structured around the same verses as is his argument in Galatians. Paul introduces Hab. 2:4 early in this letter: "For the justice of God is revealed therein, from faith unto faith, as it is written: The just man lives by faith" (Rom. 1:17).[65] As in Galatians, Paul plays out the implications of this teaching in relation to other verses that include the elements of justice and faith, especially Ps. 143:1–2 and Gen. 15:6, and in relation to Lev. 18:5—*wāḥay bāhem.*

Chapter 3 of Romans is constructed around Ps. 143:1–2: "in your faithfulness answer me in your justice. And do not enter into judgment with your servant, for none living will be just before you." Paul quotes this passage in 3:20, though his argument earlier in this chapter, and even as early as chapter 1, echoes this passage as he is interpreting it.[66] Paul cites Ps. 143:2 in Romans 3 in the same way that he does in Gal. 2:16, inserting "by the works of the law" and rendering "one living" as "flesh":[67]

> [**20**] Because <u>by the works of the law no flesh shall be justified before him</u>, for through the law is the knowledge of sin.
> [**21**] But now without the law the justice of God has been made manifest, being witnessed by the law and the prophets.
> [**22**] That is <u>the justice of God, through faith of Jesus Christ</u>, to all those who believe. . . .

It should be noted that Paul is working not only with Ps. 143:2 but also with the end of the preceding verse, as I have suggested is the case with Paul's reference to justification by the faith of Christ in Gal. 2:16. Here, Paul is contrasting the justice of God (*ṣidqātĕkhā*), which comes through faith in Jesus[68] (*beʾĕmunātekhā*), with the justification of people through the works of the law, which is impossible ("for none living will be just before you").[69]

As in Galatians 3, Paul here works out his contention that justification can come only through faith and not through law by reference to human beings' sinfulness. Paul frames the central section of this chapter with another verse that includes the root *ṣ-d-q*: *ki ʾādām ʾēn ṣaddiq bāʾāreṣ ʾăšer yaʿăśe ṭov wĕloʾ yeḥĕṭāʾ* (Eccles. 7:20).[70] Paul cites the first part of the verse in 3:10 to support his claim, in the previous verse, that "all are under sin" (3:9): "As it is written: There is none just, not one." This citation launches a catena of scriptural references, beginning, in 3:11–

12, with a reference to Ps. 14:2–3, which ends with "there is none that does good, not even one." Paul, it seems, is working through the Ecclesiastes verse bit by bit: first he cites the beginning of the verse verbatim: "There is none just" (3:10); then he echoes the second part of the verse through quoting Ps. 14:3: "there is none that does good" (3:12); finally, he returns to the theme of sin that led to citation of this verse by stating that "all have sinned" (3:23), echoing the final part of the verse. Thus, the claim in 3:9 that "all are under sin" is substantiated in 3:10 through 3:23 through a breakdown of Eccles. 7:20 in reference to other biblical verses that vividly portray human beings' sinfulness. It is toward the end of this central section of the chapter that Paul quotes Ps. 143:2: "by the works of the law no flesh shall be justified before him" (3:20). The structure of the argument, the interweaving of Ps. 143:1–2 with Eccles. 7:20[71] and related verses,[72] makes it clear that Paul is saying that it is *because* of universal sinfulness that no one can be justified by the works of the law—and, thus, that human beings need the justice of God by faith.

If it is indeed the case that Paul is working through each part of Eccles. 7:20 (and it should be noted that my analysis of Paul's argument about sinfulness and the impossibility of justification through deeds does not depend on this point), it is worth pausing to note how Paul is reading this verse and what other possible way there is to read this verse. Taken as a unit, the verse can simply mean that there is no one who is completely righteous—so righteous that he *only* does good and *never* sins.[73] Paul, though, breaks the verse into three parts and applies the negative of the first part separately to each individual part. This process generates the following three statements: "There is none just" (3:10); "there is none that does good" (3:12; quoting Ps. 14:3 but, in so doing, expressing the negative form of the second part of the verse from Ecclesiastes, as if it said *ʾēn ʾăšer yaʿăśe ṭov*); "all have sinned" (3:23; taking the negative form of the negative final part of the verse, as if it said *ʾēn ʾăšer loʾ yeḥĕṭāʾ*, and expressing it as a positive assertion).

Fragmenting the verse in this way nuances each part of the verse in a far more negative way and generates a very different reading of the verse from the one that seems to emerge from reading the verse as a single unit. In this fragmented reading, no one does good, everyone sins, and thus no one is righteous. It is this reading that allows Paul to use this verse as a demonstration that "all are under sin" (3:9). The difference between the two possible readings of this verse is that, in one, the verse is saying that no one is wholly righteous (only doing good and never sinning)[74] while, in the other, the verse is saying that no one is righteous (in that no one does good and all have sinned). Thus, for Paul, all are in the power of sin.[75]

Paul's construction of this verse encapsulates what I have argued characterizes Paul's understanding of why justification cannot be through works of the law: the fact that there is no one who does *only* good and *never* sins is equivalent, for Paul, to no one doing good and everyone sinning—to being under sin. And so it is the impossibility of perfectly fulfilling the law that underpins Paul's contention that justification cannot come through the works of the law.

Chapter 4 of Romans concludes the main part of Paul's argument in this letter that justification is by faith, not by works.[76] Here, as in Galatians 3, Paul introduces Gen. 15:6—"Abraham believed God, and it was reckoned [*wayyaḥšĕvehā*] to him as justice"[77] (Rom. 4:3)—though the argument that Paul makes based on this verse is different in Romans from in Galatians. In Romans 4, Paul introduces Gen. 15:6 to set up a stark distinction between faith and works. Analyzing the word *wayyaḥšĕvehā*, Paul argues that reckoning works differently for those who work and for those who believe but do not work. The faith of the latter is reckoned for justification through God's grace (4:5), while the works of the former are reckoned in terms of debt (4:4).

As many commentators have suggested,[78] Paul is using this distinction to set up an antithesis between faith and works (similar to his antithesis between grace and works in Rom. 11:6). But Paul seems to be going further, to be setting up the impossibility of works being reckoned for justification. Paul does this by introducing another biblical passage that includes the verb "to reckon" but in which there is a shift in the object of the verb: "Blessed are they whose lawless deeds have been forgiven, and whose sins have been covered. Blessed is the one whose sin the Lord will not reckon [*yaḥšov*]" (Rom. 4:7–8, quoting Ps. 32:1–2 [LXX 31:1–2]). Paul characterizes this passage as talking about the blessedness of the person "to whom God reckons justice without works" (4:6), which follows directly from his contrast between reckoning for the person who works and reckoning for the person who has faith (4:4–5). But whereas the contrast with which Paul begins suggests that one *could* gain reward through works, the passage that Paul now introduces suggests quite the opposite: that, if God *were* to reckon works, the person would be found to be sinful. Thus, Paul is not only setting up an antithesis between faith and works; he is suggesting that a person *cannot* be justified through works.

Having established in chapters 1–4 that justification is by faith, not by works, Paul goes on in chapters 6–8 to a new theme: the link between law, sin, and death.[79] The theme of death versus life is introduced in chapter 5, to be discussed below, and is resumed in chapter 10, when Paul explicitly cites Lev. 18:5 (Rom. 10:5). But Paul clearly is working with the Leviticus passage even before he introduces it explicitly. For example, Paul declares that "we have died to sin" (6:2): "For we are buried together with him [Christ] through baptism into death, that as Christ was raised from the dead through the glory of the Father, so we also may walk in newness of life" (6:4). This is in clear contrast to walking in the commandments (*lālekhet bāhem,* Lev. 18:4) and living by them (*wāhay bāhem,* Lev. 18:5). Because of sin, failure to obey the commandments, death has come (5:12–13);[80] by dying with Christ, through faith in him,[81] we achieve life. Paul works with the idea of Lev. 18:5 also in his striking portrayal of sin itself as being dead or coming to life, in inverse relationship to the person: "For without the law sin was dead. And I lived then without the law. But when the commandment came, sin came to life. And I died. And the commandment that was for life, itself was found to be for death to me" (7:8–10).

Finally, returning to the theme of law versus faith at the end of chapter 9 and the beginning of chapter 10,[82] Paul cites Lev. 18:5 explicitly to contrast "the justice which is of the law" with "the justice which is of faith" (10:5–6). Of the former, says Paul, "Moses wrote . . . the one that shall do it shall live by it" (10:5). Paul contrasts this with "the justice of faith" into whose mouth Paul puts an astonishing inversion of Deuteronomy's promise that the commandments,[83] which one might find inaccessible, are in fact well within reach (Deut. 30:11–14):

> [**6**] "But the justice which is of faith speaks thus: Say not in your heart, Who shall ascend into heaven? That is, to bring Christ down.
> [**7**] Or who shall descend into the deep? That is, to bring up Christ from the dead.
> [**8**] But what does it say? The word is near you, in your mouth and in your heart. This is the word of faith, which we preach."

The Deuteronomy passage talks about commandment (Deut. 30:11) and concludes its denial of the commandment's inaccessibility with the assertion that it is indeed near: "in your mouth and in your heart *to do it* (Deut. 30:14)." Paul omits the opening reference to commandment and offers an interpretation of the passage in relation to Christ. He goes on to cut off the quotation just before the end. In place of the words "to do it," Paul appends an explication of *haddāvār*—the word or thing that the biblical passage asserts is near—as referring to "the word of faith."[84] Thus, what is near is not the commandment, which one must do, but rather faith. Faith, says Paul, "comes from hearing" (10:17); to achieve the justice that is of faith (that "speaks"—10:6), one must simply hear, believe (with the heart), and confess (with the mouth) (10:8–10).

It seems clear that Paul is contrasting here the *doing* of Lev. 18:5 (Rom. 10:5) with the hearing of the word of faith.[85] It is important to note that, since the Deuteronomy passage explicitly responds to the concern that the commandments are unfulfillable, Paul's inversion of this passage not only replaces the reference to the commandments with faith but, in so doing, leaves the problem to which the Deuteronomy passage is responding unanswered. That is, by wiping out Deuteronomy's answer to the concern that the commandments are not within reach, Paul subtly suggests that, indeed, the problem to which the Deuteronomy passage is responding is simply unsolvable. Doing the commandments *is* an inaccessible goal. Thus, the promise of Lev. 18:5 is not within reach, while the word of faith is near (10:8) and, thus, can bring justification (10:4,[86] 10).

The contrast between *doing* the law and *hearing* the word of faith aligns with Paul's contrast between "the justice of God" and "their own" (Rom. 10:3). "The justice of God" is what comes through faith; "their own" is the attempt to achieve justification through doing the law.[87] Not only is the first accessible (it need simply be heard) and the second out of reach, but, Paul emphasizes, the first is offered by God while the second must come from the person. The contrast in Rom. 10:3–4 between justification from God, through faith, and (the failed attempt to achieve) justification through the person's own action once again recalls Paul's interpretation of Ps. 143:1–2: "in your faithfulness answer me in your justice. And do not enter into judgment with your servant, for none living will be just before you."[88]

Hab. 2:4, then, sets out the agenda for Paul's main line of argument in Romans. After introducing this passage in chapter 1, Paul works out the relationship between its components, focusing on justification and faith in chapters 4 and 5 and on life in chapters 6 through 8, and finally bringing all three components together in the bold argument of chapter 10. As in Galatians, Paul sets Hab. 2:4 in opposition to Lev. 18:5 in relation to the question of how one gains life, mustering Ps. 143:1–2 and Gen. 15:6, with their association of faith and righteousness, to work out why life/justification must be by faith and not by works. Paul's argument, in essence, can be reduced to a demonstration that Hab. 2:4 wins out over Lev. 18:5,[89] since the life promised in the latter through obeying the law is unattainable.

The final mishna in Makkot along with the Rabbi Simlai passage, I have noted, are structured around the same two biblical verses. And, I have argued, they address the same question: Is it possible to live by law if we inevitably fall short of fully obeying the law? For Paul, the answer is a clear no. That the law is not perfectly fulfillable leads to the conclusion that law cannot bring life. In contrast, the mishna as well as the Rabbi Akiva passage argue that even partial obedience grants life. Thus, inability to perfectly fulfill the law may require punishment (or other vehicles of atonement), but it does not lead to despair of gaining life through *mitzvot.*

Justification through Deeds

I want to turn now to the final teaching in the mishna, the teaching of Rabbi Chanania ben Aqashia: "The Holy Blessed one wanted to give merit [*lĕzakkot*] to Israel, therefore he multiplied for them Torah and *mitzvot,* as it says 'God desires for the sake of his righteousness [*ṣidqo*] to make the Torah great and to glorify it' (Isa. 42:21)."[90] *Lĕzakkot* should be understood here as meaning to justify, to declare righteous.[91] Rabbi Chanania ben Aqashia is reading the verse from Isaiah as saying that God wanted to justify Israel (no doubt reading the word *ṣidqo* as *ṣaddĕqo,* "to declare righteous") and so made Torah great—that is, made a lot of law. Thus Rabbi Chanania ben Aqashia is claiming not only that performance of *mitzvot* is the path to life but that God made many *mitzvot* in order that Israel can be justified.

Paul makes the opposite claim toward the end of a rhetorically striking passage in Romans 5, the chapter that serves as the conclusion to the argument about justification through faith rather than through works and that introduces the idea of law bringing death and faith bringing life. Rather than law being an opportunity for justification—and the more law the better—Paul declares: "Now the law entered in, that trespass might abound" (Rom. 5:20). The passage is knit together by a series of comparisons and how-much-more-so arguments:

> [**15**] But not as the trespass, so also the effect of grace. For if by the trespass of one, many died, how much more the grace of God and the gift by the grace of one man, Jesus Christ, has abounded to many.
>
> [**16**] And not as the one who sinned, the gift. For judgment was from one to condemnation, but the effect of grace is from many trespasses, to justification.
>
> [**17**] For if by the trespass of one, death reigned through one, how much more those who receive abundance of grace and of the gift of justice shall reign in life through one, Jesus Christ.
>
> [**18**] Therefore, as through the trespass of one, unto all men to condemnation, so also through the just act of one, to all men to justification of life.
>
> [**19**] For as through the disobedience of one man, many were made sinners, so also through the obedience of one, many shall be made just.

[**20**] Now the law entered in, that trespass might abound. But where sin abounded, grace overflowed in abundance.
[**21**] That as sin has reigned to death, so also grace might reign through justice to eternal life, through Jesus Christ our Lord.

The final mishna in Makkot includes a similar rhetorical strategy, leading up to Rabbi Chanania ben Aqashia's teaching about the multiplicity of law providing an opportunity for justification:

Rabbi Chanania ben Gamliel said: If one who transgresses a single transgression loses his life on account of it, one who does a single commandment—how much more so that his life will be given to him. . . .

Rabbi Shimon ben Rabbi says: Behold it says "Only be strong not to eat the blood, because the blood is the soul . . . [in order that it be good for you and for your children after you when you do what is straight in the eyes of God]" (Deut. 12:23–25)—If blood, by which a person's soul is repulsed, one who separates from it receives a reward, robbery and forbidden sexual relationships, which a person's soul desires and covets, one who separates from them—how much more so will he gain merit for him and for his generations and for the generations of his generations until the end of all the generations.

As we have seen, Rabbi Chanania ben Gamliel reverses the core asymmetry between good deeds and bad deeds, claiming rather paradoxically that, if violating a single law causes one to lose life, then how much more so does fulfilling a single *mitzva* cause one to gain life. Rabbi Shimon ben Rabbi makes a rhetorically similar argument, showing that, if keeping from a forbidden thing for which one has no desire grants merit, how much more so does keeping from forbidden things that one greatly desires. These two teachings lead up to Rabbi Chanania ben Aqashia's teaching that God desired to justify Israel and that the multitude of God's laws are designed to give Israel an opportunity for justification.

The passage from Romans, rhetorically so similar, makes an opposite claim, though one that is also based on the notion that the good is greater than the bad: if the sin of one man (here, Adam, prefiguring Christ) brings death, then how much more so does the grace of God through Jesus bring "justification of life." Justification cannot come through law; rather, "the law entered in, that sin might abound." Law is an opportunity for disobedience and death; "justice unto life everlasting" must come in a different way.

It should be noted that the Rabbi Simlai passage, which begins with Rabbi Simlai's teaching about the number of *mitzvot,* comes in this *sugya* as a commentary on Rabbi Chanania ben Aqashia's teaching: "God wanted to bring merit to Israel and *therefore* multiplied for them Torah and *mitzvot.*"[92] Rabbi Simlai, in the context of this mishna, is saying: How much did God multiply *mitzvot*? How many *mitzvot* did God give Israel as an opportunity for justification? It is perhaps noteworthy that the number of positive commandments offered corresponds to the number of a person's limbs. In effect, Rabbi Simlai is saying that every limb of a person can be called upon to perform *mitzvot*, the opposite of Paul's repeated argument that one's fleshliness inevitably entraps one in sin—"But I see a different law in my members . . . captivating me by the law of sin which is in my members" (Rom. 7:23)—so that life cannot come through law.[93]

Paul and the Law

It is important to point out that the readings of Paul that I have offered stand in stark opposition to much of the "New Perspective" on Paul that has developed in the wake of Sanders's revolutionary work on Paul and contemporary Judaism.[94] Sanders has argued that it was not a problem with law that led Paul to the conclusion that justification is through faith in Christ. Indeed, for Sanders, Paul is arguing "from solution to plight"[95]—that is, it is the fact of the Christ event[96] (along with, Sanders stresses in later formulations, the need to offer salvation to the Gentiles)[97] that motivates any argument that Paul makes in relation to law versus faith.

Further, Sanders argues against the view of contemporary Judaism as a religion of works-righteousness. For Sanders, salvation within Judaism is not dependent on obedience to the law; rather, Sanders's notion of "covenantal nomism"[98] encapsulates a view of Judaism in which covenant election and salvation precede obedience to the law and in which obedience is a response to "being in" (rather than a way of "getting in") the covenant.[99]

As a corollary to this, Sanders and his followers argue that Paul is not setting justification through faith over against works of the law in the sense of attacking the attempt to achieve salvation through obedience to the law or the attempt to achieve justification through one's own effort instead of through God's free grace.[100] And, further, it is argued that no Judaism of the time expected perfect obedience to the law or was concerned with the problem of the law being unfulfillable and, accordingly, that the issue of human inability to fulfill the law is not a core problem for Paul.[101]

This is not the place for an extensive engagement with the New Perspective on Paul, but a few comments are in order in relation to the readings of passages from Galatians and Romans that I have offered. First, it is important to distinguish between what might have motivated Paul to come to the conclusions to which he came and what Paul sets out as a core premise of his argument. While I am not arguing that what actually led Paul to his conclusion about justification through faith was a problem with law,[102] I think it is clear that Paul does pose a problem with law as a core premise of his arguments in Galatians and Romans about the inadequacy of law to grant life and the necessity of faith as the path to justification.[103]

Second, I think it goes without saying that the Judaism of Paul's time, in continuity with biblical tradition, sees obedience to the law as the means of attaining life. Sanders's important arguments against a Lutheran understanding of Jewish legalism does not exclude, as Westerholm and Byrne have argued,[104] a more nuanced understanding of obedience to law as central to the Jewish conception of righteousness and salvation—in short, of *mitzvot* as life-giving.

Finally, the fact that Jews acknowledged that people fail to obey the law perfectly and the fact that rabbinic Judaism (again, in continuity with biblical traditions) emphasized that repentance and atonement are available do not mean that rabbinic Jews had no problem with the fact that we all fail to live up to the requirements of the law. The fact that rabbinic texts offer a solution does not mean that they do not see a problem. My reading of the Makkot passage shows that they *do* see a problem, and, in fact, it seems strikingly close to the problem that Paul is addressing. And Paul's solution, as I have shown, *is* to set up justification through faith over against justification through works—Hab. 2:4 over against Lev. 18:5. It is in the particular solution that Paul offers that he differs with rabbinic Judaism. Thus, the similarities that I have pointed out between the Makkot passage and passages from Galatians and Romans argue for a reevaluation of the post-Sanders perspective on Paul and the law.

* * *

Let me sum up the main points of my argument so far, before going on to address the different philosophical underpinnings of the rabbinic and Pauline texts.

I have argued that the Makkot passage (the mishna along with the Bavli *sugya*) addresses a problem posed by the core texts and core premises of Judaism and that Paul is addressing the same problem in his arguments about law and justification. I am not suggesting that any of the statements in the mishna, any of the traditions cited in the Gemara, or the Bavli *sugya* itself are responding directly to Paul's teachings, although I am not sure that such a possibility should be ruled out. It is possible that the correspondences emerge independently from reflection upon shared biblical texts and the apparent relationship between those texts, from shared hermeneutics, from shared ideas (such as that the good with which God governs the world exceeds the bad), and from shared human concerns within the shared context of a religious tradition based on law.

I have also argued that, within its broad literary context, the final mishna of Sanhedrin-Makkot and the Rabbi Simlai passage serve as a counterpoint to a tractate-pair the greater part of which addresses the severe consequences of violation of law. I have suggested that the final *sugya* asks how we ordinary people—the majority of us who do mostly good but who occasionally fail to fulfill the Torah's precepts—can hope to live. And I have suggested that Rabbi Akiva's teaching, inserted into the center of the extended homily, offers a solution to the problem, a solution that is based on law and that demands a mechanism of atonement for violations of law, such as the mechanism suggested in the mishna's teaching about *malqut.*

In addition, I have suggested that the mishna's teaching about *malqut* propels the idea that unifies all the sections of this final *sugya*: that we are masters of our own fate and that human action as well as human interpretation defines reality. It is this point to which I will now return.

"Guilt" versus "Shame": Makkot and Paul

Earlier, I presented two brief passages from Herbert Morris's classic essay on punishment, in which he argues in favor of a system of punishment, of what he calls a "guilt morality," and presents the claim that people have "a right to punishment." Morris lays out a range of benefits that he thinks are offered by a system based on guilt and punishment, rather than alternative systems, such as one based on the notion of illness and therapy or one based on shame. One of the benefits was mentioned above: a guilt morality, Morris argues, allows a person to pay the price of his misdeed and thus to be accepted back into the community. I suggested that the mishna's teaching about the person who receives the penalty of *malqut* becoming exempt from *kārēt* fits Morris's model of a guilt morality—"once he receives *malqut,* he is like 'your brother'"—that is, not only is the person exempt from a more severe punishment, but the person is reincorporated into the community.[105]

But another benefit of a guilt morality, according to Morris, is that it takes the person seriously as a moral agent. In a system of punishment, Morris argues, "The punishment associated with these primary rules paid deference to an individual's free choice by connecting punishment to a freely chosen act violative of the rules, thus giving some plausibility to the claim . . . that what a person received by way of punishment he himself had chosen."[106] A legal system that holds people accountable for their choices, for Morris, fits with a view of human beings "as capable . . . of creating, among other things, ourselves."[107] Thus, punishment is connected with a claim about human responsibility that implies both freedom of choice and self-determination.

These ideas intersect in our *sugya*, the closing passage of the tractate-pair that deals with the subject of punishment and the legal system that determines guilt and innocence and inflicts punishment on the guilty. The final teaching about punishment in mishna Sanhedrin-Makkot is the teaching of Rabbi Chanania ben Gamliel about those who are liable for *kārēt* achieving exemption through the court-imposed punishment of *malqut*. This teaching, as I discussed above, combines the notion of the possibility of the sinner's reincorporation into the community with the idea of human beings' power to shape their destiny. The latter is expressed through the substitution of a human-imposed punishment for *kārēt*, whether *kārēt* is seen as a cutting off from the people naturally consequent upon the sinner's violation of God's command or as a punishment inflicted on the sinner by God's hand. The court's action, as envisioned in the mishna, trumps what would appear to be the inevitable consequence of sin, just as the exegesis of the Rabbis overrides the law of the Torah. And, as I pointed out, this notion of human decision making and human interpretation as determining future reality, despite scriptural passages or historical reality to the contrary, is the theme that knits together all of the parts of this final *sugya*. Thus, perhaps counterintuitively, it is in connection with the idea of the legal institution of punishment that the Gemara lays out a vision of human freedom and self-determination, in Morris's words, the idea that human beings are "capable . . . of creating, among other things, ourselves."

It is noteworthy that it is Rabbi Akiva, the sage who is known as the master of exegesis and who applies his interpretive skill at the very end of our *sugya* to reenvision the future reality, who assures Rabban Gamliel that human beings are not doomed to failure, that even less than perfect people who obey God's law less than perfectly can live before God. As discussed above, this teaching, combined with the teachings of the mishna, suggests that failings can be atoned for, through the actions of human beings, and that human actions are redemptive, as performing even a single *mitzva* brings life.

I want to turn back now to Morris's paradigms of shame and guilt in order to pinpoint what I think is the fundamental difference between the Pauline and rabbinic views of human nature and human action. In addition to the elements of these paradigms discussed above, Morris offers the following:

> [In a shame morality] conduct is evaluated through comparison and contrast with a certain model identity. . . . [T]he shame morality is a scale morality not, like guilt, a threshold morality. . . . With guilt one has either done wrong or

not. . . . [W]ith shame we may focus on failure to achieve an ideal, perfection, some maximum whereas with guilt it is a minimum demand that has not been met. . . . Shame . . . may arise through failure to do the extraordinary. . . . [T]he shame response focuses on failing to be a worthy person as one conceives it, rather than on failing to meet one's obligations. . . . [P]aying the price is not alone adequate for restoration. The disposition is to be the kind of person one values. . . . [T]he steps that are appropriate to relieve shame are becoming a person that is not shameful. Shame leads to creativity; guilt to restoration.[108]

Morris's guilt morality corresponds to the view of human nature and of the human capacity for restoration in the final *sugya* of Makkot. His shame morality, to a significant degree, corresponds to the view of the human being in Paul's letters. Here, sin signifies one's failure to be a worthy person. And this failure, as Morris points out, cannot be redressed by action alone, by "paying the price." Failure to be a worthy person, Morris emphasizes, demands transformation of the self into a person who is not shameful. While guilt demands restoration, Morris argues, shame demands creativity.

But here is where the correspondence between the rabbinic and Pauline views, on the one hand, and Morris's paradigms of guilt and shame, on the other, breaks down. It is the model of Makkot that embodies the notion of creativity, of human beings' ability to transform themselves and their destiny.[109] The restoration of the person who is liable for *kārēt* is dependent on creativity, on human interpretation and human action.

In contrast with the Makkot model, Paul's letters do not suggest the possibility of human beings re-creating themselves. As scholars have noted, Paul rarely mentions repentance.[110] The possibility of repentance is predicated on a person's capacity to change—or, alternatively, on the idea that sin does not attest to a person's true nature, that a person who has sinned can return to a pre-sin state. But Paul seems to assume an alternative view of human nature, a view that is largely deterministic. For Paul, sin demonstrates human beings' essential sinfulness, and so there is no possibility of restoration short of entering into a wholly different existence predicated on different terms of salvation—terms that, it should be noted, need to be offered from the outside.[111] If sin attests to a sinful nature, then, according to Paul, human action cannot restore the person to a state of living before God.

What separates Paul from rabbinic Judaism, I have argued, is not his concern with the human propensity toward sin or the idea that human sinfulness poses a challenge to our ability to live before God. These concerns, in fact, are expressed by Rabban Gamliel in our *sugya* and, I have suggested, underlie the teachings in our mishna. The radical disjunction between Paul and rabbinic Judaism, rather, lies in the different answers offered in response to this problem. And, I am now suggesting, the different answers that are offered in the final *sugya* of Makkot and in the Pauline letters rest on different assumptions about human nature.[112] Rabbinic Judaism's embracing of law—of *mitzva*, human action, as the path to life—is intertwined with the idea of human self-determination. Paul's rejection of law is embedded in a deterministic view of human nature.[113]

The relationship between the concept of law and the idea of self-determination in rabbinic Judaism will be the subject of the next chapter. But, before moving on, we will return for a final look at the Makkot *sugya* through the lens of Morris's paradigms. And we will see that this *sugya* does not fall as neatly into the guilt model as I have presented it in contrasting it with Paul's writings.

Law and Aspiration

Morris suggests that the guilt model is characterized by the idea of a threshold, or a minimum demand, while the shame model focuses on a maximum, an ideal toward which one strives and in relation to which one can feel shame even if one merely fails to do the extraordinary. Clearly, the former correlates with a system based on law.[114] As Morris says, "With guilt, one has either done wrong or not." A system of dos and don'ts allows one to measure clearly whether one has failed to do what one must do or has done what one is forbidden to do. The latter, in contrast, relates to ideal qualities or characteristics or modes of behaving,[115] not to specific behaviors that one either must or must not do.[116]

Turning now a final time to the Makkot *sugya*, it should be noted that, while I have presented Rabban Gamliel as crying in relation to the impossibility of doing *mitzvot*, the anecdote's place within the *sugya* suggests the need for a more complex reading.[117] Rabban Gamliel is presented as crying in response to the passage from Psalm 15,[118] a passage that lists a series of general qualities—such as walking perfectly and acting justly—as well as a few specific actions that the person has desisted from doing—such as lending money with interest or taking a bribe against the innocent. The *sugya* presents Rabban Gamliel's response after a systematic interpretation of each characteristic of the righteous person described in the psalm (see the complete passage in the Appendix). Notably, the interpretations of the specific behaviors elevate the demand well beyond the simple meaning of the scriptural passage. It is not enough not to take bribes (can one be considered righteous for simply desisting from violating this prohibition?!) or not to violate the biblical prohibition of lending with interest; the Gemara offers illustrations that go beyond the requirements of the law, generating a portrait of the person who "dwells in God's tent" as a person who is righteous in the extreme.[119] It is then that the *sugya* interposes the story of Rabban Gamliel crying. Coming from the Gemara's reading of Psalm 15, we can indeed understand why Rabban Gamliel cries. The portrait offered by the psalm, along with the Gemara's elaboration of the attributes listed by the psalmist, offers a model of the righteous person that is impossible to emulate. If it is only *such* a person that "dwells in God's tent," then none of us can live before God.

The *sugya* has made a subtle and curious move. Rabbi Simlai's homily states that Moses was given 613 *mitzvot* but that a series of later figures reduced the number progressively. A reduction of the number of *mitzvot* can be seen as a reduction in the requirements that a person must fulfill.[120] But, in fact, the progressively smaller list of requirements is progressively more focused on broad attributes that the Gemara identifies with mythically righteous figures and that seem impossible to aspire to. In a sense, the extended homily moves from Morris's minimalist model (though one that has 613 requirements) to his maximalist model (though it has only a single demand), from a threshold model in which one either has or has not obeyed the rules to a model in which one can only aspire to become more and more like the ideal person but in which one will always fall short. It is when this second model is introduced that the Gemara presents Rabban Gamliel weeping with despair.

The situation is similar in the parallel passage about Rabban Gamliel crying in bSanhedrin. Ezek. 18:10–12 is first cited in this passage in relation to the Mishna's teaching about a person who violates more than one capital offense. The list of offenses in the passage is first taken literally: "a shedder of blood" means a murderer; "his neighbor's wife he defiled" means that he has committed adultery; "to the idols he has lifted up his eyes" means that he is an idolater. A person who does these things, says Ezekiel, "shall not live; all of these abominations he has done; he shall surely die" (18:13). But the Gemara soon moves on to look at the verses in Ezekiel that describe the opposite person: "upon the mountains he did not eat, and to the idols of the house of Israel he did not lift up his eyes, and his neighbor's wife he did not defile, and to a menstruating woman he did come near. . . . He is righteous; he shall surely live" (18:6, 9). Rav Acha beRabbi Chanina offers an interpretation of each of the acts that Ezekiel describes the righteous person as not doing: Rav Acha interprets "upon the mountains he did not eat" as "that he did not eat through the merit of his ancestors"; "and to the idols he has not lifted up his eyes" as "that he did not walk with an upright (=haughty) posture"; "and his neighbor's wife he did not defile" as "that he did not enter his neighbor's profession"; and "to a menstruating woman he did come near" as "that he did not benefit from the charity fund."[121]

It is at this point that the anecdote about Rabban Gamliel crying appears. And, indeed, it is really only at this point that it makes sense. It would not be at all difficult to imagine someone who keeps all the laws that the Gemara has cited from the Ezekiel passage—someone who neither murders, nor commits adultery, nor worships idols.[122] It is only after the introduction of Rav Acha's homily, which transforms the idea of the righteous person who achieves life from one who keeps the rules to one who meets lofty aspirations of personal conduct, that it makes sense for Rabban Gamliel to weep in despair.

In both the Makkot and Sanhedrin passages, then, the Gemara introduces the story of Rabban Gamliel weeping only once there has been a shift from a focus on specific laws that one must obey to a focus on broad qualities that shape a righteous person's behavior. In Morris's terms, each of these *sugyot* shifts from a guilt morality to a shame morality. Rabban Gamliel's despair over the impossibility of achieving life is expressed not in relation to the plenitude of law but in relation to a maximalist demand of righteous behavior.

More specifically, in the Makkot *sugya* the anecdote about Rabban Gamliel interrupts the flow of Rabbi Simlai's extended homily. It appears at the moment after Rabbi Simlai has made the initial shift from a focus on *mitzvot*, the element that links this homily to the mishna, to a focus on qualities of personal conduct. The anecdote hovers between the two poles of the homily: the minimalist, guilt model and the maximalist, shame model. The interpretation that I offered earlier reads the anecdote in relation to the minimalist pole; on this reading, Rabban Gamliel despairs of the possibility of fulfilling all of the *mitzvot*. But we might alternatively read the anecdote in relation to the maximalist pole; on this reading, it is in relation to the aspiration to be perfectly righteous that Rabban Gamliel sees everyone as necessarily failing.

Rabbi Akiva's response, too, can be read in relation both to the mishna's teaching about *mitzvot* and to the conclusion of Rabbi Simlai's homily. The first of these readings, which is the one that I have been working with up to now, sees Rabbi Akiva's response as entirely consistent with Rabbi Chanania ben Gamliel's teaching in the mishna about gaining life through the performance of even a single *mitzva*. The alternative reading sees Rabbi Akiva's response as anticipating the conclusion of the homily, the reduction of the *mitzvot* to a single quality. Let us take each of these readings of Rabbi Akiva's teaching in turn and see how it can fit as a response to Rabban Gamliel's despair, recalling that we have just offered two different understandings of the cause of Rabban Gamliel's despair, as well. We will begin with our initial understanding of R. Akiva's teaching.

If we read Rabban Gamliel as crying because of an acute awareness that there is no person who does not sin, then Rabbi Akiva is saying that one achieves life nonetheless through the performance of even a single *mitzva.* This is the reading that I developed earlier, a reading that situates both Rabban Gamliel and Rabbi Akiva squarely within the "guilt" pole of the *sugya.* And, as discussed earlier, it is the paradoxical nature of Rabbi Akiva's teaching and of Rabbi Chanania ben Gamliel's similar teaching in the mishna that necessitates a mechanism for undoing the consequences of sin, such as the mechanism described in the first teaching of the mishna, the teaching that *malqut* undoes the consequences of an act that could cut one off.

If, though, we understand Rabban Gamliel's crying in relation to the *sugya*'s shift to a maximalist/shame model, then we might read Rabbi Akiva as forcing a shift back to the minimalist/guilt model. It is as if Rabban Gamliel is working with a model in which no one is ever good enough, and Rabbi Akiva responds with a model in which, though you cannot be a perfect human being, you *can* be good enough. Indeed, the suggestion that even one *mitzva* is sufficient can be seen as a hyperbolic affirmation of a minimalist model in response to the extreme maximalism suggested by the portrait of the righteous person in Psalm 15, as elaborated by the Gemara.

On the other hand, as I just suggested, Rabbi Akiva's response itself can be read in relation to the conclusion of Rabbi Simlai's homily. While Rabbi Akiva's claim about "even by means of *one* of them" echoes the teaching of the mishna about one who does even *one mitzva,* it also resonates with the end of the extended homily, in which a prophet comes and reduces all the *mitzvot* to just *one* quality. If we read Rabbi Akiva's response to Rabban Gamliel as anticipating the culmination of Rabbi Simlai's homily, then Rabbi Akiva is affirming the aspirational, maximalist model toward which the homily has been moving, the model that, on our new reading, has precipitated Rabban Gamliel's despair. Nevertheless, even within this model, Rabbi Akiva is suggesting, righteousness is within reach of the human being.

The question that I am raising is: How do we read the tradition about Rabban Gamliel's weeping and Rabbi Akiva's response within the context of the *sugya* in which it appears? While Rabban Gamliel weeps in response to different biblical passages in Makkot and in Sanhedrin, in both cases he weeps in response to a passage that has just been presented in the Gemara as describing a person who aspires to the extraordinary, within a larger *sugya* that begins as a discussion about law. In Makkot, the situation is even more complicated because Rabbi Akiva's response resonates both with the minimalist teaching of the mishna about *mitzvot* and with the climax of the homily about the reduction of *mitzvot* to maximalist principles or qualities. The shift within the *sugya,* the place of the anecdote in the middle of the homily, and the echo of Rabbi Akiva's statement with both the "one" of the mishna and the "one" at the end of the homily raise intriguing questions of interpretation and call into question a reading of the *sugya* that focuses too exclusively on law as the path to living before God.

Perhaps, ultimately, we should not choose between the alternative interpretations of the cause of Rabban Gamliel's despair and the meaning of Rabbi Akiva's response that I have just laid out. Perhaps, rather, we should read the multiple resonances of this anecdote as complementing each other, highlighting the problems and promises of a religious life that is grounded in specific actions and yet that accepts the challenge of aspiring to moral perfection.

The anecdote about Rabban Gamliel weeping and Rabbi Akiva's response to his despair hovers between the "guilt" and "shame" poles of the *sugya,* between the mishna's teachings about doing *mitzvot* (along with Rabbi Simlai's teaching about the great number of *mitzvot*) and the ending of the extended homily of Rabbi Simlai about the progressive reduction of *mitzvot* and the attendant transformation to a focus on an aspirational model of religious life. I have suggested that the thrust of the final mishna and *sugya* affirms a vision in line with Morris's description of a "guilt morality," with its assertion of human responsibility, freedom, and self-determination. The Rabbi Simlai homily, though, introduces a maximalist, aspirational perspective, and the appearance of the Rabban Gamliel anecdote in the middle of the homily highlights the challenges that this perspective poses to the person who would live before God. The resonance of Rabbi Akiva's teaching with both poles of the *sugya* suggests, perhaps, that the fundamental belief in human self-determination—in *mitzva,* human action, as the path to life—makes living before God possible even within the impossibly maximalist view of the religious life.

Chapter 6
Law, Responsibility, and Transformation

The analysis that I offered in the preceding chapter of the conclusion of Mishna and Bavli Makkot dovetails with the findings of the first four chapters in pointing toward a view of the human being and of human action that is expressed in rabbinic texts about criminal procedure and punishment. At the end of Chapter 4, I reviewed the findings of the first part of this study about the conception of law and violation of law that is expressed in rabbinic texts about punishment, and I asked what the significance is of the rabbinic construction of sinaitic law as positive law. I offered some thoughts about the implications of this view of law, focusing in particular on the words of the would-be violator of law in response to the *hatrā'ā* that is issued by the bystanders: "I know, and I do it on that condition." I suggested that these words express a view of the person as a knowing, free, and fully responsible agent who chooses to act in awareness of the consequences of his action and who accepts the consequences that his action will bring.

Such a view contrasts starkly with a view of consequences as the natural results of one's actions. Further, in the the latter view, consequences are independent of human choice: whether or not one accepts the consequences, the consequences come, and they come whether one did the action upon which they were attendant in full awareness of the wrongness of the act or not.[1] It is the inevitability of consequences that is called into question in the texts about *kārēt* and *malqut* that were discussed in Chapter 5. The shift from *kārēt* to *malqut* is, among other things, a shift from punishment as a consequence of action to punishment that is imposed in response to an action. At the same time, crucially, the punishment that is imposed functions to alter the course of events; it derails what would be the inevitable result of wrongdoing: "All those who are liable for *kārēt* who have been flogged become exempt from their *kārēt*."

With *malqut*, human beings respond to human mischoice in a way that makes the clear statement that the consequences of our actions are not final; we can step in and shape the future despite the mess that we have made. Thus, the fact that *malqut* is imposed by people, replacing the specter of *kārēt* as the inevitable consequence of sin, correlates with the notion that *malqut* makes the miscreant "your brother" again, rather than the wrongdoer being consigned by his misdeed to being cut off from his people. The idea of *malqut* is, in a sense, an expression of a bond between people who refuse to allow the future to be determined by the past and who thus respond to human action with human action, action that allows each member of the community to continue to function as a member of the community.

The assumption of human volition that is embedded in rabbinic texts about criminal procedure and punishment, then, goes hand in hand with the notion of human self-determination. This view of the person as a free, knowing, responsible, and self-determining agent, I suggest, is at the core of the rabbinic portrait of criminal procedure and punishment.

This view of human volition and self-determination through action is anything but a given, though. In fact, as I pointed out at the end of Chapter 4, it accords poorly with much of our sense of how we live in the world and how things happen in the world. Or, rather, we often find ourselves living with two contradictory sets of assumptions about ourselves and our world, one in which we are free, self-determining agents, and another in which both we and what happens to us are largely determined.

The rabbinic judicial construct, then, expresses one among other possible ways of seeing the human person and human behavior. We saw a very different view of the human being in Paul's writings, and this view of the human being, I suggested, is at the heart of Paul's rejection of human action as redemptive.

Our look at noachide law, too, disclosed an alternative view of human behavior and its consequences, a view that is expressed within rabbinic texts through an alternative construction of law. In this view, human action matters greatly, but knowledge and choice—intent to commit a wrongdoing and awareness of the consequences of behavior—are not relevant. Thus, as we saw, the requirement of *hatrā'ā* is absent for noachides. Ignorance of the law or of the consequences of breach of the law does not mitigate the consequences of one's action.[2] Punishment is the inevitable consequence of one's action. Thus, the rabbinic construction of noachide law is a portrait of a world in which people do not act as fully aware, fully free agents; the strict liability of noachide law amounts to a denial of a vision of human beings as fully self-determining moral agents, since intent and knowledge are not factors in liability. Along with this, the view of punishment as the natural consequence of wrongdoing that I suggested characterizes noachide law stands in contrast to a system in which punishment is seen as imposed by the human court,[3] as freely accepted by the violator, and as anything but inevitable.[4]

It is important to recall my argument that noachide law is a form of natural law. Thus, the view of the human being as less than a fully free moral agent is linked, within this construct, to a view of the person as part of the natural order and of the natural order itself as normative and determined. The reason that violation of noachide law is not mitigated by lack of awareness—the reason that punishment does not depend on intent to violate the law—is that violation of law is nothing more than violation of the natural order, violation that inevitably leads to destruction.

The notion of law as a part of the natural order—as a part of the world as it is—that I have argued is expressed in the rabbinic construct of noachide law is, indeed, known to us from sources outside of rabbinic literature. It is just such a view that characterizes the dominant philosophical schools of the Greco-Roman world.[5] While it may seem intuitive that, within Judaism, a conception of law as based in command is inevitable—after all, laws in the Torah are almost always presented as the commands of God[6]—this, in fact, is not the case. The book of Jubilees makes it clear that even a group who accepts the notion of law as revealed by God and as expressed in God's command can accept as well a view of nature and of human history as normative. The commands of the Torah, then, are not the ultimate *source* of law; they are expressions of laws that have been embedded in the world since the beginning of time and that may have been observed *as laws* throughout pre-sinaitic history.[7] A few examples will suffice to make this point clear.

In the first week Adam was created and also the rib, his wife. And in the second week he showed her to him. And therefore the commandment was given to observe seven days for a male, but for a female twice seven days in their impurity.

And after forty days were completed for Adam in the land where he was created, we brought him into the garden of Eden so that he might work it and guard it. And on the eightieth day his wife was also brought in. And after this she entered the garden of Eden. And therefore the command was written in the heavenly tablets for one who bears, "If she bears a male, she shall remain seven days in her impurity like the first seven days. And thirty-three days she shall remain in the blood of her purity. And she shall not touch anything holy. And she shall not enter the sanctuary until she has completed those days which are in accord with (the rule for) a male (child). And that which is in accord with (the rule for) a female is two weeks—like the first two weeks—in her impurity. And sixty-six days she shall remain in the blood of her purity. And their total will be eighty days."

And when she finished those eighty days, we brought her into the garden of Eden because it is more holy than any land. And every tree which is planted in it is holy. Therefore the ordinances of these days were ordained for anyone who bears a male or female that she might not touch anything holy and she might not enter the sanctuary until these days are completed for a male or female. This is the law and the testimony which is written for Israel so that they might keep it always.

(Jubilees 3:8–14)[8]

This passage tries to make sense of a law in Leviticus that has challenged people throughout the ages who have tried to find rationales for the laws of the Torah. But it is important to note the *kind* of explanation that is offered for this law in the book of Jubilees. Jubilees locates the source of this law in the way the world came to be. If we look at the very beginnings of humankind, we can see embedded in the story of the creation of the first human beings the law that is revealed in the Torah about the periods of impurity and separation from holiness after a woman gives birth to a male or a female child.[9] There are three critical points about law in this passage; while the points overlap and may perhaps seem identical at first glance, it is important to spell them out individually in anticipation of the discussion that will follow. First, as just mentioned, law emerges from the way the world came to be. Second, the rule does not come into being later in human history (at Sinai); the rule is there from the beginning of time—there is no sense in this passage that the requirements change at some point in history. Third, the rule as law—as command—preexists Sinai: "the command was written in the heavenly tablets."

The relationship between the view of law as always there—as embedded in the way the world came to be—and the revelation to the Israelites at Sinai is addressed in the following passage, which follows the description of God's covenant with Noah and his children after the flood:

> Therefore, it is ordained and written in the heavenly tablets that they should observe the feast of Shavuot in this month, once per year, in order to renew the covenant in all (respects), year by year. And all of this feast was celebrated in heaven from the day of creation until the days of Noah, twenty-six jubilees and five weeks of years. And Noah and his children kept it for seven jubilees and one week of years until the day of the death of Noah. And from the day of the death of Noah, his sons corrupted it until the days of Abraham. . . . But Abraham alone kept it. And Isaac and Jacob and his sons kept it until your days, but in your days the children of Israel forgot it until you renewed it for them on this mountain.
>
> And you, command the children of Israel so that they might keep this feast in all of their generations as a commandment to them. One day per year in this month they shall celebrate the feast. . . . Just as it is written and engraved concerning it, observe it. This is because I have written it in the book of the first law, which I wrote for you, so that you might observe it in each of its appointed times, one day per year. And I have told you its sacrificial offering so that the children of Israel might remember them and observe them in their generations in this month one day each year.
>
> (Jubilees 6:17–22)

The law of Shavuot does not come into human practice until the time of Noah; it is not practiced by human beings since the beginning of time, since it marks the covenant that God makes with Noah and his sons after the flood. Nevertheless, the law was always there. Before Noah, the festival was observed in heaven, "from the day of creation." In this case, then, the law emerges from an event in human history—from primeval history, it should be noted, but not from the initial beginning of humankind at creation. But the law is there before the event in human history that propels it into human experience. It is as if the history of the world itself follows a primordial template, the very same template that generates law. Thus, we see here the same three points noted in relation to the passage about impurity after childbirth but in a more complex interrelationship: the existence of law from the beginning of creation, the relationship between law and the way the world comes into being, and law articulated as command before the revelation of the commandments to the Israelites at Sinai.

What, then, is the purpose of the revelation of God's commandments at Sinai? The revelation of the commandments certainly does not *make* law; law is already there—its existence is already expressed in the commandments written on the heavenly tablets and in its observance in heaven from the time of creation.[10] The revelation of the commandments does not *obligate* one to observe the law; people are obligated to observe the law from the time that it emerges into human experience with the primordial event that propels it into earthly expression. What this passage suggests, rather, is that the revelation of the commandments at Sinai is fundamentally a reminder, and it is a reminder for those who are committed to following the laws. After Noah's death, his sons corrupted the law. Abraham, though, kept the law, and so did Isaac and Jacob and Jacob's sons. Thus, the law that is a part of the coming into being of all of humankind becomes the domain of the descendants of Abraham, Isaac, and Jacob. Nevertheless, the Israelites forgot the law, and thus Moses needs to articulate it for them *again* at Sinai. The sinaitic revelation, then, is neither the origin of law nor the basis of obligation to observe the law. It is nothing more than a rearticulation of the law to those who have forgotten it yet who are committed to observing what they rediscover to have been the law all along.

It is immediately after this passage that Jubilees moves on to outline the structure of the 364-day year and to plead for the observance of this calendar:

> And on the first of the first month and on the first of the fourth month and on the first of the seventh month and on the first of the tenth month are the days of remembrance and they are the days of appointed times in the four parts of the year. They are written and inscribed for an eternal witness. And Noah ordained them for himself as feasts for eternal generations because they were a memorial for him. And on the first of the first month, he was told to make an ark. And on it the land dried up, and he opened and saw the land. And on the first of the fourth month, the mouths of the deeps of the abysses which were

beneath were shut. And on the first of the seventh month, all of the mouths of the depths of the earth were opened, and the water began to go down into them. On the first of the tenth month the heads of the mountains appeared, and Noah rejoiced. And therefore he ordained them for himself as feasts of remembrance forever, and thus they are ordained. And they set them upon the heavenly tablets. . . . Thus it is engraved and ordained on the heavenly tablets, and there is no transgressing in a single year, from year to year.

And you, command the children of Israel so that they shall guard the years in this number, three hundred and sixty-four days, and it will be a complete year. . . . But if they are transgressed, and they do not observe them according to this commandment, then they will corrupt all of their (fixed) times, and they years will be moved from within this (order), and they will transgress their ordinances. And all of the sons of Israel will forget, and they will not find the way of the years. And they will forget the new moons and (appointed) times and sabbaths. And they will set awry all of the ordinances of the years. . . .

And there will be those who will examine the moon diligently because it will corrupt the (appointed) times and it will advance from year to year ten days. Therefore, the years will come to them as they corrupt and make a day of testimony a reproach and a profane day a festival, and they will mix up everything, a holy day (as) profaned and a profane (one) for a holy day, because they will set awry the months and sabbaths and feasts and jubilees.

(Jubilees 6:23–38)

The calendar, of course, is the focal point of Jubilees and, no doubt, a central identity marker of the group from which this book emerged. The calendar is described here immediately after the passage that makes clear the relationship between the primordial law and the sinaitic revelation and between both of these and the world's coming into being. The passage about the calendar makes it clear that the natural order, the beginnings of human history, and the law that is ordained on the heavenly tablets are one and the same. Those who "examine the moon diligently" and observe a year of twelve lunar months will be corrupting time *as it is*: violating the natural order of the year, the structure of the reemergence of the world after the flood, and the ordinance in the heavenly tablets.

The argument for the observance of this calendar is an argument about law,[11] and it is the argument that we have seen in each of the passages that we have looked at. We see then that the legacy of sinaitic revelation, the possession of a foundational text in which hundreds of laws are articulated as commands given by God to Moses, does not dictate the development of a group's conception of law. What Jubilees shows us is that one need not be a pagan to believe in natural law. Jews could simultaneously hold on to sinaitic revelation and articulate a concept of law as embedded in the world as it is and as it came to be.

If this is the case, it becomes clear not only that the rabbinic view of sinaitic law as positive law is in stark contrast to the Greco-Roman tradition of natural law but that such a view is in no way necessitated by the biblical facts of sinaitic revelation and bodies of revealed commandments. In other words, the rabbinic conception of sinaitic law is one option among other possible options. I have suggested that the Rabbis demonstrate awareness of the possibility of alternative conceptions of law in their construction of noachide law, and we now see that a view of law as a kind of natural law, widespread in the Greco-Roman world, appears in Jewish writings as well as in the writings of pagan philosophers.

I suggested earlier that, within the construct of noachide law, the idea of law as embedded in nature is tied to a view of the person as part of a normative and determined natural order. This relationship between natural law and a view of the person as less than a fully free moral agent appears, in fact, in a variety of non-rabbinic and non-Jewish circles throughout the cultural world in which rabbinic Judaism took shape.[12] For example, Stoicism, the philosophical school in which a conception of natural law was fully articulated, struggled with the question of how human beings can be free and, thus, morally responsible if they are fully determined creatures.[13] The book of Jubilees, too, reflects a deterministic view of the human being. Mastema, we are told, controls a portion of humankind, with the help of cruel spirits.[14] And, of course, central Qumran texts that share the basic ideas about law and nature that are articulated in Jubilees[15] express a striking portrait of human beings as predestined to be good or evil.[16]

While I do not want to suggest that these groups shared identical worldviews, a look at the writings of these groups suggests a correlation between a deterministic view of the world, a limited view of human freedom, and a view of law as embedded in the natural world.[17] While the relationship between these views may not be a necessary one,[18] the clustering of these views in the writings of each of these groups suggests that these ideas were seen within the cultural world of the Rabbis as integrally connected to one another. And, it bears reemphasizing, the conception of law that is reflected in these writings can coexist with the biblical tradition of sinaitic revelation.

We see then that the Rabbis' view of law is one option among other options—options that not only are logically possible but that are attested within the Rabbis' cultural framework. We see, too, that the opposing view of law correlates with crucial ideas about the world and about human nature. Both these points find expression in the famous passages to which I will now turn, passages in which a Rabbi has a conversation with a pagan about law. These passages, I will argue, demonstrate the Rabbis' awareness of the distinctive nature of their view of law and, in addition, point us toward what the Rabbis see as crucial ideational corollaries of *their* view of law.

And this question the evil Turnusrufus asked Rabbi Akiva: "If your god is a lover of poor people, then why doesn't he support them?"

He said to him: "So that we may be saved from the judgment of hell."

He said to him: "On the contrary! It is this that condemns them to hell. I will give you a parable—to what is this similar? To a king of flesh and blood who became angry at his slave and confined him in prison and commanded concerning him not to feed him and not to give him drink. And a certain person went and gave him food and gave him drink. When the king hears, wouldn't he be angry at him? And you are called slaves, as it says: 'For to me are the children of Israel slaves' (Lev. 25:55)."

Rabbi Akiva said to him: "I will give you a parable, to what is this similar? To a king of flesh and blood who became angry at his son and confined him in prison and commanded concerning him not to feed him and not to give him drink. And a certain person went and gave him food and gave him drink. When the king hears, wouldn't he send him a gift? And we are called sons, as it says: 'You are children of the Lord your God' (Deut. 14:1)."[19]

He said to him: "You are called sons and you are called slaves. When you do the will of God you are called sons and when you don't do the will of God you are called slaves, and now you are not doing the will of God!"

He said to him: "Behold, it says: 'Is it not to extend your bread to the hungry, and to bring to the house the cast out poor' (Isa. 58:7)—when are there cast out poor to bring to the house? Now! And it says: 'is it not to extend your bread to the poor'!"

(bBava Batra 10a)

The evil Turnusrufus asked Rabbi Akiva: "Which works are more lovely, those of the Holy Blessed One or those of flesh and blood?"

He said to him: "Those of flesh and blood are more lovely."

The evil Turnusrufus said to him: "Behold the heaven and the earth—can you make things the likes of them?!"

Rabbi Akiva said to him: "Do not speak to me of something that is higher than humankind, over which they have no control, but of things that are found among human beings."

He said to him: "Why do you circumcise yourselves?"

He said to him: "Indeed I knew that you were going to say this to me, that is why I said at the beginning that the works of flesh and blood are more lovely than those of the Holy Blessed One.

"Bring me stalks of wheat and white bread!"

He said to him: "These are the works of the Holy Blessed One and these are the works of flesh and blood—aren't these more lovely?

"Bring me bundles of flax and garments from Beit She'an!"

He said to him: "These are the works of the Holy Blessed One and these are the works of flesh and blood—aren't these more lovely?"

Turnusrufus said to him: "Since he desires circumcision, why doesn't the person come out of his mother's womb circumcised?"

Rabbi Akiva said to him: "And why does his umbilical cord come out with him?—should his mother not cut his cord?! And why doesn't he come out circumcised?—because the Holy Blessed One gave *mitzvot* to Israel only to refine them, thus David said: 'the saying of God is refined . . .' (Ps. 18:31)."

(Tanchuma, Buber ed., *Tazria* 7)[20]

Each of these passages describes an argument that, ultimately, is an argument about law. While in each case, Turnusrufus begins with a different question—Why does God not support poor people? Are the deeds of God or people more lovely?—he soon shows his real hand. He is challenging the observance of law: Why do you give *tzedaka*? Why do you circumcise yourselves? But his opening questions spell out the basis to his challenge to the Jews' observance of their laws. Turnusrufus looks at the world around him—at the natural world and at the social order—and takes this world to reflect the normative order.[21] If poor people are poor, it must be that this is how society should be. If men are born uncircumcised, it must be that this is the way men should be. Rabbi Akiva's responses are a sharp rejection of the basic assumption of his challenger. Neither nature nor the social order is normative; neither is a reflection of God's will.[22]

It is noteworthy that, in several parallels to the passage about circumcision, another challenge appears: If God wants circumcision, why was it not commanded to Adam?[23] This question recalls the worldview of Jubilees as well as the assumptions about noachide law that we saw in Chapters 2 and 3. And this precise challenge to circumcision appears in Christian writings as well.[24] The assumption behind this question is that law derives from what is good to do or what is bad to do, what is in sync with the world as it was created and meant to be or what is in opposition to the natural order. This, I suggested, is why noachide law is presented as having been in place from the beginning of human history. This is why the Bavli can argue that brother-sister intercourse is permitted to noachides based on the narrative of the beginnings of humankind: "Once it was permitted, it was permitted." And this is why, in Jubilees, Shavuot is celebrated in heaven from the time of creation and by Noah and the patriarchs well before the revelation at Sinai. Law, in such a view, cannot punctuate history. According to the Rabbis, sinaitic law does precisely that.

Not only is law independent of nature, the social order, and history but, Rabbi Akiva argues in each of these passages, law is transformative. Law transforms the natural world, improving upon the world of nature, making things more lovely. Circumcision improves upon the natural state of the human being just as processing grain into baked goods and processing flax into garments improves upon the raw products. And law also transforms the social order, rejecting the givens of society and seeking to improve the state of those who are on the margins of society. But, in addition to transforming the world in which the doer of law is situated, law transforms the doer of law. This is most clear in the case of circumcision, where improving upon the state of nature is a fixing of the natural state of the human being himself.[25] But in the passage on circumcision, law is transformative in another sense: Rabbi Akiva emphasizes that God gives commandments in order to refine the doers of law.[26] Thus, there is a conflation between law's transformation of the world and law's transformation of the doer of law—obedience to God's commands both improves the world and improves the human being who is commanded to improve the world.

A similar point is made in the *tzedaka* passage. Here, Rabbi Akiva argues that the opportunity to support the poor is an opportunity for the salvation of the performer of this act. God, according to Rabbi Akiva, pulls back from doing what God wills—supporting the poor—because God wants to give that opportunity to human beings. Again, transforming the world is an opportunity for self-transformation. But Rabbi Akiva's argument here raises an additional, related idea: that one of the purposes of law is to invite human participation in shaping the world. God, we are left feeling after reading both passages, intentionally does not perfect the world. God leaves the world in an unfinished, unperfected state because God wants human beings to participate in creating the world. And this point brings us full circle. We cannot read what *ought to be* off of what *is*—off of nature, the social order, or history—because God has not fully realized God's will in the world as it is. God has left the world in a state that requires human participation to improve it. The world needs transformation, and law expresses God's command to human beings to transform the world and, in so doing, to transform themselves.

The expression of these ideas in the form of a debate between a Rabbi—*the* Rabbi—and a pagan makes it clear that the Rabbis saw these ideas as central to their self-definition. Whether those ideas and that self-definition took shape over time in relation to other Jewish groups, to paganism, or to Christianity—or to all of the above—I cannot say. Nor do I want to suggest that this cluster of rabbinic ideas and their expression in a conception of law and punishment emerged as a reaction to the competing ideas of other groups. What I am arguing, rather, is the following: that the cluster of ideas that characterize rabbinic texts about law and punishment stands in sharp contrast to alternative possible constructs of law and human nature; that the Rabbis are aware of alternative possible conceptions of law and their ideational corollaries; and that the Rabbis see their own view of law with its corollaries as central to their self-definition.

The rejection of natural law for the Rabbis is a rejection of a view of the world as determined, of the human being as less than fully free, of the way things should be as reflected in the ways things are. The Rabbis' rejection of natural law expresses a view of the world—the natural world and the social order—as imperfect and as demanding improvement, of human beings as being called to action, action that improves the world and that refines the person who acts. This view, for the Rabbis, takes expression in the notion of command, of God's will as expressed through a call to action. And it is this notion of law as command—and of the person as a fully autonomous actor—that takes expression in the rabbinic construction of criminal procedure and punishment.

Appendix

bMak 23b–24a

Rabbi Simlai expounded: 613 *mitzvot* were given to Moses: 365 negative commandments, corresponding to the number of days in a solar year, and 248 positive commandments, corresponding to the number of limbs of a person.

Rav Hamnuna said: What is the scriptural source? "Moses commanded us the Torah as an inheritance" (Deut. 33:4)—Torah in *gematria* equals 611. "I" and "there shall not be for you" we have heard from the Almighty.

David came and reduced them to eleven, as it is written: "A psalm of David: God, who will dwell in your tent? Who will dwell in your holy mountain? One that walks in perfectness and works righteousness and speaks truth in his heart; has no slander on his tongue, has not done evil to his fellow, and has not borne disgrace against one who is close to him; in whose eyes a contemptible person is repulsive and who honors those who fear God; who swears to his detriment without retracting; his money he did not give with interest, and a bribe against the innocent he did not take. One who does these will never be moved."

"One that walks in perfectness"—this is Abraham, as it is written: "Walk before and be perfect" (Gen. 17:1);
"works righteousness"—like Abba Chilqiyahu;
"and speaks truth in his heart"—like Rav Safra;
"has no slander on his tongue"—this is our father Jacob, as it is written: "Perhaps my father will feel me and I will be in his eyes as an errant one" (Gen. 27:12);
"has not done evil to his fellow"—that he did not infringe on his fellow's trade;
"and has not borne disgrace against one who is close to him"—this is one who brings his relatives near;
"in whose eyes a contemptible person is repulsive"—this is King Chizqiya, who dragged the bones of his father on a bier of ropes;

"and who honors those who fear God"—this is Yehoshafat, king of Judah, who, when he would see a scholar, would stand from his throne and embrace him and kiss him and call him "my teacher, my teacher, my master, my master";
"who swears to his detriment without retracting"—like Rabbi Yochanan, for Rabbi Yochanan said: "I will remain in a fast until I come to my home";
"his money he did not give with interest"—even in interest from an idolater;
"and a bribe against the innocent he did not take"—like Rabbi Yishmael son of Rabbi Yose.

It is written: "One who does these will never be moved." When Rabban Gamliel would reach this scriptural passage he would cry. He said: "It is only the person who does *all* of these who will not be moved, thus [the person who does] *one* of them will be moved!"

They (ms. Munich—Rabbi Akiva) said to him: "Is it written 'one who does *all* of them'?! 'One who does them' is written—even by means of *one* of them.

"For if you do not say this, another scriptural verse is written: 'Do not become defiled by means of any (*kol*—which can mean 'any' or 'all') of these' (Lev. 18:24)—there, too, is it the one who touches *all* of these who is defiled, but [one who touches] *one* of them not?! Rather, no, [a person is defiled] by means of *one* of all of these—here, too, by means of *one* of all of these."

Isaiah came and reduced them to six, as it is written: "One who walks in righteousness and speaks in straightness, despises the gain of oppressions, shakes his hands from grasping bribery, closes his ear from hearing bloodshed, and shuts his eyes from seeing evil" (Isa. 33:15).

"One who walks in righteousness"—this is our father Abraham, as it is written: "For I have known him that he will command [his children and his household after him and they will keep the way of God to do righteousness and justice] (Gen. 18:19);
"and speaks in straightness"—this is one who does not embarrass his friend in public;
"despises the gain of oppressions"—like Rabbi Yishmael son of Elisha;
"shakes his hands from grasping bribery"—like Rabbi Yishmael son of Rabbi Yose;
"closes his ear from hearing bloodshed"—that he did not hear a

derogatory remark about a scholar and remain silent, like Rabbi Eleazar son of Rabbi Shimon;
"and shuts his eyes from seeing evil"—in accordance with the teaching of Rabbi Chiya son of Abba, for Rabbi Chiya the son of Abba said: "This is one who does not look at women while they are standing at the wash."

And it is written: "He will dwell on high" (Isa. 33:16).

Micah came and reduced them to three, as it is written: "He has told you, oh human being, what is good and what God seeks of you: only doing justice and loving-kindness and walking humbly with your God" (Mic. 6:8).

"doing justice"—this is judgment;
"loving-kindness"—this is performing acts of kindness;
"and walking humbly"—this is taking out the dead [for burial] and bringing in the bride [for marriage]. And isn't this an a fortiori argument: If, concerning matters that it is not their way to be done in private, the Torah says "and walk humbly," in matters that it is their way to be done in private—how much more so.

Isaiah came again and reduced them to two, as it says: "Thus said God: Keep justice and do righteousness" (Isa. 56:1).

Amos came and reduced them to one, as it says: "Thus said God to the house of Israel: Seek me and live" (Amos 5:4).

Rav Nachman son of Yitzchaq challenged: I could say "seek me" by means of all of the Torah! Rather—

Habakkuk came and reduced them to one, as it says: "but the righteous shall live by his faith[fulness]" (Hab. 2:4).

Notes

Preface

1. The expression is borrowed from Clifford Geertz, *The Interpretation of Cultures* (New York: Basic Books, 1973), 5: "The concept of culture I espouse . . . is essentially a semiotic one. . . . I take culture to be those webs [of significance], and the analysis of it to be therefore . . . an interpretive one in search of meaning."

2. Geertz, *The Interpretation of Cultures,* 10.

3. Which is not to say that any given text constructs ex nihilo; see below, in relation to rabbinic traditions, and Chapter 1, in relation to biblical texts.

4. Geertz, *The Interpretation of Cultures,* 13.

5. See Sacha Stern, *Jewish Identity in Early Rabbinic Writings* (Leiden: Brill, 1994), xxvi–xxvii, for the Mishna as "a work of the present" to the Amoraim; Stern comments that "the *Amoraim* and Talmudic redactors treated Tannaitic sources, to some extent, as their own." Looking at the Bavli along with the Mishna and the *baraitot* that it cites does not, of course, suggest that the Bavli does not often present a different understanding from that reflected in these tannaitic sources.

6. See, for example, the analysis of the Bavli *sugya* on noachide law in Chapter 2.

7. For example, Avraham Walfish, "Creative Redaction and the Power of Desire: A Study of the Redaction of Tractate Qidushin: Mishna, Tosefta, and Babylonian Talmud" (Hebrew), forthcoming in *Jewish Studies, an Internet Journal* (*JSIJ*).

8. See, for example, the discussion in Chapter 1 of Rabbi's derivation of *ḥeneq.*

9. See, for example, the mention of *śērēfā* as leaving no mark in bSan 52b, discussed in Chapter 1, n. 17. Of course, a statement that originates as a thematically peripheral rhetorical move often later becomes part of the formative discourse (see Chapter 1, n. 35), much as post hoc explanatory characteristics of a case often become generative categories within halakhic discourse.

10. See Chapter 5, n. 3.

11. See the discussions and critiques of the extreme documentarian approach associated with Neusner in Daniel Boyarin, "On the Status of the Tannaitic Midrashim," *Journal of the American Oriental Society* 112 (1992), 455–65; and Christine Hayes, *Between the Babylonian and Palestinian Talmuds: Accounting for Halakhic Difference in Selected Sugyot from Tractate Avodah Zarah* (New York: Oxford University Press, 1997), 3–26.

12. See bShabbat 23a, where the commandedness of rabbinic *mitzvot* is grounded in the biblical law requiring adherence to the teachings of human authorities. Thus, acts whose normativeness derives from rabbinic decree are

preceded by the same blessing as acts whose normativeness derives from the Torah: "Blessed are you . . . who sanctified us with his commandments and commanded us to do such-and-such."

13. The following anecdote offers an example of the kind of stance that I am talking about. A Shabbat guest who had called in advance to tell me that he was a vegetarian told the following story over lunch. A few weeks before, he had been set up for a Shabbat meal in a different community. Then, too, he called his hostess in advance to tell her that he was a vegetarian. Her response: "I hope not on moral grounds!"

The hostess's comment implies the assumption that law is all-inclusive and self-sufficient. To look outside of law for a guide to behavior is not only unnecessary; it poses a challenge to law. It is as if to say that law does not include within itself everything that we need to know in order to behave properly. Thus, choosing to act in a certain way because of one's understanding of the dictates of morality is an affront to law. In addition, such a choice grants importance to one's own viewpoint, which might be seen to pose an additional challenge to the normativeness of law. Better to take a stance of moral passivity and to see law as telling us everything that we need to know about how to act.

Of course, the issue of the self-sufficiency of law is particularly acute when we are talking not about morality complementing law but about morality posing a direct challenge to law—that is, when we think that a particular law goes against the dictates of morality. On this, see below.

14. H. L. A. Hart has argued eloquently against the position that positivism entails the denial of a relationship between law and morality; see *The Concept of Law* (New York: Oxford University Press, 1997), 185–212. See also his "Positivism and the Separation of Law and Morals," *Harvard Law Review* 71 (1958), 593–629.

15. This term was made famous by Lon Fuller; see his *The Morality of Law* (New Haven, Conn.: Yale University Press, 1964).

16. For an excellent discussion, see Aharon Lichtenstein, "Does Jewish Tradition Recognize an Ethic Independent of Halakha?" in Marvin Fox, ed., *Modern Jewish Ethics: Theory and Practice* (Columbus: Ohio State University Press, 1975), 62–88.

17. Rivan (R. Yehuda ben Natan) on bMak 24a, s.v. *wĕheʿĕmidān ʿal ʾaḥat ʿeśrē*, suggests that the homily is talking about a progressive reduction in demands that one must comply with in order to be vindicated ("to be justified," in the vocabulary of Chapter 5); see the discussion in Chapter 5 of the reading of this passage that highlights the impossibility of doing all of the *mitzvot*. But clearly, that is different from an understanding of the homily as saying that the larger body of *mitzvot* is no longer obligatory.

18. For a recent example of this interpretation, see Yoel Bin-Nun, "*ʾĔmunā ʾel mul hăfākhehā,*" in M. Halbertal, D. Kurzweil, and A. Sagi, eds., *ʿAl hāʾĕmunā* (Jerusalem: Keter, 2005), 196–98.

19. See Yaakov Gartner, "*ʿIbbud bavli šel dĕrāšat rabbi śimlay ʿal taryag miṣwot,*" *Sinay* 96 (1985), 236–49, for a comparison of the homily as it appears in the Bavli with parallels in Tanchuma Buber *Shoftim* 10 and Midrash Tehillim 15. Both the Amos and Habakkuk verses appear in the parallels, but only in the Bavli does the Habakkuk verse appear as a replacement for the Amos verse that is necessitated by a problem that is raised about that verse.

20. See Bin-Nun, "*ʾĔmunā ʾel mul hăfākhehā,*" 19–97; and see below, Chapter 5, n. 1.

21. See Hart, *The Concept of Law,* 207–12; and see next note. Hart also points out the possibility of law challenging and influencing conventional morality (176–77).

22. But the point is that law can be immoral. For Hart, what is at stake in what is often called "the separation of law and morals" is the preservation "of the sense that the certification of something as legally valid is not conclusive of the question of obedience, and that, however great the aura of majesty or authority which the official system may have, its demands must in the end be submitted to a moral scrutiny. This sense, that there is something outside the official system, by reference to which in the last resort the individual must solve his problems of obedience, is surely more likely to be kept alive among those who are accustomed to think that rules of law may be iniquitous, than among those who think that nothing iniquitous can anywhere have the status of law" (Hart, *The Concept of Law,* 210).

23. Ibid., 175–78, on deliberate change as one of the distinguishing features of law, as opposed to morality.

24. See Lichtenstein's disagreement with K. Kahana's claim that "in Jewish civil law there is no separation of law and morals and . . . there is no distinction between what the law *is* and what the law *ought* to be." ("Does Jewish Tradition Recognize an Ethic Independent of Halakha?," 68; it should be noted that Lichtenstein supports the idea of ethics as a "complement" to halakha but not as functioning to "override" halakha.) And compare what Hart describes as one of the "great battle-cries of legal positivism," J. C. Gray's comment: "The law of a State is not an ideal but something which actually exists. . . . it is not that which ought to be, but that which is" (Hart, *The Concept of Law,* 207).

Chapter 1

1. For some approaches to critical questions related to *mitot bēt din*, see, in addition to the sources that will be cited below, Victor Aptowitzer, "Observations of the Criminal Law of the Jews," *Jewish Quarterly Review,* n.s., 15 (1924–25), 55–118; Ephraim E. Urbach, "Courts of Twenty-Three and Laws of Judicial Execution" (Hebrew), in *Hahălākhā: Mĕqorotehā wĕhitpatḥutah* (Jerusalem: Yad Latalmud, 1984), 47–53; and the review of the secondary literature and approaches in Yair Lorberbaum, *Ṣelem ʾĕlohim* (Tel Aviv: Schocken, 2004), 173–75 and nn. 10–11. For one approach to crucifixion in relation to *mitot bēt din,* see David Halperin, "Crucifixion, the Nahum Pesher, and the Rabbinic Penalty of Strangulation," *Journal of Jewish Studies* 32 (1981), 32–46; and the discussion in Lorberbaum, *Ṣelem ʾĕlohim,* 200–203. See also the discussions of "hanging" in Joseph Baumgarten, "Does TLH in the Temple Scroll Refer to Crucifixion?," *Journal of Biblical Literature* 91 (1972), 472–81; Joseph Heinemann, "Early Halakha in the Palestinian Targum," *Journal of Jewish Studies* 24 (1974), 114–22; and Yigal Yadin, *Mĕgillat hammiqdāš* (Jerusalem: Israel Exploration Society, 1977), 1:285–89. See the censored aggada in bSan 43a on the execution of Jesus and the discussion by Jacob Z. Lauterbach, *Rabbinic Essays* (Cincinnati: Hebrew Union College Press, 1951), 490–500.

2. See the reports of *śĕrēfā* as actual immolation of the body in mSan 7:2, tSan 9:11, bSan 52b, and ySan 7:2/24b. Urbach, "Courts of Twenty-Three," assumes that there were simultaneous divergent practices in different local courts. Others take these reports to reflect actual practice and the rabbinic description of

the *ʾarbaʿ mitot* to represent a revision of judicial execution as actually practiced. See Chanokh Albeck, *Sēder nĕziqin* (Jerusalem: Dvir, 1953), 448; and Lorberbaum, *Ṣelem ʾĕlohim*, 179–84. Rabbinic sources talk of capital trials ceasing to take place forty years before the destruction of the Temple; see ySan 1:1/18a and 7:2/24b, bSan 41a, bShab 15a.

3. The impractical nature of capital punishment is less extreme in the Mishna than in other rabbinic texts. At least two requirements that are elaborated in other rabbinic texts would seem to make conviction impossible: the very strict requirements of *hatrāʾā* (warning), including specification of the penalty by the person delivering the warning, explicit acceptance of the warning on the part of the one about to commit the crime, and the requirement that *hatrāʾā* take place immediately preceding commission of the crime (see, for example, tSan 11:2–3, bSan 8b, 40b, 72b, 81b, ySan 5:1/22c–d; and see the discussion below); and the requirement that witnesses see the actual crime in an indisputable manner (bMak 7a—to the point of needing to have verified, for example, that there was no fatal wound previously extant in the spot where a murder victim was stabbed; see also *Mekhilta deRabbi Yishmael, Kaspa* 20 (ed. Horowitz-Rabin, 327), tSan 8:3, ySan 4:11/22b, bSan 36b). While *hatrāʾā* and clear firsthand testimony are required by the Mishna (mSan 4:5, 5:1), these requirements are not elaborated in the Mishna in a way that would make them impossible to fulfill.

4. mMak 1:10.

5. See, for example, tSan 12:6–7, mSan 9:5, and bSan 81b on punishing a person who has committed a capital offense but who cannot be prosecuted because of the strict requirements of criminal procedure. See bSan 46a for a broad mandate for courts to punish acts that are not ordinarily punishable as violations of Torah law, and compare yHag 2:2/78a, which mentions also deviations from standard criminal procedure.

6. The famous eleventh homily in *Derashot HaRan* emphasizes the impossibility of maintaining social order through the exclusive means of judicial procedure as described in rabbinic sources. The Ran distinguishes between "true justice" and social need, the latter requiring a more extensive power to punish and mandating a separate jurisdiction (that of the *melekh*, as opposed to that of *šofĕṭim*). Whether the Ran sees the political leader as having only extrajudicial emergency powers or, rather, whether he envisions two distinct systems—each with its own goal and its own procedures and penalties—is debated. See, for example, Gerald Blidstein, "On Political Structures: Four Medieval Comments," *Jewish Journal of Sociology* 22 (1980), 47–58; and Warren Z. Harvey, "Liberal Democratic Themes in Nissim of Gerona," in Isadore Twersky and Jay Harris, eds., *Studies in Medieval Jewish History and Literature* (Cambridge, Mass.: Harvard University Press, 2000), 3:197–211. See also the comments of the Rashba cited in Blidstein, "On Political Structure," 53 and nn. 22 and 23.

The power of the king/government to impose punishment is mentioned in rabbinic sources: see tSan 9:10 (see Lorberbaum, *Ṣelem ʾĕlohim*, 215 n. 174), ySan 7:1/24b. Maimonides codifies both the power of the king to punish and the extrasystemic power of the courts to impose sanctions; see *Hilkhot Melakhim* 3:8–10, *Hilkhot Sanhedrin* 18:4–5 and 24:4–10, *Hilkhot Rotzeach* 2:4–5. Maimonides seems to distinguish between three types of power to punish outside of the rubric of standard *dinē nĕfāšot*: the power of the king (which he can impose to protect his own honor or for the benefit of social order; the latter seems limited largely to responding to the crime of murder, though see *Hilkhot Sanhedrin* 18:6 [see the discussion of murder in Chapter 4, and see the review of possible understandings of Maimonides' position in J. David Bleich, "Capital Punishment in the Noachide Code," in *Contemporary Halakhic Problems* (New York: Ktav, 1982), 2:341–67 n. 11]); extrajudicial emergency powers of the court (*horāʾat šāʿā*—to be applied only when contemporary circumstances necessitate emergency action); and regular powers of the court that extend beyond the rules of *dinē nĕfāšot* to allow for broad-ranging penalties for lawbreakers (so that courts may uphold adherence to the law among the general population).

7. See Gerald Blidstein, "Capital Punishment: The Classic Jewish Discussion," *Judaism* 14 (1965), 159–71. Blidstein elegantly states the case for a theoretical rather than a practical understanding of the rabbinic portrait of capital punishment: "Indeed, Jewish law abolished capital punishment in fact not by denying its conceptual moral validity but rather by allowing it *only* this conceptual validity" (164). See also the discussion in Aaron Kirschenbaum, *The Criminal Confession in Jewish Law* (Hebrew) (Jerusalem: Magnes, 2005), 419–41; and Arnold Enker, *"Yĕsodot bĕmišpāṭ happĕlili hāʿivri," Mišpāṭim* 24 (1994), 177–206.

8. For some classic modern discussions of punishments and surveys of basic approaches to punishment and its goals, see H. L. A. Hart, *Punishment and Responsibility: Essays in the Philosophy of Law* (New York: Oxford University Press, 1968); Herbert Morris, *On Guilt and Innocence: Essays in Legal Philosophy and Moral Psychology* (Berkeley: University of California Press, 1976); Jeffrie G. Murphy, *Punishment and Rehabilitation*, 3rd ed. (Belmont, Calif.: Wadsworth, 1995); and Michael Davis, "Punishment Theory: Making Sense of What We Know About Punishment," *NYSBA Law Studies* 22 (1998), 3–10.

9. The idea that "talmudic penology" reflects an ideal unconstrained by practical realities but that it is constrained to some degree by biblical sources is discussed by Haim H. Cohn, "The Penology of the Talmud," *Israel Law Review* 5 (1970), 53–74.

10. See, for example, Lorberbaum, *Ṣelem ʾĕlohim*, 178–84 (on *śĕrēfā*) and 234–40 (on *sĕqilā*); Albeck, 448 (on *śĕrēfā*) and 457 (on *sĕqilā*). See Moshe Halbertal, *Interpretive Revolutions in the Making* (Hebrew) (Jerusalem: Magnes, 1997), 152–53. Whether sources such as Jubilees, Philo, and Josephus represent actual practice in the period of their authorship or in the recent past or, rather, their authors' understandings/interpretations of the biblical text is debatable. In any event, as Halbertal notes, these sources minimally show that the rabbinic descriptions of execution are interpretive choices among other possible interpretations of the biblical material.

11. A third Israeli scholar, Peretz Segal, has also interpreted the rabbinic system of *ʾarbaʿ mitot* as shaped by a fundamental idea. Segal sees each of these *mitot* as interpreted within rabbinic sources to simulate divinely imposed death, *mitā biydē šāmayim*, with the notion of atonement, such as that achieved through sacrifice, being central to execution. See *"Ḥiyyuv biydē šāmayim": Ḥiyyuvē mitot bēt din wĕḥiyyuvē mitā lĕšāmayim"* (Ph.D. diss., Hebrew University, 186) and his abstract published as "Postbiblical Jewish Criminal Law and Theology," *Jewish Law Annual* 9 (1991), 107–21.

12. Halbertal, *Interpretive Revolutions*, 145–67. The notion that the goal of the design of some or all of the modes of execution was to minimize damage to the body was already suggested over a century ago by Nechemia Brüll, "Miscellaneous Notes" (Hebrew), *Bēt talmud* 4 (1885), 7–11; and again some years later by A. Büchler, but with a different rationale—to preserve the body intact for resurrection; see Lorberbaum, *Ṣelem ʾĕlohim*, 173.

13. Lorberbaum, *Ṣelem ʾĕlohim*, 170–249; for Lorberbaum's characterization of his understanding of *ṣelem ʾĕlohim*, see especially 18–19.

14. The passage in which this phrase appears will be quoted and discussed below.

15. It should be noted that *hereg*—execution by sword—also seems to be a rabbinic innovation as a form of *judicial* execution administered by the *bēt din*, though killing by sword does appear in the Torah in relation to the citizens of *ʿir hanniddaḥat* (Deut. 13:16). (Note that it is only for this case and for murder that rabbinic sources mandate *hereg*; see the discussion of *hereg* as the punishment for murder in Chapter 4.) A number of scholars have pointed out that the Torah's command to kill the residents of *ʿir hanniddaḥat* seems less a case of judicial execution than a kind of war; compare the killing by sword that takes place after the sin of the Golden Calf (Exod. 32:27). See Albeck, *Sēder nĕziqin*, 453; Moshe Weinfeld, *Deuteronomy and the Deuteronomic School* (Oxford: Oxford University Press, 1972), 91–100; Halbertal, *Interpretive Revolutions*, 123–44; Lorberbaum, *Ṣelem ʾĕlohim*, 216, and "Blood and the Image of God: The Punishment of Beheading in Early Rabbinical Literature" (Hebrew), *Meḥqĕrē mišpāṭ* 15 (2000), 429–56, especially n. 34. Maimonides, *Hilkhot Sanhedrin* 14:1, includes only *sĕqilā* and *śĕrēfā* as explicit in the Torah; *ḥeneq* as the default *mitā* is described as learned "from Moses our master"; *hereg* for murder and *ʿir hanniddaḥat* is simply stated as such. While *ḥeneq* appears to have no such basis in biblical sources, some have argued that this form of execution does have its roots in the biblical mention of hanging (Deut. 21:22–23); see, especially, Halperin, "Crucifixion"; the discussions by Lorberbaum, *Ṣelem ʾĕlohim*, 198–203; and Aharon Shemesh, "*Kāmā mitot nimsĕru lĕvēt din wĕlāmā himṣiʾū ḥāzāl et mitat ḥeneq*," *Meḥqĕrē mišpāṭ* 17 (2002), 509–29.

16. Lorberbaum acknowledges the existence of other motives, as well; see, especially, "Blood," in which the notion of *ṣelem ʾĕlohim* is seen by Lorberbaum as requiring decapitation of the murderer, despite the damage thus done to the body. In this case, though, Lorberbaum still maintains that *ṣelem ʾĕlohim* is the formative principle; how that concern is expressed in the case of punishing a murderer simply differs from the way it is usually expressed—by preserving the integrity of the body. Lorberbaum also acknowledges, for the Bavli but not for the Yerushalmi, a secondary concern with minimizing pain; see *Ṣelem ʾĕlohim*, 244–45.

17. Rabbi Yoshiya is working with the assumption that *ḥeneq* is the most lenient form of execution, an assumption debated by R. Shimon in mSan 7:1. In addition, as the Bavli points out, his position only makes sense if one already has the notion that there is a fourth form of execution in addition to *sĕqilā*, *śĕrēfā*, and *hereg*. See n. 57, below. In other words, Rabbi Yoshiya is not explaining the source of the existence of this fourth *mitā*; according to the Bavli, there must be a preexisting tradition that there *are* four *mitot*. Maximally, Rabbi Yoshiya is identifying what that fourth *mitā* is—it must be something more lenient than the other three, and the most lenient form of death is death by strangulation. Minimally, and I think most probably, he is working with the assumption not only that there is a fourth *mitā* but that this fourth *mitā* is *ḥeneq*; once we know that *ḥeneq* exists, we can infer that *ḥeneq* is the default mode of execution to be administered when the Torah does not specify a particular *mitā*. Rabbi, on the other hand, seems to be deriving the notion of strangulation from the verse cited, basing this derivation on the symmetry between divinely imposed and judicially imposed death. The Bavli, though, appears to see Rabbi not as deriving the idea of strangulation but as simply identifying what *mitā* the verse is referring to; the Bavli asks, according to Rabbi, why we might not see the verse as referring

to *śĕrēfā*, since, as rabbinically understood, this form of execution, too, leaves no mark on the body of the criminal. (The notion of *śĕrēfā* as leaving no mark on the body, though, is clearly derivative; it is not the essential definition or the essential characteristic of *śĕrēfā* in rabbinic sources, as it is of *ḥeneq* [see n. 35, below, on later interpretations of the purpose of the cloth in *śĕrēfā* that take the notion of not leaving a mark on the body in *śĕrēfā* as formative in regard to at least this detail of *śĕrēfā*].) In the parallels in Sifra and Mekhilta (see n. 19), we have the term *mikkā'n 'āmĕru*—implying that these sources see Rabbi's teaching as the source of *ḥeneq* as a mode of execution or, at least, as the source of the particular way in which *ḥeneq* must occur, as described in the Mishna. (See Lorberbaum, *Ṣelem 'ĕlohim*, 207–8, for a different understanding of the implication of *mikkā'n 'āmĕru* in these sources.)

18. It is not clear how Rabbi Yonatan derives the punishment of *ḥeneq* from the verse's reference to death. It should be noted, though, that Rabbi Yonatan and Rabbi Yoshiya disagree about the semantic meaning of the verse. Rabbi Yoshiya takes the verse's reference to death as unspecific; since the Torah does not specify the manner of death, we must choose (or design—see the preceding note) the most lenient form of death. Rabbi Yonatan, in contrast, takes the verse's reference to death as referring to a specific mode of death, which he asserts is *ḥeneq*. According to bSan 53a, Rabbi Yonatan and Rabbi are of the same opinion, and Rabbi is merely elaborating on Rabbi Yonatan's reasoning. In ySan 7:4/24b–c, R. Yonatan is cited as disagreeing with R. Yoshiya, but Rabbi's comment is not cited.

19. See parallels in Sifra on Lev. 20:10 (ed. Weiss, 92a); *Mekhilta deRabbi Yishmael, Neziqin* 5 (265–66, 267); and also ySan 7:1/24b and 7:4/24b–c (the Yerushalmi passages do not include the entire range of opinions).

20. Lorberbaum, *Ṣelem 'ĕlohim*, 206–7. See n. 53, below, for a discussion of what "death . . . by the hand of heaven" Rabbi might be referring to; the accompanying text discusses how we might understand this form of death and its simulation by *ḥeneq*.

21. Lorberbaum reads Rabbi's formulation as stating a general principle and cites the version of the argument in *Mekhilta deRabbi Yishmael, Neziqin* 5 (266), in support of this reading; see n. 17, above. Halbertal sees Rabbi's formulation as referring specifically to *ḥeneq* but understands this to reflect a general desideratum that influenced the redesign of *sĕqilā* and *śĕrēfā* as well (*Interpretive Revolutions*, 155–56). Halbertal sees R. Yoshiya as agreeing in principle with Rabbi (whom he takes to be in agreement with R. Yonatan), understanding R. Yoshiya's description of *ḥeneq* as a lenient form of execution as a reference to the body being left intact. It should be noted, though, that Halbertal brings no support for this interpretation: "It would appear that the leniency of *cheneq* is not connected to the degree of pain . . . . *Cheneq* is the most lenient [form of execution] because . . . it does not harm the body and does not destroy it" (155).

22. Lorberbaum's conviction of the general nature of this principle leads him to raise this as the basis for analysis of what, given this principle, is the outrageous deviance of the penalty of *hereg*—a form of execution imposed by rabbinic sources that does, indeed, leave a significant mark on the body of the condemned; see "Blood."

23. Segal ("Postbiblical Jewish Criminal Law") explains Rabbi's argument as deducing *ḥeneq* "from natural death at the hand of heaven without a mark," while Lorberbaum rejects the notion that *mitā biydē šāmayim* here refers to natural death (*Ṣelem 'ĕlohim*, 207).

24. See n. 2, above, for sources that discuss actual burning of the body.

25. See Lorberbaum, *Ṣelem ʾĕlohim,* 195–96; and Halbertal, *Interpretive Revolutions,* 147–49.

26. Lorberbaum (*Ṣelem ʾĕlohim,* 195) argues against the possibility that internal *śĕrēfā* was chosen because it was seen as a quicker and, thus, less painful form of death, quoting the statement of Urbach ("Courts of Twenty-Three") that such determinations are subjective. Note, though, that the Bavli does explain the choice of internal *śĕrēfā* in relation to it bringing death more quickly than immolation of the body; see n. 33, below. An interesting parallel to the contrast in immediacy between internal and external burning, especially given one of the Sifra's descriptions of the death of Nadav and Avihu (Sifra *Milu'im* 23 on Lev. 10:2 [45a] and 34 on Lev. 10:2 [45b]), found also in bSan 52a—"two threads of fire came out from inside the Holy of Holies and were divided into four; two went into the nose of one and two into the nose of the other"—is the description by Helen Prejean of the problematic nature of electrocution as currently implemented in *Dead Man Walking: An Eyewitness Account of the Death Penalty in the United States* (New York: Vintage, 1994), 18–20. Prejean argues that, while the goal of electrocution is to achieve immediate and therefore painless or near-painless death, the fact that the electrical charge is administered externally makes death take several minutes. In the description of the burning of Nadav and Avihu, in contrast, the divinely sent fire is delivered directly to the interior of the bodies of the men.

27. *Śĕrēfā*—bSan 52a; *sĕqilā*—bSan 45a, discussing the question of whether a woman should be stoned naked to minimize discomfort to the body or clothed to minimize humiliation and also, on the same page, explaining the law that the condemned is cast from higher than the minimum height that can be fatal because of the principle of "choosing a fine death." See n. 33, below.

28. See n. 33, below.

29. Segal, as noted above, n. 11, sees the description of *śĕrēfā* as well as of all the other *mitot* as reflecting divinely imposed deaths; see *Ḥiyyuv biydē šāmayim* and "Postbiblical Jewish Criminal Law."

30. bSan 52a; see Sifra *Milu'im* 23 on Lev. 10:2 [45a], 27 on Lev. 10:5 [45a], 34 on Lev. 10:2 [45b], and 41 on Lev. 10:6 [46a] and parallels discussed in Lorberbaum, *Ṣelem ʾĕlohim,* 186–91. These sources include conflicting opinions about the nature of these miraculous deaths: (1) the bodies were burned but the clothes were not; (2) the *nešāmā* was burned but the body remained intact. It is based on the second conception that the analogy to *śĕrēfā* as internal burning is drawn. Lorberbaum sees this second tradition as earlier and more authentic. The inconsistency in the Sifra is already noted by Tosafot on bSan 52a, s.v. *hahiʾ śĕrēfā mammāš hāvē.* It is discussed by Lorberbaum, *Ṣelem ʾĕlohim,* 190 n. 71. See also Avraham Goldberg, *"Haddĕrāšot hakkĕfulot bimĕkhiltā dĕmilu'im," Sinay* 89 (1981), 115–18.

31. The idea that *śĕrēfā* imitates divinely imposed death, though, would be different from the similar idea in relation to *ḥeneq,* since in *ḥeneq* we seem to be approximating natural death while in *śĕrēfā* we seem to be approximating miraculous death. See Lev. 9:24 and Num. 16:35, where the fire is of divine origin. While the way in which this fire kills might, nevertheless, be understood simply as natural immolation, it is not too great a step to move from the idea of a miraculous fire of divine origin burning naturally to the idea of a special fire that kills in a miraculous kind of way. See also the divine fire in Num. 11:1–3 and the "fiery" snakes in Num. 21:6–9.

Alternatively, we might see the description of the deaths of Nadav and Avihu and of Qorach's congregation as *nĕšāmā niśrefet wĕguf qayyām* as a different form of "natural" death—perhaps more similar to death that results from illness/ fever. (I use "natural" here only in the sense of how people die absent an externally imposed physical cause; it is, in fact, an unfortunate choice of words in that "natural" and *biydē šāmayim* represent radically different conceptions of how death is caused.) See Lorberbaum, *Ṣelem ʾĕlohim,* 191–92 n. 77, and Aptowitzer, "Observations," 62 n. 27, who cite the description of the death of a sick person in bAvoda Zara 20b: "the Angel of Death . . . , at the time that a sick person departs, stands at his head, and his sword is drawn in his hand, and a drop of gall hangs from it; when the sick person sees him, he is shaken and opens his mouth, and he throws it into his mouth—from it he dies." See also the description of illness as fire from heaven in bNed 41a.

Lorberbaum (*Ṣelem ʾĕlohim,* 188–91) rejects the notion that, in rabbinic sources (as opposed to in Syriac Barukh 63:8; see James H. Charlesworth, *The Old Testament Pseudepigrapha* [Garden City, N.Y.: Doubleday, 1983], 1:643), internal burning is described to emphasize the miraculous nature of the deaths of Nadav and Avihu and others. For Lorberbaum, the rabbinic sources emphasize the merciful nature of these deaths, in that God preserves the bodies of the victims. Lorberbaum dismisses as erroneous Sifra *Milu'im* 27, which sees God's mercy in preserving the clothes of Nadav and Avihu while their bodies were burned, since Lorberbaum assumes that preservation of dignity is coterminous with preservation of the body (see, though, n. 28, above, and the discussion below; clearly, rabbinic sources recognize other ways than preservation of the body that dignity can be preserved, including being clothed).

32. As noted below in the context of Rabbi's derivation of *ḥeneq,* it is difficult to know whether one should take details of an argument like this to be merely formal elements or whether one should see them as disclosing fundamental conceptual elements of the argument. A strong reading of the *sugya* might give some weight to all of the analogies that the *sugya* brings, including those that do not end up generating the conclusion of the argument (such as the analogies to the death of Aaron's sons and of Qorach's congregation) as well as those that are rejected along the way (such as the rejected analogy of *śĕrēfā* to *pārim hanniśrāfim;* compare bSan 42b, where this analogy is accepted in relation to the location of *bēt hassĕqilā*). See further n. 72, below.

33. Halbertal, *Interpretive Revolutions,* 147–49, discusses this *sugya* and notes that, according to its conclusion, the case of Qorach's congregation simply extends the semantic range of *śĕrēfā* but that it is the principle of *bĕror lo mitā yāfā* that determines the choice of how the biblical requirement of *śĕrēfā* will be interpreted. Halbertal, though, identifies the determining value here as avoidance of damage to the body, not as hastening death/minimizing pain (see also Lorberbaum, *Ṣelem ʾĕlohim,* 195–96 n. 91). It should be noted, though, that the Gemara makes it clear that, had we not been able to derive the acceptability of internal burning as a fulfillment of *śĕrēfā,* the principle of *bĕror lo mitā yāfā* would mandate adding flammable materials that would hasten the person's death. Thus, *bĕror lo mitā yāfā* is applied within this argument in reference to minimizing the person's suffering (if we were to implement actual immolation), and there is every reason to assume that, when the Gemara applies this principle in order to explain the choice of the option of internal burning, the kind of *mitā yāfā* that is achieved is death with the most minimal pain. See the discussion below of R. Nachman's teaching in relation to the height of the platform in *sĕqilā*

(bSan 45a). It is absolutely clear that *mitā yāfā* in that context entails minimizing suffering by hastening death (as noted by Rashi, s.v. *mitā yāfā*: "that he die quickly"). It is important to emphasize that I am not arguing that *mitā yāfā* exclusively entails minimizing pain; see the discussion below of the competing considerations in the design of *sĕqilā*. But it is clear that this is one element of *mitā yāfā*, and I think that it is also clear that this is the element that the Gemara considers central to the choice of internal burning for *śĕrēfā*.

34. It should be noted that the term that the Gemara uses—*nivul*—does not connote disfigurement per se. It means being made repulsive or being degraded in some way, and in our passage that no doubt derives from the damage to the body that would occur were the person to be cast from a very high platform. Compare bArakhin 7b: a pregnant woman about to be executed is first struck across the abdomen so that she not be disgraced in the course of execution by signs of labor. Here the anticipated *nivul* again has to do with the woman's body, but it is not an instance of damage to the body. Even more broadly, *nivul* could refer to something that is considered disgusting for reasons other than the state of the body. See the dispute about the manner of implementing *hereg* in mSan 7:3, in which the sages argue about which way of performing the execution is a greater form of *nivul*. It is hard to construe them as arguing about which does more damage to the body, as both are forms of decapitation. They could be arguing about something else in relation to the body (such as in the bArakhin passage, where the concern relates to the woman's physical state but not to disfigurement), or they could be arguing about other considerations that might render one form or another of decapitation more degrading. For an interpretation along the lines of this latter possibility, see Tosafot on bSan 52b, s.v. *rabbi yĕhudā ʾomēr nivul huʾ ze*. Tosafot argues, based on a *baraita* introduced in the Bavli in relation to this mishna, that R. Yehuda says that decapitating in the way the (non-Jewish) government does is *nivul* because it violates *uvḥuqqotēhem loʾ tēlēkhu*, "and by their laws you shall not go" (Lev. 18:3).

35. It is worthwhile addressing here another detail of the Mishna's description of both *śĕrēfā* and *ḥeneq* that Lorberbaum explains as designed to minimize damage to the body. The procedure for both of these forms of execution includes placing a rough cloth inside a soft cloth, placing them in this arrangement around the neck of the condemned person, and having two people pull on either side of the cloth (mSan 7:2–3). Lorberbaum (*Ṣelem ʾĕlohim*, 196 and n. 94) assumes that the reason for the soft cloth in *ḥeneq* and *sĕqilā* is to prevent a mark from being left on the person's body; this is the explanation that Rashi (bSan 52a, s.v. *qāšā lĕtokh hārakkā*) offers in relation to *śĕrēfā*. The Yerushalmi offers a different explanation for the soft cloth in the case of *śĕrēfā*: to ensure that the condemned not die of strangulation, which could happen if the executioners were to use only a rough cloth (ySan 7:2/24b). Lorberbaum rejects this explanation because he feels that the explanation for the soft cloth should apply to both forms of execution in which it is used, and the Yerushalmi's explanation obviously could not apply to *ḥeneq*. In relation to Rashi's explanation of the soft cloth in *śĕrēfā*, though, it should be noted that Rashi gives a similar explanation for another detail of *śĕrēfā*: the sinking of the lower part of the condemned person in dung. Rashi (bSan 52a, s.v. *mašqiʿin ʾoto*) says that the purpose of this is to immobilize the condemned so that the wick not fall on the outside of the body. (Though whether Rashi sees the Mishna as concerned to avoid *nivul* or pain is unclear here. In any event, it should be noted that the Bavli already sees *śĕrēfā* as leaving no mark [bSan 52b; see above, n. 17], and it may be because of this,

rather than because of a general concern, that Rashi interprets one or more of the details of *śĕrēfā* as designed to avoid disfigurement. See the Yad Rama [100, s.v. *miṣwat hanniśrāfin*], who articulates the interpretation offered by Rashi for the soft cloth in *śĕrēfā* as a function of the Gemara's characterization of *śĕrēfā* as leaving no mark on the body.) Rashi's explanation of the requirement of sinking the person's body in *śĕrēfā* cannot be used to account for the requirement of this same procedure in *ḥeneq*, since there is no wick that might fall on his body should he move during the process of execution. The Yad Rama (100, s.v. *miṣwat hanniśrāfin*) suggests an alternative explanation for sinking the person's body that could apply to both *śĕrēfā* and *ḥeneq*: to preserve the dignity of the condemned person should he soil himself during the execution. (See Prejean, *Dead Man Walking*, 92, for a contemporary measure to address this concern; and see mMak 3:14 on the possibility that this might occur during *malqut*.) And it is, of course, possible to explain the use of the soft cloth in both *śĕrēfā* and *sĕqilā* as designed to minimize pain.

36. It is, in fact, not absolutely clear that the Gemara sees the concern for *nivul* as falling under *bĕror lo mitā yāfā*, as it clearly does for the issue of being naked. This depends on how we read the conclusion of the discussion about the height of the stoning platform. One possibility is to read the steps of the argument of the Gemara thus:

(1) Why do we need a height greater than the minimum height that can be fatal?
(2) Because of Rav Nachman's requirement that we choose a good (i.e., least painful) death.
(3) Then why do we not make the platform higher, in order to make sure that he dies immediately?
(4) Because Rav Nachman's requirement to choose a good death also includes executing in a way that is not disgraceful (in this case, that does not make the person's body disgusting).

An alternative reading replaces the final element of this argument with the following:

(4) Because (in addition to Rav Nachman's requirement to choose a good death) we have the competing requirement to avoid making a person's body disgusting.

This reading would locate the requirement to avoid *nivul* within the general rubric of *kĕvod habbĕriyyot*. While I have adopted the first reading in my discussion, it should be emphasized that, on either reading, the avoidance of *nivul* is only one way in which we adhere to a broader imperative. It is not an independent requirement, it is not limited to damage to the body (see n. 34, above), and it stands alongside other (sometimes competing) demands to treat the person with consideration and respect.

37. Threats or acts of spontaneous stoning or burning occur in Exod. 17:4, Num. 14:10, 1 Sam. 30:6, 1 Kings 12:18, and Judg. 12:1, 14:15, 15:6, respectively. Akhan (and his family and property) are both stoned and burned, and then left under a pile of stones, in Josh. 7:25–26. See bSan 44a on this combination of acts. For additional, nonbiblical sources, see Albeck, *Sēder nĕziqin*, 457.

38. *Sĕqilā* is specified in the Bible for crimes having to do with idolatry, necromancy, and blasphemy (Lev. 20:2, if this is understood to refer to an idolatrous

practice, 20:27, 24:14, Deut. 13:11, 17:5); violation of Shabbat (Num. 15:36); the rebellious son (Deut. 21:12); and two specific sexual offenses (Deut. 22:21, 24); plus the ox that gores (Exod. 21:28). *Śĕrēfā* is specified for two sexual offenses (Lev. 20:14, 21:9). See also Gen. 38:24 (and see Shemesh, *"Kāmā mitot,"* for how this passage was incorporated into the criminal law of Jubilees). Many scholars believe that *sĕqilā* is assumed by the Bible as well as by its early interpreters to be the standard form of execution, except for special cases (limited, perhaps, to particular sexual violations?) that are punishable by *śĕrēfā*. See, for example, Albeck, *Sēder nĕziqin*, 457; Aptowitzer, "Observations"; and Shemesh, *"Kāmā mitot."* Nevertheless, most of the crimes for which *sĕqilā* is explicitly specified constitute major offenses against communal norms in response to which the community is asked to participate in destroying the criminal: crimes against God (idolatry, necromancy, blasphemy), sexual offenses, and violation of Shabbat. See the discussion of major sins in bSan 74a. For murder, see the discussion in Chapter 4. At least one of the two sexual offenses for which *sĕqilā* is mandated is described as a violation of the violator's father (Deut. 22:13–21); compare the case of the rebellious son (Deut. 21:18–21), and note the involvement of both father and mother in both of these cases. Perhaps the rabbinic list of crimes punishable by *sĕqilā* (mSan 7:4) can be somewhat accounted for based on these categories; see also n. 48, below.

39. Some biblical passages describe judicial (or quasi-judicial) procedures quite extensively, while others simply state the penalty. There is also a range of people designated as in charge of the proceedings (for example, *ziqnē hāʿir* in Deut. 21:20 and 22:15 and also in Deut. 19:12, as opposed to *hāʿēdā* in Num. 35:24–25) as well as a range of locations for the execution (for example, *šaʿar mĕqomo* in Deut. 21:19; *petaḥ bēt ʾāvihā* in Deut. 22:21; *miḥuṣ lammaḥăne* in Lev. 24:14—see mSan 6:1, tSan 10:10, ySan 6:1/23b, yKet 4:5/28c–d, bSan 42b, bKet 45b); see Halbertal, *Interpretive Revolutions*, 146.

40. Cohn, "The Penology of the Talmud," emphasizes the shift from public act to exercise of judicial duty as accounting for elements of the redesign of *sĕqilā*, along with considerations of minimizing pain and mutilation of the body.

41. See the biblical passages in nn. 37 and 38, above, for the participatory nature of *sĕqilā*, in particular. See Halbertal, *Interpretive Revolutions*, 149–53, on the shift in rabbinic sources away from community participation in *sĕqilā*. Halbertal attributes this shift, though, to the desire to minimize damage to the condemned criminal's body. Note Halbertal's citation (152) of Philo, *Life of Moses* 2:202, who sees the biblical punishment of *sĕqilā* as expressly designed to allow community participation in the response to the outrageous crime that has been committed (referring to the blasphemer in Lev. 24:14).

Rabbinic sources retain the theoretical possibility of communal participation in *sĕqilā*, in the event that the condemned is killed neither by being pushed off the platform by the first witness nor by having the stone cast down by the second witness; see mSan 6:4. The Bavli denies that the condemned ever survived to the point of the general community participating in the process of stoning; see bSan 45b. While retaining the possibility of community participation in *sĕqilā* may simply be necessary to fulfill the requirement of the biblical sources (see mSan 6:4, citing Deut. 17:7), it is also possible that rabbinic sources actively retain the conception of crimes punishable by *sĕqilā* as violations of communal norms the penalty for which ought to express—at least as constructed, if not necessarily as implemented—communal outrage.

Note that it is only in the case of *sĕqilā* that the Mishna makes it clear that it is the witnesses who perform the execution, though Maimonides takes this to be the case for all modes of execution (*Hilkhot Sanhedrin* 13:1), as may be implied by the challenge posed by the citation of mMak 1:10 in bSan 45b (depending on whether the Gemara understands mMak 1:10 as speaking specifically about the case of murder or as referring to any capital offense: if the former, then the Gemara seems to assume that even in *hereg* the witnesses perform the execution; if the latter, then the Gemara might not be assuming that the witnesses perform the execution in any case other than *sĕqilā*, and the challenge is posed in relation to *sĕqilā*, as one of the cases included in the Mishna's general law). Again, the Mishna's specification of the participation of the witnesses in *sĕqilā* could be seen simply as a constraint of the biblical sources, or we might see this detail as integral to the rabbinic conception of *sĕqilā* and the crimes that it punishes. If we see the notion of communal participation as integral still to the rabbinic conception of *sĕqilā*, there might be greater reason to try to account for the rabbinic list of crimes punishable by *sĕqilā* in the way mentioned in n. 38, above.

In tSan 9:6, R. Shimon describes the casting of the stone as a required component of the procedure and as simply mandated by the biblical prescription—*kĕdē lĕqayyēm bo miṣwat sĕqilā*—just as the very minimal hanging of the executed criminal is performed *kĕdē lĕqayyēm bo miṣwat tĕliyyā*. In contrast, the Bavli asserts that pushing the person off the platform qualifies as a fulfillment of the biblical requirement and that casting a stone is not necessary; see bSan 45a. The Tosefta mentions neither the possibility of the community participating nor the specification that the execution be performed by the witnesses. While both the Mishna and the Tosefta, then, have the casting of the person as well as (the possibility of) throwing a stone upon the condemned, only the Mishna explains the course of events in reference to the participation of both the witnesses and the community.

42. See Michel Foucault, *Discipline and Punish: The Birth of the Prison*, trans. Alan Sheridan (New York: Knopf, 1995), especially 32–69, for an interpretation of execution as a spectacle.

Biblical sources emphasize the public awareness of execution, if not its spectacular nature, as a deterrent; see Deut. 13:12, 17:13, 19:20, and 21:21. See the dispute in tSan 11:7 as to whether certain criminals should have their executions delayed in order to allow for public execution at the time of the festivals in Jerusalem or whether simply publicizing their crimes and punishments qualifies as a fulfillment of these biblical sources. A *baraita* that appears immediately after a parallel to this *baraita* in the Bavli (bSan 89a) states that the execution of four kinds of criminals requires publicity: the *mēsit* (inciter), the *ben sorēr umore* (rebellious son), the *zāqēn mamrē* (rebellious elder), and *ʿēdim zomĕmim* (plotting witnesses). The Gemara points out that these are the four crimes about which the Torah says that, upon the execution of the perpetrator, the people will hear and be afraid (see the biblical sources cited above). It is interesting that mSan-Mak devotes special attention to each of these four crimes: *mēsit* in mSan 7:10; *ben sorēr umore* in mSan 8:1–5; *zāqēn mamrē* in mSan 11:2–4; and *ʿēdim zomĕmim* in mMak 1:1–7. It is as if the Mishna itself, as each of these crimes is listed in relation to its punishment, is calling our attention to the crime—in effect, fulfilling the requirement to publicize the crime and its punishment on the literary level. Note that the *baraita*'s list of the four crimes that require publicity reflects the order in which they appear in the Mishna, rather than, say, the order in which they appear in the Torah.

43. See Halbertal, *Interpretive Revolutions*, 145–46 (*sĕqilā*) and 152 (*śĕrēfā*).

Note the burying of Akhan, his family, and his possessions under a mound of stones in Josh. 7:25–26; the swallowing up of Qorach, Datan, and Aviram and their families and possessions in Num. 16:32, followed by the immolation of Qorach's congregation in 16:35; and the burning of *ʿir hanniddaḥat* and its possessions in Deut. 13:17.

Note the frequent mention of *uviʿartā hārāʿ miqqirbekhā* in Deuteronomy in the context of execution (13:6, 17:7, 17:12, 19:19, 21:21, 22:21, 22:22 [*miyyiśrāʾēl*], 22:24, 24:7). The execution of the criminal, in these passages, serves in some way to set the community right, beyond by ridding the community of the danger posed by the criminal or by deterring similar criminal activity on the part of others. This may be through removing the criminal as the embodiment of evildoing from the community, by reaffirming the community's values through the condemnation expressed through punishment of the violator, or by restoring the balance of the community by doing harm to the wrongdoer. For a concise summary of conceptions of punishment that goes beyond the standard categories of retribution, rehabilitation, and deterrence, see Davis, "Punishment Theory."

44. The focus on the person is apparent, as well, in several passages in mSan-Mak, such as mSan 6:2, about confession and the atonement achieved through death, and mMak 3:1, about the atonement achieved through *malqut* (see the discussion in Chapter 5), as well as mSan 6:1, where the condemned criminal appears as a person who can advance claims in his own defense.

45. Note the injunction to bring the person about to be stoned "outside of the camp" in the stories of the blasphemer (Lev. 24:14) and the wood gatherer (Num. 15:35). The former passage is cited in mSan 6:1 as the source of the location of the stoning platform outside of the court. See the discussion of this passage in bSan 42b; among other ideas, the Gemara suggests that the court wants to distance itself from the execution—"so that the court not appear to be murderers"—a notion quite different from the distancing of the condemned criminal from the society whose norms he has violated. The Bavli also introduces a *baraita* that says that the criminal is executed outside of the "three camps" (=outside of the city; see Rashi, s.v. *ḥuṣ lĕšālоš maḥănot*, and Tosafot, s.v. *bēt hassĕqilā hāyĕtā ḥuṣ lĕšālоš maḥănot*) and compares this to the sacrifice brought when the entire community sins. This suggests that one of the functions of execution is to restabilize the community, perhaps along the lines suggested in n. 43, above.

46. This means, among other things, that the court takes full responsibility for the execution as part of its judicial responsibility (notwithstanding the distancing from the court mentioned in the preceding note) and also that the responsibility for the condemned person's death is not shrouded behind the anonymity of a group killing. In contrast, stoning by the community as described in the Torah, while it involves the entire community in the destruction of the criminal, at the same time leaves no individual responsible for the actual death of the condemned person. The latter characteristic of stoning can be found in modern times in the practice of execution by firing squad or in methods of execution that devise ways to make it impossible to know who has actually caused the death. As noted above, n. 41, it is not entirely clear in rabbinic sources who performs the execution, except in the case of *sĕqilā*, where the witnesses do (for who performs *hereg* in the case of the execution of a murderer, see the discussion in Chapter 4). Are we to see the witnesses as representatives of the community, as agents of the court, as representing the interface between the community and the court—or, perhaps, as a representation of the criminal's self-condemnation

through choosing to act as he has done, since it is the witnesses who attest to the criminal's commission of the act pursuant to his acceptance of the *hatrā'ā*? See nn. 84 and 85, below.

47. It should be noted that both Halbertal and Lorberbaum focus on tannaitic sources about capital punishment, but each also cites selected passages from the Bavli and other rabbinic texts in developing his interpretation of the tannaitic material. My discussion, as noted earlier, focuses on the construction of punishment in the Bavli (including the tannaitic sources on which it comments and which it cites). While it has been suggested to me that Halbertal and Lorberbaum's thesis might offer a valid interpretation of the tannaitic materials, if not of the Bavli, this seems to me not to be the case. In fact, as I have pointed out, it is more difficult to find any reference to minimizing damage to the body as a concern within tannaitic sources than within the Bavli.

48. Though designated as the default mode of execution, *ḥeneq* is not the form of execution that is mandated in rabbinic texts for every crime for which the Torah does not specify the mode of execution. Several crimes are assigned in mSan 7:4 to *sĕqilā*, some, but not all, of which are linked in the Torah to the words *dāmayv bo*, which are taken in rabbinic sources to indicate *sĕqilā* (see Sifra on Lev. 20:9, 11, 13, 16 [92a–b] and, especially, 27 [93b], *Mekhilta deRabbi Yishmael, Neziqin* 5 (268), *Mekhilta deRashbi* on Exod. 21:17 (ed. Epstein-Melamed, 173), bSan 66a; see Shemesh, *"Kāmā mitot"*). In addition, with respect to a number of crimes, there are debates within rabbinic sources about which mode of execution is to be imposed.

49. See Halperin, "Crucifixion," and related sources cited in n. 15, above.

50. *Ḥeneq* is described as more lenient (or lighter—*qal*) in the *baraita* quoted above and parallels. According to the Mishna's list of modes of execution in order of decreasing severity (mSan 7:1), *ḥeneq* is last in the list according to the majority opinion and third in the list according to the dissenting opinion. According to both positions, then, *ḥeneq* is less severe a punishment than the biblical modes of execution, *sĕqilā* and *śĕrēfā*. Even according to the position that *ḥeneq* comes third in the list, with *hereg* appearing as most lenient, it should be noted that *hereg* is limited to a very small number of crimes; thus, it is still possible to suggest that *ḥeneq* was introduced as a less painful, broadly applied alternative to *sĕqilā* and *śĕrēfā*.

It is not entirely clear in what way this mode of execution is considered lenient; see Shemesh, *"Kāmā mitot,"* n. 9. As noted above, n. 21, Halbertal assumes that this is a function of *ḥeneq* leaving the body intact, but he brings no evidence in support of this understanding.

51. Shemesh, *"Kāmā mitot."*

52. Halbertal and Lorberbaum also take Rabbi's teaching as their starting point. The other two positions in the *baraita* are difficult to pin down; see the discussion above in nn. 17, 18, and 50. To sum up the main points: the statement of R. Yoshiya's position does not make clear in what way he sees *ḥeneq* as most lenient, and the statement of R. Yonatan's position does not make clear how the Torah's reference to death implies *ḥeneq* (as noted above, the Bavli takes R. Yonatan and Rabbi as articulating the same interpretation, with Rabbi merely spelling out how R. Yonatan arrived at this interpretation). Rabbi's teaching serves as a useful starting point, because it is this teaching that says something substantive about the nature of *ḥeneq*, which can be read as offering a source for the existence of this mode of execution (as opposed to as merely offering a source for the choice of this mode of execution in unspecified cases; see n. 17,

above), and which can be read as providing the background for the Mishna's teaching that describes how *ḥeneq* is implemented (note the term *mikkāʾn ʾāmĕru* in the Mekhilta and the Sifra; see n. 17, above).

53. What precisely Rabbi is referring to by the phrase *mitā biydē šāmayim* is unclear: is he referring to a particular instance of divinely imposed death described in the Torah, or is he referring to biblical references to dying in general? Rashi (bSan 52b, s.v. *wĕneʾĕmār mitā biydē šāmayim*) understands the phrase in the first of these ways, citing the causative form *wayyāmet* in Gen. 38:10. Onan, like his brother Er (Gen. 38:7), is "caused to die" by God in response to God's judgment that his action was evil. This source is particularly apt since the death is in response to an evil act and since the form of the verb here has death being caused, rather than the person simply dying. Thus, the *mitā biydē šāmayim* here parallels the *yumāt* in Lev. 20:10, where a person "shall be caused to die" in response to a criminal act. It is possible, though, that Rabbi is simply referring to any death that the Torah mentions as occurring without apparent cause; such a death can be said to be "at the hands of heaven," even if God is not mentioned as causing the death, as in the case of Er and Onan. My use of the term "natural death" here is not meant to favor one over the other of these interpretations of Rabbi's reference. It seems to me that, whether we understand Rabbi to be referring to particular cases where God is said to impose death for a misdeed or whether we understand Rabbi to be referring to any case where a person simply dies, the idea is that *mitā* connotes death that has no apparent physical cause; the person has simply stopped breathing. See bSan 52a, where the word *wayyāmutu*, used of Aaron's sons, is understood to suggest that their *śĕrēfā* was "like *mitā*"—that is, it was not simply that they died, but that their manner of death was *like mitā*, in that there was no apparent physical cause of death.

54. Or a sickness/fever that "burns" the body from the inside; see n. 31, above.

55. In rabbinic sources, death is determined by cessation of breathing; see, for example, bYoma 85a. This is not to say that all deaths are seen to be caused by lack of breathing; but lack of breathing is, always, a sign of death, and, in cases where there is no apparent cause of death, expiration is the cause—or, perhaps better, the definition—of death. Note the use of *wayyigwaʿ* to describe the deaths of the patriarchs in Gen. 25:8, 35:29, and 49:33. And see Gen. 7:21–22, where death by drowning in the floodwaters is described with the word *wayyigwaʿ*; note the designation of the creatures that died as "all which had the breath of the spirit of life in its nostrils." For the flood in relation to *ḥeneq*, see Chapter 2, n. 43 and accompanying text.

56. See A. Kosman, "Kissing the Dead—Transformation of a Custom" (Hebrew), *Tarbiṣ* 65 (1996), 483–508, especially the appendix, 504–8 and also n. 42, about death by a divine kiss as a taking back of the breath of life. Kosman notes Rashi's comment in bBava Batra 17a, s.v. *kĕdēʾāmĕrān*, contrasting death by a divine kiss with death at the hands of the Angel of Death described in bAvoda Zara 20b. See n. 31, above. A similar conception, of course, lies behind the offering of good wishes to a person who sneezes, forcibly expelling breath, and behind the phrase "to give up the ghost," among many other examples.

57. bSan 53a. Rava makes this claim in response to a difficulty with R. Yoshiya's position in the *baraita* about *ḥeneq* quoted above: How can R. Yoshiya explain the law that *ḥeneq* is the default mode of execution by saying that, unless the Torah specifies otherwise, we must impose the most lenient mode of execution? If this is the case, then R. Yoshiya ought to assume that, when the Torah does

not specify a mode of execution, the court must impose the punishment of *hereg*, the most lenient of the known modes of execution. How do we know, the Gemara asks, that the punishment of *ḥeneq* exists at all?

58. mSan 6:5.

59. bSan 47a. The Bavli initially explains the division into two burial places by saying that more evil and less evil people ought not to be buried together. This leads to the obvious question: Why not have four different burial places, one for each of the modes of execution? The Gemara responds in the same language with which Rava explains the source of the notion that there are four *mitot*: *šnē qĕvārot gĕmārāʾ gĕmirē lēh.*

60. mSan 7:1.

61. These ways of killing also appear as spontaneous acts of violence against those who have violated norms of the community; see above, n. 37.

62. For *hereg* as judicial execution as an innovation within rabbinic sources, see above, n. 15.

63. See mSan 7:3, tSan 9:10, ySan 7:1/24b. This will be discussed further in Chapter 2.

64. bSan 56a, 57b, 71b.

65. What exactly is being burned in *śĕrēfā* is unclear. The Mishna (mSan 7:2) seems clearly to suggest a physical burning of the internal organs. The Bavli (bSan 52a), in comparing execution by *śĕrēfā* to the deaths of Nadav and Avihu and Qorach's congregation, describes it as *śĕrēfat nĕšāmā wĕguf qayyām.* See the passages in the Sifra, cited above, n. 30; and see Lorberbaum, *Ṣelem ʾĕlohim*, 190, nn. 71–72. Halbertal (*Interpretive Revolutions*, 147) and Lorberbaum (191) both emphasize the *guf qayyām* element of this formulation.

66. For *hereg* as a spilling of blood, see the discussion in Chapter 4 of the assignment of this punishment to murder. See also Chapter 2, n. 44.

67. See Chapter 4, n. 19.

68. See the conclusion of the description of *ḥeneq* in mSan 7:3: *ʿad šennafšo yoṣēʾā.*

69. *Sĕqilā*, as noted above, nn. 37, 38, and 41, is a way in which groups of people kill. (This is true, as well, of burning as it appears in biblical texts but not of *śĕrēfā* as redefined by the Rabbis.) Note also the explicit retaining of the community's participation in *sĕqilā*, minimally by the witnesses and maximally by the entire community, discussed above, n. 41.

See Chapter 4, n. 43 for *h-r-g* as the word used for killing by a human being. In fact, the use of this word by Moses in his plea to God to kill him (Num. 11:15) prompts a comment by Nachmanides, who notes that *h-r-g* generally connotes killing by a human being, not being caused to die by God. See the discussion in Chapter 4 of who implements *hereg* in the case of a murderer. As noted in n. 41, above, rabbinic texts are silent about who performs the execution in cases of *śĕrēfā* and *ḥeneq.*

70. See the three-way dispute in bSan 84a about the connotation of *yumāt* in Num. 18:7. R. Yishmael believes that *yumāt* (passive form) and *yāmut* (active form) have the same connotation: death by the hand of heaven. R. Akiva and R. Yochanan ben Nuri, on the other hand, believe that *yumāt* connotes execution by a court. Rabbi's interpretation of *yumāt* in Lev. 20:10 seems to mediate between these two options: the person is put to death by human hands but in a way that approximates divinely caused death.

71. See Halbertal, *Interpretive Revolutions*, 155–56.

72. See above in relation to the Bavli's discussion of *śĕrēfā*: Are the cases of

Aaron's sons and Qorach's congregation being brought simply to expand the semantic range of the word *ś-r-f*, or is the text making a point about the punishment of *śĕrēfā* in relation to these two biblical narratives? It should be noted, though, that, in the Bavli's discussion of *śĕrēfā*, the cases of internal burning are an intermediate, though extended, step in the argument, with the conclusion about the mode of *śĕrēfā* coming from the principle of *mitā yāfā*, and thus there may reason to give less weight to the substantive content of this step of the argument. Here, in contrast, the case of *mitā biydē šāmayim* is brought to yield the conclusion—that we should execute in a similar way, by means of *ḥeneq*—and this suggests that we should take the substantive content of this argument seriously. Nevertheless, the methodological question remains, both in cases of halakhic and aggadic exegesis. Often, the interpreter treads a tricky line between the temptation of reading in, on the one side, and the danger of missing the point, on the other.

73. I am using this term to designate the body of law that is seen in rabbinic sources as having its roots in sinaitic revelation as opposed to other bodies of law, such as noachide law, which will be discussed in Chapter 2.

74. This conception of law is known as legal positivism. For a basic introduction to positivism and to alternate conceptions of law, see P. J. Fitzgerald, *Salmond on Jurisprudence*, 12th ed. (London: Sweet and Maxwell, 1966), esp. 15–53. The classic work on legal positivism, with a review and critique of earlier versions of positivism, is H. L. A. Hart's *The Concept of Law* (New York: Oxford University Press, 1997). For other descriptions of the rabbinic conception of law as essentially positivist, see Yochanan Silman, "Halakhic Determinations of a Nominalistic and Realistic Nature: Legal and Philosophical Considerations" (Hebrew), *Dinē yiśrāʾēl* 12 (1984–85), 251–66; and Daniel Schwartz, "Law and Truth: On Qumran-Sadducean and Rabbinic Views of Law," in D. Dimant and U. Rappaport, eds., *The Dead Sea Scrolls: Forty Years of Research* (Leiden: Brill, 1992), 229–40; see Jeffrey Rubenstein's response to Schwartz, "Nominalism and Realism in Qumranic and Rabbinic Law: A Reassessment," *Dead Sea Discoveries* 6 (1999), 157–83. For an extreme statement of this understanding of the *mitzvot*, see Maimonides' commentary to the passage in mChulin 7:6 concerning the prohibition of eating *gid hannāše*. The positivist view of the *mitzvot* raises the question of the status of these laws before Sinai. How, for example, are we to understand the nature of the patriarchs' observance of the *mitzvot* that is asserted in many midrashic texts? For a discussion of the issue of the status of law before Sinai in nonrabbinic texts, see Gary A. Anderson, "The Status of the Torah Before Sinai," *Dead Sea Discoveries* 1 (1994), 1–30, and "The Status of the Torah in the Pre-Sinaitic Period: St. Paul's Epistle to the Romans," in M. Stone and E. Chazon, eds., *Biblical Perspectives: Early Use and Interpretation of the Bible in Light of the Dead Sea Scrolls* (Leiden: Brill, 1998), 1–13.

75. By "explicitly," I do not mean that it is explicit in the common sense of the word; in fact, often the *ʾazhārā* or *ʿoneš* is derived through scriptural exegesis. The point is, though, that the *ʾazhārā* and *ʿoneš* must have a scriptural source that is seen as applying specifically to the law in question; neither the *ʾazhārā* nor the *ʿoneš* can be derived by means of logical inference. For further discussion of this principle, see Chapter 3.

76. For sources, see n. 3, above.

77. See bSan 8b, 41a, 72b, bMak 6b, 9b. Note that the term *šogēg* (as opposed to *mēzid*) ordinarily can apply both to situations where the violator is not aware of the prohibition (for example, he does not know that it is forbidden to write

on Shabbat) and to situations where the violator is aware of the prohibition but is not aware that the situation at hand falls under that prohibition (for example, he mistakenly thinks that it is a weekday, not Shabbat). It would appear that the position that a *ḥāvēr* does not need a *hatrā ʾā* is focusing on this first kind of *šōgēg*, on the assumption that a *ḥāvēr* would be aware of the existence of the prohibition. Presumably, it would still be necessary to ascertain whether the *ḥāvēr* knows that the situation at hand falls under the prohibition. See Chapter 2 on *hatrā ʾā* in relation to noachide law and on Maimonides' distinction between the two kinds of *šogēg* with respect to a noachide.

78. *Mekhilta deRabbi Yishmael, Kaspa* 20 (327), tSan 11:2–3, ySan 5:1/22c, bSan 72b. See Meir Ish-Shalom, "Essay on the Issue of *ʿĒdim Zomĕmim* and the Issue of *Hatrā ʾā*" (Hebrew), part 2, *Bēt talmud* 5 (1886), 259–61, for the idea of warning as a primary meaning of *lĕhā ʿid*.

79. See mMak 1:10, discussed briefly above, pp. 1–2. The same argument has been made about the strict rules of testimony. For these rules, see n. 3, above; for the argument and for a substantive interpretation of the very limited scope of acceptable testimony, see below, n. 84.

80. The same would apply as well, for example, to the strict limitations in rabbinic texts on the case of *ben sorēr umore* (the rebellious son) (see mSan 8:1–4 and especially the *baraita* with R. Yehuda's teaching on bSan 71a). While it can be argued that these are designed to make the law inapplicable in practice—or to make the point that the biblical passage ought not be understood as articulating a real-world law—the particular limitations that the Rabbis construct should be explored to disclose the values and ideas of the constructors. See the claim in bSan 71a that there never was and never will be a *ben sorēr umore* (the Gemara includes an opposing opinion as well) and that the purpose of the inclusion of the passage about *ben sorēr umore* in the Torah is to invite exegesis. Is the purpose of that exegesis only to render the law inapplicable, or is it to generate meaning from the biblical text?

81. How explicitly and in what form the prohibition must be articulated is discussed by commentators. See, for example, Tosafot on bMoʿed Qatan 2b, s.v. *miššum may matrinān*—"he must clearly spell out the name of the prohibition"; and Rashi on bShev 20b, s.v. *wĕʾazhārātēh milōʾ tiššavĕʿu višmi lāššāqer* and *ʾākhalti wĕloʾ ʾākhalti*—the person who issues the warning must quote the biblical verse that states the prohibition.

82. bSan 40b. Rashi (s.v. *qibbēl ʿālayv hatrā ʾā* and *hittir ʿaṣmo lĕmitā*) understands the first of these two elements, the acceptance of the *hatrā ʾā*, as referring to knowledge of the prohibition; and the second element, giving himself over to death, as referring to acceptance of the punishment.

83. bSan 41a. In ySan 5:1/22c, this phrase is taken as the source of the requirement that the would-be criminal be told the specific penalty for the crime he is about to commit.

84. Note that this reduces the conception of the role of the witnesses significantly. This may explain why the witnesses can do no more than report the fact of the crime in a way that allows for no interpretation of the events (see above, n. 3). This strict requirement can be explained as nothing more than a device for rendering conviction impossible (see the discussion of this explanation for the strict requirements of *hatrā ʾā*, above) or, instead, as fundamentally necessary to avoid convictions based on human error. (For both of these possibilities, see Blidstein, "Capital Punishment." See also bMak 7a, where extreme limitations on acceptable witness reports are offered as ways in which courts could, in prac-

tice, abolish execution.) But perhaps it ought to be seen as a way of reducing the role of the witnesses and of the court in determining the defendant's guilt. The defendant, in fact, has rendered himself guilty and has acceded to his own sentence. The role of the witnesses is nothing more than to bring this to the attention of the court. (For a similar interpretation of the limited role of the witnesses and of the court, see Enker, "*Yĕsodot.*")

85. The notion that the evildoer is considered already to be dead appears also in aggadic statements based on this same verse (Deut. 17:6). See bBer 18b and also Devarim Rabba *veZo't haBerakha*, s.v. *wayyo'mer*; Tanchuma and Tanchuma Buber *veZo't haBerakha* 7. This notion is juxtaposed with the legal requirement of "giving oneself over to death" in Midrash Tannaim to Deut. 17:6 and Yalqut Shim'oni *Shoftim*, 909.

86. See Lev. 20:14 and 21:9 and mSan 9:1.

87. For a suggestion that, in the rabbinic assignment of *sĕqilā* to particular crimes for which *sĕqilā* is not explicitly mandated in the Torah, we might see a reflection of the rabbinic conception of the nature of those particular crimes and of that particular punishment, see nn. 38 and 41, above.

88. Note that only *ḥeneq* and *hereg*, the two nonbiblical modes of judicial execution, are assigned by rabbinic sources to systems of law: *ḥeneq* to sinaitic law (as the default *mitā*) and to Tanna deve Menashe's version of noachide law; and *hereg* to the Sages' version of noachide law and to (Jewish and non-Jewish) governmental execution (for the latter, see the sources in Chapter 4, nn. 42 and 43). This is another indication that *sĕqilā* and *śĕrēfā* should be seen as constraints generated by biblical sources; when rabbinic sources assign modes of execution to different systems of law, their choices are limited to *ḥeneq* and *hereg*. See the discussion of the assignment of these two modes of execution to the two versions of noachide law in the Bavli in Chapter 2.

Chapter 2

1. It is, of course, debatable how much consistency (and what kinds of consistency) we should expect in rabbinic sources. In this case, one could accept that the punishment of *ḥeneq* expresses the rabbinic conception of sinaitic law without necessarily expecting that punishments assigned in rabbinic sources to alternate bodies of law express the rabbinic conception of those bodies of law. Nevertheless, the possibility that a jurisprudential analysis of punishment can be extended beyond the case of *ḥeneq* bears investigation. And it should be noted that the main rabbinic sources that will be discussed in relation to the three main topics addressed in this and the following two chapters are from bSanhedrin, as are the main sources discussed in Chapter 1 in relation to *mitot bēt din* and the rabbinic conception of sinaitic law. Nevertheless, it could still be argued that one should not expect the kind of consistency even within a single tractate that I am looking for here. See the brief discussion of these methodological questions in the Preface.

2. For a review of some of the extensive literature on noachide law, see Suzanne Stone, "Sinaitic and Noahide Law: Legal Pluralism in Jewish Law," *Cardozo Law Review* 12 (1991), 1157–1214. See David Novak, *The Image of the Non-Jew in Judaism* (New York: Edwin Mellen, 1983), for a survey of understandings of noachide law and of the specific laws.

3. Louis Finkelstein, *Pharisaism in the Making* (New York: Ktav, 1983), 226–27.

4. Saul Lieberman, *Greek in Jewish Palestine* (New York: Jewish Theological Seminary, 1942), 81–82. Lieberman proposes that disagreement within and between rabbinic sources about the number and content of noachide laws "mirrors the facts of actual life": different semi-converts observed different laws.

5. For a discussion of Mendelssohn's approach, see Novak, *Image*, 369–83.

6. The brief discussion here of the approaches of Selden, Grotius, and Cohen is based on Stone, "Sinaitic," 1165, and Novak, *Image*, 386–90.

7. Nachum Rakover, "Jewish Law and the Noachide Obligation to Preserve Social Order," *Cardozo Law Review* 12 (1991), 1073–1136.

8. Though this is not exclusively the case; see below.

9. See my "Vineyard, Farm, and Garden: The Drunkenness of Noah in the Context of Primeval History," *Journal of Biblical Literature* 113 (1994), 193–207, for a discussion of the shift in the nature of human responsibility and autonomy between the antediluvian and postdiluvian worlds.

10. See Bereshit Rabba 16:6 and the note on parallels in the Theodor-Albeck edition, 149–50.

11. See Gen. 9:3 in contrast with Gen. 1:29. See bSan 59b, and see Rashi on bSan 57a, s.v. *lĕmiśrē bāśār hu*ʾ *dĕ*ʾ*ātā*, and Tosafot on bSan 56b, s.v. ʾ*ăkhol to*ʾ*khēl wĕlo*ʾ ʾ*ēver min haḥay*, on how this commandment could possibly apply to Adam, an argument necessitated by the Bavli's linking of all seven *mitzvot* with the first human being, to be discussed below.

12. See, for example, Bereshit Rabba 34:8 and the note on parallels in the Theodor-Albeck edition, 316–17.

13. See, for example, the parallel in Bereshit Rabba 34:8, where this same list appears, followed by four opinions about additional laws and a biblical source for the details of one of these laws, all of which appear following the presentation of the first list of seven laws in the Bavli passage.

14. Compare Bereshit Rabba 16:6 and parallels. As noted above, these lists omit the prohibition against eating a limb from a living animal. See, though, the end of the Bereshit Rabba passage for an additional opinion that sees Gen. 2:16 as hinting at this prohibition.

15. Along with Seder Olam, chap. 5, which bears other resemblances to the Bavli's presentation of noachide law, as discussed below.

16. As in Bereshit Rabba 34:8.

17. It is, of course, possible that the Bavli knows a tradition attributed to Tanna deve Menashe, even though no such tradition is preserved outside of this passage in the Bavli. By talking about the Bavli's two traditions as having been constructed by the Bavli, I do not necessarily mean that the second tradition, that of Tanna deve Menashe, was invented by the Bavli, although this is entirely possible and, perhaps, likely; I mean, rather, that by setting these two lists side by side and by emphasizing their derivations from entirely different sources, the Bavli is constructing these two lists as representing different traditions about noachide law that are based, as I will argue, in different conceptions of law.

18. Note that, in the Hebrew, the word "commanded" appears as the first word in the verse. A second opinion derives *dinin* from ʾ*ĕlohim*, which is the derivation that appears in Bereshit Rabba 16:6 and parallels (with the exception of Seder Olam, chap. 5, which derives *dinim* from *wayyĕṣaw*); in most of these sources, the order of the laws is, correspondingly, different, with *dinin* not appearing as the first item on the list (with the exception of tAvoda Zara 9:7, which does not associate the laws with Gen. 2:16). These two derivations of *dinin* may express different conceptions of the basis, and perhaps of the content, of

law; for one such interpretation, see Responsa of Rabbi Moses Isserles 10 and the discussion in N. Rakover, "Jewish Law," and in Stone, "Sinaitic," 1173–74.

19. For a discussion of the meaning of *dinin* in rabbinic sources and the elaboration of this concept in later Jewish thought to include not only the establishment of a judicial system but also the mandate to develop systems of conventional law, see Stone, "Sinaitic," 1171–75.

20. It is interesting that this injunction is a prohibition against eating something, given in the context of a statement of permission to eat everything else (Gen. 9:3), which is similar to God's command to Adam not to eat of the fruit of the tree of knowledge (Gen. 2:17), given in the context of a statement that Adam may eat from all of the other trees in the garden (Gen. 2:16):

2:16—you may eat from all of the trees
2:17—but not from the tree of knowledge
9:3—you may eat all animals
9:4—but not the blood

It is possible that, as an exception to what is permitted, the limitation that is understood as expressed in Gen. 9:4 is construed in this Bavli passage as something other than a command. In this regard, it is noteworthy that the *mitzvot* that are derived from the verse in the Adam story are themselves not derived from 2:17, the verse that expresses the prohibition against eating from the tree of knowledge. Instead, they are derived from 2:16, a verse that we tend to read as concessive, not as articulating a command. In other words, we tend to read 2:17 as the command—"you shall not eat of the fruit of the tree of knowledge"—and 2:16 as an introductory concessive—"although you may eat of the fruit of all the other trees in the garden." But the word *wayyĕṣaw* begins the first of these verses, and thus it is the first of these verses that is parsed by the Rabbis to generate a series of commands. The second verse is either understood within this interpretation as a command specific to Adam in the garden, and thus not generative of general commands for humankind, or as not containing a command at all (similar to what I have suggested in relation to 9:4), the command(s) being contained, instead, in the preceding verse. Understanding the command(s) as being contained in 2:16 might also generate the idea of God's command to Adam as a positive command ("you shall . . ."); it should be noted that the Sages' list of laws, associated by the Bavli with the *wayyĕṣaw* verse, contains a positive command. This command, the obligation of *dinin*, begins the list of noachide laws according to the Sages, and it can well be seen as a kind of super-law, in that it allows for implementation of the remaining six laws (which themselves are prohibitions).

A second item on Tanna deve Menashe's list, the prohibition against murder, is derived in the Gemara from a verse that can be read as a legal statement (Gen. 9:6), but this verse does not take the form of a command not to murder. Rather, it speaks of the penalty for or consequence of murder. This verse will be discussed below, in Chapter 4. Note that the verses about murder immediately follow 9:4, the limitation on eating the blood of an animal; and the prohibition against murder is expressed, like the prohibition against eating blood, as a limitation on the permission granted in 9:3:

9:3—you may eat animals
9:4—but not the blood

9:5—and also the blood of human beings, if spilled, will be sought out by God
9:6—a person who spills the blood of human being, that person's blood will be spilled

21. The other item from the Sages' list omitted in Tanna deve Menashe's list is blasphemy—*birkat hāššēm.* Perhaps we ought to see blasphemy as linked to *dinin*; see the midrash that an unfavorable court decision is what led to the blasphemy described in Lev. 24:11 (Sifra on 24:10 [ed. Weiss, 104b]) and the two interpretations of *ʾĕlohim loʾ tĕqallēl* (Exod. 22:27) in *Mekhilta deRabbi Yishmael, Kaspa* 19 (317): that this is a statute prohibiting blasphemy, the punishment for which is stated in Lev. 24:16; or that this is a prohibition against cursing judges, interpreting *ʾĕlohim* as in Exod. 22:8. On the other hand, blasphemy is listed among the five examples of reasonable laws in Sifra on Lev. 18:4 [86a] and bYoma 67b (see n. 48, below), in the absence of *dinin*; in the Sifra, it comes right after idolatry (though in bYoma these two items are not proximate), and perhaps blasphemy should simply be seen as a fundamental religious prohibition alongside idolatry.

22. On crossbreeding as a violation of the order of creation, see Nachmanides' commentary on Lev. 19:19.

23. See Gen. 1:11–12, 21–22, 24–25, 28.

24. In Bereshit Rabba 34:8, castration and crossbreeding are similarly derived from "by their families" in Gen. 8:19. (See also Bereshit Rabba 7 and yKil 1:6/27a for the link between crossbreeding and "according to their kinds" in the creation story; see also bBava Qama 55a.) Crossbreeding is also mentioned in the Bavli as a possible addition to the Sages' list of noachide laws (bSan 56a); see below.

25. For the flood as an un-creation followed by a re-creation of the world, see Steinmetz, "Vineyard" and the literature cited there.

26. The word *wattiššāḥēt* might be less literally translated as "was corrupted" or the like; I am using the translation "was destroyed" in order to retain the link with other uses of *š-ḥ-t* in this passage, especially in Gen. 6:13, to be discussed below.

27. It should be noted that a similar verse from the story of creation (Gen. 1:28) is understood in rabbinic texts as the source for an obligation that applies to Jews, the obligation to reproduce. (See mYev 6:28, where specifics of this obligation are derived from this verse as well as from the narrative of Gen. 5:2.) Note, though, that the Bavli presents Tanna deve Menashe as deriving a *prohibition* from this verse; for those commanded at Sinai, though, this prohibition is derived from a verse that is formulated as an *ʾazhārā*, a negative command (see, for example, bShab 110b in relation to Lev. 22:24).

See also the discussion in bSan 59a–b about whether *mitzvot* that were given to noachides, including the obligation to reproduce, are binding on both Jews and non-Jews. In this passage, the obligation to reproduce is based on Gen. 9:7, God's words to Noah and his sons. The Bavli argues that this obligation applies only to Jews, but it recognizes the *mitzva* as having its basis in noachide obligation.

28. Stone, "Sinaitic," reviews some of the literature on noachide law and natural law and rejects the notion that noachide law is a form of natural law. Her analysis, though, is focused on the Sages' list of noachide laws, especially on *dinin*, and does not address Tanna deve Menashe's position as an alternate conception of noachide law. For the debate on whether the notion of natural law

exists within rabbinic thought, see the sources cited in Stone, "Sinaitic," 1167–68 nn. 36–37. And see especially Marvin Fox, "Maimonides and Aquinas on Natural Law," *Dinē yiśrā'ēl* 3 (1972), v–xxxvi (see the discussion below); Aharon Lichtenstein, "Does Jewish Tradition Recognize an Ethic Independent of Halakha?," in Marvin Fox, ed., *Modern Jewish Ethics: Theory and Practice* (Columbus: Ohio State University Press, 1975), 62–88; J. David Bleich, "Judaism and Natural Law," *Jewish Law Annual* 7 (1988), 6–42; David Novak, "Natural Law, *Halakhah*, and the Covenant," *Jewish Law Annual* 7 (1988), 43–67; and Rakover, "Jewish Law."

29. For an introduction to different theories of natural law from ancient to contemporary times, see Lloyd L. Weinreb, *Natural Law and Justice* (Cambridge, Mass.: Harvard University Press, 1987); see chap. 1 for the classical version of natural law as it was developed within Stoic philosophy and articulated by Cicero. See also Michael B. Crowe, *The Changing Profile of the Natural Law* (The Hague: Martinus Nijhoff, 1977), chap. 2. Crowe discusses Ulpian's contribution to classical natural law theory in detail on 41–51. Ulpian famously defined natural law as "what nature has taught all animals": "For this law is not proper to man but is common to all animals whether born on land or in the sea, and birds also. Whence comes the conjunction of male and female, which we call marriage; whence the procreation of children." This definition aligns closely with the Bavli's construction of Tanna deve Menashe's view; note, in particular, that the source of the prohibition against sexual misconduct—"The earth was *destroyed* before God . . . for all flesh had *destroyed* its way"—appears to describe the world-destroying behavior that is forbidden in Tanna deve Menashe's view as common to all creatures, not only to human beings.

30. For a brief discussion of classical and later approaches to natural law, see Jeffrie G. Murphy and Jules L. Coleman, *Philosophy of Law: An Introduction to Jurisprudence* (Boulder, Colo.: Westview, 1990), 12–16. Alternatively, we might productively see the conception of law that is expressed in the Sages' version of noachide law in relation to the classical notion of *jus gentium*, which is closely related to the notion of natural law but which is seen, especially after Ulpian's distinction between *jus gentium* and *jus naturale*, as a category of law specific to human beings, consisting of those laws to which people universally assent. See Crowe, *Changing Profile*, 41–46.

31. See Bernard S. Jackson, "Secular Jurisprudence and the Philosophy of Jewish Law: A Commentary on Some Recent Literature," *Jewish Law Annual* 6 (1987), 3–44, especially section 5. While the content of law can be a constraint within positivist theories as well, that would be so only if such a constraint is built in to the rules of legislation within a given system of law.

32. For the post-talmudic notion that noachide law is to be expanded to meet the needs of society, see n. 19, above, and especially pp. 1174 and 1181–83 in Stone, "Sinaitic."

33. In a passage absent from standard editions of *Mishne Tora*, Maimonides emphasizes the social aspect of noachide law. Maimonides says that, if a noachide saw another noachide violating a noachide law "and did not judge him and kill him," then that person is himself to be killed (see Kapach edition, *Hilkhot Melakhim* 9:19, corresponding to 9:14 in the standard edition). The obligation to maintain adherence to the law and to punish violations of the law, according to Maimonides, falls on every member of society. Maimonides uses this principle to explain why all the inhabitants of Shekhem were deserving of death (Genesis 34). See Nachmanides' response in his comment on Gen. 34:13

for an alternative understanding of *dinin* and of the responsibility of individual noachides to respond to criminal acts.

34. See the brief discussion above of the approaches of Selden, Grotius, and Cohen to noachide law and, especially, to *dinin.*

35. See especially Fox, "Maimonides."

36. Though not of Tanna deve Menashe's. It is important to note that much of the literature about noachide law, and especially the arguments against noachide law as a form of natural law, has focused on the Sages' version and parallels.

37. Such a notion would be comparable to the conceptions of natural law as law of the state in the writings of Hobbes and Locke; see Weinreb, *Natural Law,* 68–83. See also H. L. A. Hart's discussion of "the minimum content of Natural Law," in *The Concept of Law* (New York: Oxford University Press, 1997), 193–200.

38. bSan 56b.

39. bSan 60a. The fact that the Bavli offers two different sources for crossbreeding for the Sages and for Tanna deve Menashe is especially significant, because it supports the idea that the Bavli's assignment of alternative sources for Tanna deve Menashe for the shared items on the two lists of seven *mitzvot* is not just an artifact of the Bavli's assumption that Tanna deve Menashe cannot be using the *wayyĕṣaw* verse as the source of his seven laws. In other words, one could argue that the reason that the Bavli needs to offer alternative sources for all of the seven *mitzvot* for Tanna deve Menashe is that the Bavli is forced to conclude that Tanna deve Menashe does not derive his laws from the *wayyĕṣaw* verse since, if he did, he would have to derive even *dinin* and blasphemy from that verse. Such an argument could be seen to be suggested by the Bavli's introduction to Tanna deve Menashe's sources: "The tanna from the school of Menashe—if he interprets *wayyĕṣaw,* then those also [i.e., he should include also *dinin* and blasphemy]; if he doesn't interpret *wayyĕṣaw,* then whence does he derive these [i.e., the commandments included in his own list of seven *mitzvot*]?" I have argued, though, that the Bavli's assignment of different sources for even the *mitzvot* that Tanna deve Menashe shares with the Sages suggests that the Bavli is presenting different conceptions of the nature and sources of law for these two lists. The fact that the Bavli offers two different sources for crossbreeding, a law that does not appear in the Sages' basic list of seven laws and, thus, is not derived from the *wayyĕṣaw* verse, supports the idea that the Bavli's intention is to offer different sources for the *mitzvot* of Tanna deve Menashe and the Sages, and that this is not merely an artifact of other constraints.

40. Interestingly, Rashi and Tosafot take a similar approach when explaining the Bavli's derivation of idolatry and sexual misconduct, as they appear in Tanna deve Menashe's list, from the phrase "the earth was destroyed before God." Rashi comments (bSan 57a, s.v. *wattiššāḥēt hāʾāreṣ*: "From the fact that he was punished for them, we can infer that he was commanded concerning them." Compare Tosafot (s.v. *dikhtiv wattiššāḥēt*): "And he would not have punished without having prohibited [*hizhir*]." Both Rashi and Tosafot interpret the verse describing the destruction of the world as a punishment that, of necessity, implies that, prior to that, God must have articulated a prohibition to humankind. Rashi and Tosafot, then, are interpreting the Gemara's explanation of Tanna deve Menashe's position in a way that makes it consistent with the Sages' position—that God has legislated for humanity and that people are punished when they violate those commands. In fact, the Gemara makes exactly this argument in relation to the source for details of a possible addition to the Sages' list

of laws (bSan 56b; this also appears in tAvoda Zara 9:7). But while such an argument fits the Sages' conception of noachide law, it does not fit Tanna deve Menashe's conception. The simple meaning of the Bavli's derivation of idolatry and sexual misconduct for Tanna deve Menashe has nothing to do with an assumption of prior legislation, since legislation is not the basis of law in this second conception of noachide law. Rather, as I have suggested, "the earth was destroyed before God" suggests, within the Bavli's explanation of the sources for Tanna deve Menashe's *mitzvot*, that human beings have engaged in destructive acts and that destruction naturally comes upon them in consequence; these acts are forbidden not in that they have been prohibited by God's command but in that they are destructive of God's world.

41. bSan 57b (and 71b). The Bavli gives as the source for this position a reading of Gen. 9:6 *bā'ādām dammo yiššāfēkh*—taking *bā-* as meaning "inside," generating the idea of an internal spilling of blood.

42. bSan 56a. What the Bavli takes to be the source of the Sages' position is unclear. It would be reasonable to assume that the source for this punishment, like the source that the Bavli brings for Tanna deve Menashe's position, is Gen. 9:6. In this case, the preposition in *bā'ādām* would mean "by means of," generating the idea that the murderer's blood is spilled by a human being. Indeed, Rashi offers this as the source for the punishment of *hereg* for noachides (bSan 56a, s.v. *'ēnah 'ellā sayyif*). According to Rashi's interpretation of *qaṭlayhu hu' dĕqā-mĕgāllē* (bSan 57a), this derivation is stated in the Gemara (see Rashi on bSan 57a, s.v. *qaṭlayhu qā mĕgāllē*), though these words can alternatively be read as saying only that Gen. 9:6 mandates execution for violations of noachide law, rather than as specifying the form of execution (see Yad Rama, 108). In fact, the alternative readings of Gen. 9:6 offered on bSan 57b do not include this possibility; both readings take *bā'ādām* as meaning "inside a human being," the difference between them being whether the word goes with the first part of the verse or the second part of the verse. The latter generates the idea of punishment by *ḥeneq*, Tanna deve Menashe's position, and the former generates the idea that a noachide is punished even for killing a fetus—spilling the blood of a "human being *inside* a human being." See further n. 46, below.

43. For drowning as *ḥeneq*, see bSan 37b and the sources cited in Yair Lorberbaum, *Ṣelem 'ĕlohim* (Tel Aviv: Schocken, 2004), 210 n. 157. Victor Aptowitzer, "Observations of the Criminal Law of the Jews," *Jewish Quarterly Review*, n.s., 15 (1924–25), 55–118, correlates the two traditions about how Cain, the first murderer, was killed—in the flood, at the hand of God, or by an arrow, at human hands—with the two opinions about how noachides are killed for violating the law, *ḥeneq* or *hereg*.

44. Descriptions of human slaying of other human beings are characterized by uses of *h-r-g*, the motif of "spilling blood," and mention of weapons that pierce the body, such as sword and arrows. For just a few examples, see Gen. 4:14 (Cain's fear that he will be killed for having spilled his brother's blood—see Gen. 4:10); Gen. 4:23 (Lemekh's boast of having killed [or of being capable of killing] someone who has wounded him [or by means of inflicting a wound]); Gen. 27:41–42 (Esau's plan to kill his brother—see Gen. 27:40 for his living by his sword); Gen. 34:25–26 (the killing of the inhabitants of Shekhem and its leaders "by sword"—see also Gen. 48:22); Gen. 37:20, 22 (the plan to kill Joseph and Reuben's plea not to spill blood). Contrast the death—*mitā*—caused by God in Gen. 38:7, 10 (the death of Er and Onan), the passage cited by Rashi to explain the term "death by the hand of heaven" in Rabbi's explanation of the

source of *ḥeneq* (see Rashi on bSan 52b, s.v. *neʾěmar mitā biydē šāmayim*, and the discussion in Chapter 1, n. 53).

45. Note that *hereg* is also the mode of execution that rabbinic sources assign to secular government (see Chapter 4, nn. 42 and 43). See the discussion in Chapter 4 of *hereg* as the punishment for murder in the sinaitic system.

46. See the discussion of Gen. 9:6 in Chapter 4 in the context of the punishment for murder. According to the standard rabbinic understanding of *bāʾādām* as "by means of a human being" (though see n. 42, above, for the absence of explicit mention of this understanding of the verse in the Bavli *sugya* on noachide law), the verse emphasizes the idea that violation of human society results in the killing of the violator at the hands of human society. Note that Cain expresses concern that this will be his fate (Gen. 4:14); his crime is, perhaps, alluded to in Gen. 9:5—"at the hand of each man's brother." Note that, if *bāʾādām* is understood as "*by means of* a human being," there is a juxtaposition in Gen. 9:5–6 between God seeking justice—*ʾedroš*—and human beings carrying out justice by killing the criminal—*bāʾādām*. (Such a reading raises the possibility that we might read the end of Gen. 9:6—"for in the image of God the human being was made"—not only as an explanation for why murder of a human being is punishable by death—because the murdered human being is created in God's image—but also as an explanation of why the human being is to carry out the justice that God has just said is in God's domain—because the human being, having been created in God's image, has the responsibility to carry out justice. See Steinmetz, "Vineyard.") This juxtaposition of God's responsibility with human responsibility parallels the notion that *wayyĕṣaw*, God's command, generates the imperative of *dinin*, human judicial activity.

47. See Chapter 4 on murder as an exception to this generalization.

48. See Sifra on Lev. 18:4 and bYoma 67b for five of the Sages' seven noachide laws (all except for *dinin* and eating the limb of a living animal) as "things that, had they not been written, it would have been reasonable for them to have been written"; this supports the notion that the criminal nature of these acts derives from their wrongfulness rather than from an awareness that one is violating a law. (See Fox, "Maimonides," for an alternate understanding of this source.) It is perhaps noteworthy that, while the noachide laws are called *mitzvot*—"commandments"—and the standard formula describes the noachides as having "been commanded"—*niṣṭawwu*, bAvoda Zara 64b uses the term "accepted": "whoever accepted upon himself the seven *mitzvot* that the noachides accepted upon themselves" (see also bBava Qama 38a and bChul 92a).

49. bSan 57b; yQid 1:1/58c; Bereshit Rabba 34:14 and 52:5 and 8. Note the derivation of this rule in the Bavli: " 'from the hand of every living being' (Gen. 9:5)—even without a *hatrāʾā*." The idea that God seeks out the spilled blood of a human being from *any* living being, human and animal alike, serves as the source of the rule that a noachide does not require a *hatrāʾā* in order to be punished. See in relation to this Ulpian's definition of natural law, in n. 29, above.

It is noteworthy that Maimonides, in *Hilkhot Melakhim* 10:1–2, distinguishes between two kinds of *šogēg* with respect to noachides: if the noachide did the act unintentionally, he is not to be punished; if he did the act intentionally but without intent to violate the law, of which he was ignorant, he is liable. The notion that ignorance of the law (*ʾomēr muttār*) is not an excuse for violation of the law, unless we take that principle to be founded on the notion that it is one's responsibility to learn the contents of the law, correlates with the view of noachide law suggested here. Maimonides does say that the person ought to have learned the law, quoting a phrase that appears in bMak 9b (and bBava Qama 92a), but since this responsibility is limited to noachide law, it would seem to reflect the notion that the content of noachide law is something that one is simply expected to know. This is in stark contrast with sinaitic law, the content of which one might well not know (see the discussion of the prohibition of brother-sister intercourse in Chapter 3) and violation of which is only punishable when the stated intent is to violate the command (see the discussion of the requirement to accept the *hatrā'ā* in Chapter 1). Note that the passage in bMakkot on which Maimonides seems to be basing his principle about the two different kinds of *šogēg* for noachides does not, in fact, make the distinction that Maimonides makes between excusable errors of fact and inexcusable ignorance of the law (in fact, the phrase that Maimonides quotes—"he should have learned and he did not learn"—refers in the Bavli to the noachide's obligation to know the facts of the situation, thus making the point that ignorance of the facts is no excuse, while Maimonides uses the phrase to mean that ignorance of the *law* is no excuse).

For a review of the thorny issue of Maimonides' approach to the basis on which the noachide observes the noachide laws, see Stone, "Sinaitic," 1168–69. And see Steven S. Schwarzschild, "Do Noachites Have to Believe in Revelation?" *Jewish Quarterly Review* 52 (1961–62), 297–308, continued in vol. 53 (1962–63), 30–65; Fox, "Maimonides"; Jacob Dienstag, "Natural Law in Maimonidean Thought and Scholarship (On *Mishneh Torah, Kings* VIII.11)," *Jewish Law Annual* 6 (1987), 64–77; and Oliver Leaman, "Maimonides and Natural Law," *Jewish Law Annual* 6 (1987), 78–93.

50. Note the formulation of the acceptance of the *hatrā'ā*: "I know, and I do it on that condition." See the discussion and sources in Chapter 1.

51. Whether an act that does not meet the minimum degree that makes it punishable is, in fact, forbidden is an interesting question in relation to positivist legal theory, since at least some versions of positivism see sanctionability, along with command, as a defining characteristic of law. See the discussion in bYoma 73b.

52. See bSan 57a–b for the idea that any violation of noachide law is punishable by death—even, for example, stealing less than the value of a *pĕruṭā*, a degree of theft not actionable under sinaitic law. Stone, "Sinaitic," sees the minimum degrees of criminal acts in sinaitic law as a dispensation—a leniency granted to those who are in other ways bound to a more stringent system of law—rather than as representing the fuller articulation as a legal system of sinaitic law in contrast with the minimal legal character of noachide law, even according to the Sages' conception.

53. For the question of whether sinaitic legislation supersedes or supplements noachide law, see Stone, "Sinaitic."

54. Note the description of pre-sinaitic law as *miṣwot golĕmiyyot* in Shemot Rabba 30:9.

55. In fact, the traditional linking of law to noachides most probably does derive from the idea that, with the flood, there was a change in the way that the world runs and, thus, in the responsibilities and rights of human beings; see my reading of the biblical narrative in "Vineyard." Such a view could be consistent with natural law, yet the Bavli seems to go out of its way to see present noachide law as unchanged from the beginning of human history, a view that is representative of natural law and that presents a sharp contrast with positive law.

56. Thus, perhaps, the wide range of competing accounts of noachide law in

the scholarly literature. Often these deal with noachide law as a general construct, without distinguishing between the different presentations of noachide law that appear in rabbinic sources.

57. *Śĕrēfā* is limited to those cases specified in the Torah and *sĕqilā* to a handful of others; see Chapter 1 for details and for the hypothesis that *sĕqilā* is the default mode of execution in the Torah.

58. See the sources and discussion in Chapter 4. See n. 44 there for the possibility that the mandate to secular authorities is, in fact, an expression of noachide law.

Chapter 3

1. See below for a qualification of this generalization.

2. Thus, the Sifra repeatedly says, in its discussion of the laws of chap. 20, "We have heard the *ʿoneš*; the *ʾazhārā* we have not heard," followed by a citation of the relevant prohibition from chap. 18. Even though the prohibitedness of the act is perfectly inferable from the fact that the person who does the act is to be punished, the Rabbis maintain that it is essential for the Torah to articulate the command prohibiting the act. See the discussion below of the idea that a prohibition cannot be based on an inference.

3. By "explicitly," I do not mean that the Torah's articulation of the prohibition and punishment is stated clearly. Often, in fact, the Rabbis derive prohibitions and punishments through exegesis of the biblical text. I mean only that the Torah must be understood to be stating the prohibition and punishment in relation to the act in question; a prohibition or punishment cannot be deduced by means of a *qal wāḥomer*—an a fortiori argument—from the existence of a prohibition or punishment for a different act.

4. It should be noted that, according to the Bavli, whether an *ʿoneš* can be inferred is disputed. The Bavli emphasizes, though, that even those who think that an *ʿoneš* can be inferred agree that an *ʾazhārā* cannot be inferred. See bSan 54a, bMak 17b, bZev 106b.

5. Lev. 18:9 is cited as the source of the principle *ʾēn mazhirin min haddin* in Sifra *Qedoshim* 10:12 on Lev. 20:17 [92b]; in bYev 22b and bMak 5b, the principle is derived from Lev. 18:9 along with Lev. 18:11. The principle is mentioned several other times in the Bavli, but no other verse is ever cited as its source.

6. Lev. 20:17 is cited as the source of the principle *ʾēn ʿonĕšin min haddin* in Sifra *Qedoshim* 10:10 on Lev. 20:17 [92b], bMak 5b and 14a, bKar 3a. *Midreshe halakha* on several other verses include an argument similar in form to the Sifra's comment on Lev. 20:17: a suggested logical inference of an *ʿoneš*, the objection "if you say thus, then you have punished based on a logical inference," and, finally, a statement that the verse that the midrash is addressing comes "to teach you that we do not punish based on a logical inference." See *Mekhilta deRabbi Yishmael, Neziqin* 7 (272–73), 11 (288), 12 (291), Sifre beMidbar 1 (ed. Horovitz, 2), 23 (28), Midrash Tannaim, Deut. 17:2 (99). In each of these cases, though, while the biblical phrase is stated to be the source of the principle, the principle actually functions to justify the Torah's inclusion of the phrase in question—that is, the principle is invoked to solve an exegetical problem, rather than the verse being invoked to generate the principle. It should be noted that the situation in the Bavli is different in two ways. First, Lev. 20:17 is the *only* verse cited in the Bavli as the source of the principle. Second, the verse is invoked as the source

of the principle when the issue under discussion is the principle, not the verse. See bMak 5b, where Lev. 20:17 is not under discussion; the verse is cited only because it is the source of the principle that is being invoked in the context of a different law entirely. Thus, while there is a strong link between the verses about brother-sister intercourse and this pair of principles in earlier sources, it is in the Bavli that the verses about brother-sister intercourse are presented as the unique source of these fundamental principles of sinaitic positive law.

7. This interpretation differs from the proposal recently set forth by Azzan Yadin in *Scripture as Logos: Rabbi Ishmael and the Origins of Midrash* (Philadelphia: University of Pennsylvania Press, 2004), 83–86. Yadin sees the principle *ʾēn ʿonĕšīn min haddin*, as articulated in the *midreshe halakha* of the school of Rabbi Yishmael, as one of several ways in which this midrashic school seeks to limit the freedom of the interpreter.

8. bMak 13a–b. This source is discussed further in Chapter 6.

9. bMak 13b–14a.

10. The positions are stated in bKet 32a, 32b, 33b.

11. bKet 32b.

12. See the discussion in Chapter 6.

13. bKar 12b.

14. bKar 2b.

15. This rule is articulated in mShab 7:1.

16. Tosafot, s.v. *minnayin lĕhatrā ʾā min hattorā*, points out that this question must be understood as going beyond the basic need to determine whether the person intends to perform the act. Tosafot takes it as a given that one cannot be punished for an unintentional act; this would not need to be derived from a biblical source. The principle to be derived, rather, is that a person whose intention to act is clear nevertheless cannot be punished without a *hatrā ʾā*. Alternatively, Tosafot suggests, the principle to be derived is the requirement that the crime be committed immediately following the *hatrā ʾā*.

17. *ʿAd šĕyyarʾuhu ṭaʿămo šel dāvār* (bSan 40b): the fact that the act is prohibited or, perhaps, the source of the prohibitedness of the act. See Chapter 1, n. 81 as to whether the actual biblical source must be cited by the witnesses when issuing the *hatrā ʾā*.

18. bSan 40b.

19. ySan 5:1/22c.

20. This is the reading of the Pene Moshe. The teaching of R. Bun does, in fact, occur in a different context in yYev 11:1/11d. According to this reading, the passage should be punctuated differently: "From where do we derive *hatrā ʾā*? R. Shmuel bar Nachman said in the name of R. Yonatan: 'And a man who takes his sister . . . .' 'it is *ḥesed*'—R. Bun said: Cain married his sister, Abel married his sister; I [says God] did an act of kindness [*ḥesed*] with the first ones so that the world would be built from them—'For I said: The world shall be built through *ḥesed*.' "

21. Sifra *Qedoshim* 10:11 on Lev. 20:17 [92b].

22. Although it is possible that this passage views *hatrā' ā* as having only the function of distinguishing between *šogēg* and *mēzid*, and not any additional function beyond that. See the discussion of the two approaches to *hatrā ʾā* in Chapter 1; and see n. 16, above. This question, though, has no bearing on my argument about the fundamental similarity between the Sifra passage and the Bavli and Yerushalmi passages.

23. bSan 57b–58b. As noted, the discussion is not limited to intercourse

between a brother and sister; rather, it relates to the entire category of relationships in which a sibling relationship is involved. It seems clear, though, that the other relationships are derivative of the brother-sister relationship. That is, if a man is not forbidden to sleep with his sister, then he cannot be forbidden to sleep with his aunt. The Gemara treats all of these relationships as a single category in the series of challenges that it brings to one or the other of the positions about sibling relationships, as the first challenge relates to the case of intercourse with an aunt, while the other two relate to intercourse with a sister.

24. bSan 58b.

25. Note that this claim is different from the similar claim in bQid 21b, where the phrase is used to argue that a woman who has been captured in war by a *kohēn* is permitted to her captor after the first act of intercourse. The argument that an object or a person remains permissible to a particular person is very different from the argument that the Gemara is making here: that an act that is permissible at one point in time must remain permissible for all time. (My thanks to Shabtai Rappaport for this point.) This latter argument, as I noted in Chapter 2, makes sense only from a natural law perspective; it makes no sense from a positivist perspective.

26. Note that this claim should not be taken to mean that the Rabbis saw this act as "natural" in the sense of normal or regular or acceptable. My claim should be understood in the limited way that I have articulated it: from the perspective of natural law as defined in my analysis of noachide law, brother-sister intercourse is not forbidden.

It is interesting that, in rabbinic sources, brother-sister intercourse is sometimes presented as something likely to occur, if only by virtue of the proximity of the people involved; see, for example, bNaz 23a, bKar 17b. Rabbinic sources, of course, see as desirable a man marrying his sister's daughter, just one step away from the prohibited relationship; see, for example, mNed 8:7 and 9:10, yYev 13:2/13c, bYev 62b, bGit 17a, bSan 76b.

27. Note that, in the Bavli, this act is allowed within a social context—Adam allows Cain to do this. Thus, Cain's act not only allows the generation of human society; it is an act that is encouraged *within* human society.

28. In the Yerushalmi passage, the *ḥesed* is God's kindness in having permitted this act. In the Bavli passage, the *ḥesed* appears to be Adam's, in allowing Cain to take his sister rather than Adam taking his daughter for himself, as well as, perhaps, God's, in allowing this act. (See Rashi on bSan 58b, s.v. *ḥesed yibbāne* and Yad Rama, 111.) In the Sifra passage, it is not clear whose *ḥesed* is being referred to; quite possibly *ḥesed* is being taken here to describe the nature of the act of brother-sister intercourse, through which the world was built. Note the appearance of the word *ḥesed* in relation to Abraham presenting Sarah as his sister in Gen. 20:13, and note the reference to this story in the Bavli passage, immediately before the discussion of Cain's marriage to his sister.

29. Awareness of the prohibition of brother-sister intercourse is presented within a rabbinic idiom as a paradigm for that which is clearly known: "if the thing is as clear to you as your sister that she is prohibited to you, say it, and, if not, do not say it." See, for example, bShab 145b, bSan 7b.

30. It is worthwhile in this context to note an extended passage in Bereshit Rabba 18 (parallel in yQid 1:1/58b–c), also dealing with sexual behavior, which highlights the distinction that I have drawn between noachide and sinaitic law in this and the preceding chapter. (See the discussion of this passage in relation to Qumran and New Testament passages in Aharon Shemesh, "4Q271.3: A Key

to Sectarian Matrimonial Law," *Journal of Jewish Studies* 49 [1998], 244–63 [section A].) The passage makes the following points:

(1) Based on "and he shall cleave to his wife" (Gen. 2:24), a noachide becomes married only through the act of sexual intercourse; there is no (legal) state of betrothal for noachides (this is articulated in terms of the absence of sanctions for a man who sleeps with a woman betrothed to another man).
(2) Based on *wĕhi' bĕʿulat baʿal* (Gen. 20:3), sexual intercourse creates a state of marriage even without (legal) intent on the part of the man to acquire the woman as a wife.
(3) There is no such thing as divorce for noachides (according to the primary interpretation that is offered and developed in the passage).
(4) The forbiddenness to noachides of adultery, of homosexuality, and of bestiality derive from "and he shall cleave to his wife."
(5) A noachide is culpable for anal sex with his wife; this prohibition derives from "and he shall cleave to his wife and they shall become one flesh" (the same verse given as the source of the rules in [1] and [2]). In this context, an obscure statement appears that says that noachides are not under the rubric of positive or negative commandments. This might mean that all violations of noachide law lead to death, unlike sinaitic law, which has violations that lead to death as well as violations that do not (see the note in the Theodor-Albeck edition, 168), or it might mean that noachide prohibitions do not derive from statutory articulations of the law but rather from narrative—the example being the verse cited here as the source of the prohibition of anal sex.

Sinaitic law differs on each of these points:

(1) The legal act of betrothal creates the status of marriage (with attendant prohibitions and sanctions).
(2) Sexual intercourse creates marriage only with accompanying legal intent.
(3) The state of marriage can be dissolved by means of legal acts that effect a change in legal status (with attendant voiding of the prohibitions and sanctions brought into effect by the act of betrothal).
(4–5) Acts are prohibited if and only if they are articulated as prohibited in a statutory formulation.

Note that the first three points relate to a different element of legal systems from the element of the statutory formulation of prohibitions on which we have focused and to which the last two points relate. See, in this regard, H. L. A. Hart's discussion of the place of legal powers and "power-conferring rules" within the framework of a positivist conception of law in *The Concept of Law* (New York: Oxford University Press, 1997), 27–42.

Chapter 4

1. mSan 9:1.
2. See Chapter 1, n. 15, about whether the Torah's command to kill the inhabitants of *ʿir hanniddaḥat* by sword ought to be seen as a judicial punishment. See also n. 41, below.

3. Gen. 9:6. It is not entirely clear what those consequences are; see n. 12, below.

4. For the sources of these punishments for violation of noachide law, see Chapter 2, nn. 41–42.

5. See Sifre beMidbar 161 (222), tKar 4:3, bKet 37b, and bSota 47b, which derive this law from Num. 35:33, a verse that will be discussed shortly, and ySota 9:6/23a, Rashi on Deut. 31:9, and Maimonides, *Hilkhot Rotzeach* 10:8, for a derivation from the verse that concludes the *ʿeglā ʿărufā* passage. See below for how the Bavli sees the *ʿeglā ʿărufā* ritual as informing the procedure for execution of a murderer.

6. Other crimes, especially sexual offenses, also affect the land and the people's ability to remain on the land—see, for example, Lev. 18:25–28—but murder is unique in that atonement is required for the land. For some examples of the juxtaposition of murder and sexual offenses, see Ezek. 16:38, 22:1–13, and 23:45; and the exegesis of Deut. 22:26 in bSan 73a.

7. See Devarim Rabba 2 on murder as the only crime (that is, the only violation of the six *mitzvot* commanded to Adam) that cannot be forgiven; the murderer's blood must be shed. See the story told there about the seething blood of a murder victim that is calmed only when the murderer has been killed.

8. On the different biblical passages about the city of refuge and their different foci, see Moshe Greenberg, "The Biblical Concept of Asylum," *Journal of Biblical Literature* 78 (1959), 125–32; and Alexander Rofe, "On the Origins of the Cities of Refuge in Biblical Law" (Hebrew), *Bēt miqrāʾ* 31 (1985–86), 110–33.

9. See Sifre beMidbar 160 (220) on why the unintentional murderer must stay in the city of refuge until the death of the high priest (Num. 35:25): "Rabbi says: A murderer defiles the land and causes the divine presence to depart, and a high priest causes the divine presence to rest on the human being in the land; it is not reasonable that the person who defiles the land and causes the divine presence to depart be in the presence of the person who causes the divine presence to rest on the human being in the land."

10. See below on exile as the primordial punishment for murder.

11. The elements of atonement and exile are highlighted in rabbinic discussions of the city of refuge. A result of seeing exile to the city of refuge as atonement is the development, within rabbinic sources, of categories of killers who do not go to a city of refuge: someone who kills by a completely unforeseeable accident and someone who bears a significant measure of responsibility for the killing. The former does not require atonement, and the latter does not deserve it. Note that the person who is not aware that killing is prohibited falls within the latter category; see n. 45, below.

12. The meaning of *bāʾādām* in this verse has been the subject of dispute from ancient times to the present. See Chapter 2, n. 41, for an exegesis in bSan 57b that takes this preposition to mean "within," and note also the interpretation in bSan 58b that, parsing the verse differently, takes *hāʾādām bāʾādām* to refer to the killing of a fetus, a human being "within" another human being. The standard rabbinic understanding of *bā-* is "by means of" (see, for example, the comment of Rashi on bSan 56a, cited in Chapter 2, n. 42, and a variety of classical midrashim, commentaries, and targumim). An alternate rendering of *bā-* is "instead of" or "on account of" (see LXX); that is, the murderer's blood is to be spilled *on account of* the human being who has been murdered, a reading that leaves the subject of the spilling of the murderer's blood unstated and that, possibly, clears up the fact that the previous verse has God as the seeker of justice

(see Chapter 2, n. 46, for an understanding of the relationship between these two verses according to the reading of *bā-* as "by"). For these two readings argued by contemporary scholars, see the dispute between Bernard S. Jackson, *Essays in Jewish and Comparative Legal History* (Leiden: Brill, 1975), 46–47, and Moshe Greenberg, "More Reflections on Biblical Criminal Law," in Sarah Japhet, ed., *Studies in Bible* (Jerusalem: Magnes, 1986 [= *Scripta Hierosolymitana* 31]), 15–16 and nn. 29–30. In any event, it seems clear that Num. 35:33 is reading Gen. 9:6 as requiring a human being to shed the blood of the murderer. Since this is the standard rabbinic interpretation of Gen. 9:6, as noted, it is reflected in my translation and discussion of this verse as a key part of the biblical background to the rabbinic treatment of murder and its consequences.

13. See Yair Lorberbaum, "Blood and the Image of God: The Punishment of Beheading in Early Rabbinical Literature" (Hebrew), *Meḥqĕrē mišpāṭ* 15 (2000), 429–56.

14. For a discussion of Cain's elaboration of the consequences of his act, see Devora Steinmetz, "Vineyard, Farm, and Garden: The Drunkenness of Noah in the Context of Primeval History," *Journal of Biblical Literature* 113 (1994), 193–207.

15. Note the mention of "his brother" in the preceding verse; see Chapter 2, n. 46. For a discussion of this passage as representing a shift in human responsibility and in governance of the world after the flood, see Steinmetz, "Vineyard."

16. Compare the conception of the *gō'ēl haddām* as a plaintiff who loses if the person on trial for murder is found innocent in bSan 33b; the notion of a plaintiff who loses if the defendant wins is seen as unique, in trials for capital offenses, to the case of murder. See n. 39, below, for the idea that serving as plaintiff is one of the central roles of the *gō'ēl haddām* for the purpose of which the court must appoint a surrogate *gō'ēl* if no *gō'ēl* exists.

17. See below on the role of the *gō'ēl haddām* in rabbinic sources and on the *gō'ēl haddām* as a possible paradigm for the judicial and communal response to murder.

18. The term *gō'ēl haddām* underscores the notion of restoration effected by the punishment of the murderer; compare the redeemer in Leviticus 25 and the idea of returning to one's portion of land in Leviticus 25 and in Num. 35:28. My thanks to David Silber for this point.

19. For one such analysis and a discussion of some of the literature related to this subject, see Lorberbaum, "Blood." Lorberbaum sees the blood specifically as incorporating the human being's shared essence with God, a view that I do not share. On the contrary, blood seems to represent, in the Torah, the life force that human beings share with other living creatures. Animal blood, thus, must not be consumed by a human being; it must either be returned to God, by being placed on the altar, or returned to the earth. (See Ezek. 34:6–8 for blood that is left exposed; note that here, pouring blood on the earth is equivalent to—or leads to—the blood being covered. For the difficulties in interpreting and reconciling the laws concerning slaughtering of animals and treatment of the blood in Leviticus 17 and Deuteronomy 12 and the differences in the way that these laws were understood in rabbinic and Qumran texts, see Cana Werman, "The Law of Covering Blood and Eating It in Priestly Halakha and the Halakha of the Sages" [Hebrew], *Tarbiṣ* 63 [1994], 173–83. For the suggestion that the understanding of blood underwent a transformation in the rabbinic period, see Noam Zohar, "Ancient Rituals Transmitted by R. Judah: Evidence of a Transformed Understanding of 'Blood Is Life' " [Hebrew], *Tarbiṣ* 58 [1989], 525–30. On the

significance of blood in the primeval narrative, see Tikva Frymer-Kensky, "The Atrahasis Epic and Its Significance for Our Understanding of Genesis 1–9," *Biblical Archaeologist* 40 [1977], 147–55.) But the fact that this animating substance is shared by animals and human beings suggests that we cannot look to this substance as the locus of *ṣelem ʾĕlohim*. See Gen. 9:3–6, where all blood is off-limits, but only the human being's blood cannot be shed; if it is shed by a human being, then that person's blood is shed, because the human being is created in *ṣelem ʾĕlohim*. It cannot be, then, that blood is the locus of the human being's shared essence with God, since the special quality of blood is shared by human beings and animals, while *ṣelem ʾĕlohim* is unique to human beings. In fact, neither passage that describes the creation of the human being—neither Genesis 1, where *ṣelem ʾĕlohim* is mentioned but the materials out of which the human being is created are not, nor Genesis 2, where the materials are mentioned but *ṣelem ʾĕlohim* is not—includes any mention of blood.

20. bSan 52b, commenting on mSan 9:1.

21. For the juxtaposition of murder and *nĕqāmā* in the story of the first murder in the Torah, see Gen. 4:15, 24.

22. This reciprocity is suggested by the phrase *yirṣaḥ ʾet hāroṣēaḥ* (Num. 35:30) in addition to the biblical sources mentioned above (see Gerald Blidstein, "Capital Punishment: The Classic Jewish Discussion," *Judaism* 14 [1965], 169 n. 7); see *Mekhilta deRashbi* on Exod. 21:12 (169) and the *baraita* in ySan 7:3/24b. See Aharon Shemesh, "*ʾĒlu hēn hanneherāgin: ʿIyyun bĕfereq mittorat hāʿonĕšim šel ḥazal*," *Šĕnāton hammišpāṭ hāʿivri* 21 (1998–2000), 267–90, for the hypothesis, based on a reading of the tannaitic sources, of an early rabbinic position that the murderer was to be killed in the way that he killed. Whether or not the sources suggest that such a position was in fact maintained, they certainly present such a position as a theoretical possibility (such an idea occurs in non-rabbinic sources; see Jubilees 4:31–32, and see Victor Aptowitzer, "Observations of the Criminal Law of the Jews," *Jewish Quarterly Review*, n.s., 15 [1924–25], 55–118; Chanokh Albeck, *Sēder nĕziqin* [Jerusalem: Dvir, 1953], 453; and Samuel Kraus, "*Pereq biysurē hagguf*," *Dĕvir* 1 [1923], 88–112); see especially *Mekhilta deRashbi* on Exod. 21:12 (169) and ySan 7:3/24b, the two sources that work with *yirṣaḥ ʾet hāroṣēaḥ*. And perhaps we should read the conclusions of these *baraitot*, that the murder is to be "avenged" by sword, as sustaining the notion of reciprocal vengeance but generalizing and institutionalizing it in the form of *hereg*—the paradigmatic way that human beings kill. (See below on the degree to which the execution of the murderer may not, in fact, be fully institutionalized and formalized.) Peretz Segal argues the exact opposite, that the citation of the *ḥerev noqemet* brought by God in Lev. 26:25 suggests that in *hereg*, as, he argues, in all other forms of *mitat bēt din*, judicial execution is understood in rabbinic texts as similar to ways in which God kills and as having the function of atonement; he sees this as a rejection of an older talionic view. For Segal, then, the two derivations of *hereg* discussed in the preceding note *both* emphasize atonement, rather than highlighting two aspects of the sanction for murder, as I have argued; see Segal, "*Ḥiyyuv biydē šāmayim: ʿIyyun bĕfereq mittorat hāʿonĕšim šel ḥazal*" (Ph.D. diss., Hebrew University, 1986), 116, and "Postbiblical Jewish Criminal Law and Theology," *Jewish Law Annual* 9 (1991), 107–21.

23. See also ySan 7:1/24b and 7:3/24b, *Mekhilta deRabbi Yishmael, Neziqin* 4 (261–62) (here the initial derivation of *hereg* is from Gen. 9:6) and 7 (273) and *Mekhilta deRashbi* on Exod. 21:12 (169).

24. *Mekhilta deRabbi Yishmael, Kaspa* 20 (327), tSan 11:4, ySan 5:1/22d, bSan

72b; and see Avot deRabbi Natan a, 16. This verse is also cited as the *ʿoneš* for murder in *Mekhilta deRabbi Yishmael, baChodesh* 8 (232). In *Mekhilta deRashbi* on Exod. 20:13 (152), though, the biblical source that serves as the *ʿoneš* is the much more likely *mot yumāt hāroṣēaḥ* (Num. 35:16).

25. It is especially striking that the *hatrāʾā* begins with a statement that the intended victim is an Israelite, a prerequisite for punishment of the murderer by the *bēt din*, and yet goes on to cite a verse that reflects a universal context.

26. See Chapter 2, nn. 41 and 42. One could argue that the citation of this verse has nothing to do with the elements noted here, that it is cited simply because it is more explicit about the mode of execution than any alternate verse: "his blood shall be spilled" implies *hereg*. Reference within the *hatrāʾā* to the specific mode of execution is required by R. Yehuda in bSan 8b and 80b (R. Yose beR. Yehuda in tSan 11:1). But even according to this opinion, it would presumably suffice to state the punishment without reference to an explicit biblical text; otherwise, it would be impossible to give a *hatrāʾā* for most capital offenses, since most do not have the mode of execution explicitly specified in the Torah.

27. Though even this requirement is not absolute in the case of murder; see the following paragraph.

28. bSan 45b, 53a, 72b; see also bBava Metzia 31b and nn. 31 and 41, below.

29. mSan 9:5. While this could be seen as a form of restraint—essentially, imprisonment of the criminal for the protection of society—the Bavli sees this as a way of killing the murderer outside of the rubric of the *ʾarbaʿ mitot* (bSan 81b). In the Mishna, murder is the only capital offense for which *kippā* is mandated if the person cannot be prosecuted because of lack of witnesses. (*Kippā* is also mandated for repeat committers of noncapital offenses in mSan 9:5, though how the person is treated in the *kippā* is described differently in these two mishnayot. The Bavli, though, takes the treatment of the two kinds of criminals to be the same. For a discussion of the two cases of *kippā* in this mishna, see Jackson, *Essays in Jewish and Comparative Legal History*, 187–93.) In contrast, the Tosefta (tSan 12:7) mandates *kippā* for all repeat violators of capital offenses who cannot be prosecuted under regular judicial procedure; it does not single out the murderer. The Bavli, though, interprets this source as referring to noncapital offenses. Similarly, the Tosefta (tSan 12:6) says that a person condemned of any capital offense can be killed in any way, if the court is unable to impose the mandated form of execution; the Tosefta cites *uviʿartā hārāʿ miqqirbekhā* as the basis of this mandate. In contrast, the Bavli limits this mandate to the crime of murder (see sources cited in preceding note). It is only in the Bavli combined with the Mishna, then, that all three dispensations discussed here appear as unique to murder: killing in any way, killing by anyone (for this dispensation, see the following paragraph in this note, and see n. 31 as well as the discussion of the *goʾēl haddām*, below), and condemnation to *kippā* in the absence of witnesses to the crime.

Note that Maimonides, *Hilkhot Rotzeach* 4:8–9, follows the Mishna and Bavli in limiting *kippā* to murder, commenting that no other crime entails *hašḥātat yiššuvo šel ʿolām*—the destruction of civilization or the social order—as murder does. On the other hand, Maimonides rules in *Hilkhot Sanhedrin* 14:8 that a criminal convicted of any capital offense can be killed in any way necessary. See the commentaries on the difficulty of reconciling this position with the Bavli. Maimonides does distinguish, however, between murder and other capital offenses with regard to who can implement the execution; only for murder can anyone kill the criminal if he cannot be killed by the designated executioner; see *Hilkhot Sanhedrin* 14:8 and 13:1. See the discussion below of who is to kill the murderer; for Maimonides' position, see n. 39, below. As noted in Chapter 1, n. 6, Maimonides also cites murder as the crime that a king is mandated to punish, if it is not punishable by the *bēt din*; see especially *Hilkhot Rotzeach* 2:4 and *Hilkhot Melakhim* 3:10, in both of which Maimonides cites the goal of *tikkun ʿolām*, the rectifying of the destruction mentioned in *Hilkhot Rotzeach* 4:9.

30. bSan 45b; compare Sifre beMidbar 160 (219) and Sifre Devarim 186–87 (ed. Finkelstein, 226). In the Bavli passage, the court is said to appoint a surrogate *goʾēl haddām*; see the discussion, below, on what function of the *goʾēl haddām* is referred to in this provision.

31. The first and third laws mentioned here are juxtaposed in the Bavli (bSan 45b) in a way that renders these dispensations exclusive to the cases of *roṣēaḥ* and *goʾēl haddām* (*šnē kĕtuvin habbāʾin kĕʾeḥād*). (But see n. 41, below, and see also bSan 53a and the commentaries on Maimonides, *Hilkhot Sanhedrin* 13:1, 7 and 14:8 as to whether these dispensations are, in fact, exclusive to these cases; see n. 29, above. Of course, both of these cases refer to murder, and thus what emerges is that it is only in the case of murder that anyone can kill the criminal in any way possible. It is noteworthy that elsewhere, the Bavli derives this same pair of dispensations for the case of the *bāʾ bĕmaḥteret* (bSan 72b); this perpetrator is assumed to pose a threat to the life of the householder (bSan 72a), and thus he may be killed by anyone in any way possible. It should be noted that the Gemara's assumption that there needs to be a biblical source allowing the perpetrator to be killed in any way possible suggests that the law permitting the slaying of this perpetrator, while exceptional (in that the slaying occurs before any capital offense has been committed and is preventive rather than punitive) and nonjudicial, can nevertheless be analyzed from the perspective of judicial criminal procedure. (This is reflected, as well, in other elements of the Gemara's discussion of the *bāʾ bĕmaḥteret*, such as the question of whether he can be killed on Shabbat [bSan 72b], the application to this case of the principle that a person liable for the death penalty does not incur a monetary penalty [bSan 72a; see mSan 8:6], and the question of whether a *hatrāʾā* is required in order for someone to kill a pursuer to save the intended victim [bSan 72b].)

This same *sugya* includes the *hatrāʾā* from Gen. 9:6 in two sources (the second is essentially the same as tSan 11:4, while the first is unique to this passage), the first relating to the pursuer and the second relating to murder to be punished by the court, but both of which the Bavli interprets (at least initially) as relating to the case of a pursuer. The first of these sources includes, after the quotation of Gen. 9:6, what the verse is being cited to suggest: "save this person's blood with this person's blood." The verse is being understood thus: "He who intends to spill the blood of a human being on account of a human being his blood shall be spilt." (See Rashi on bSan 72b, s.v. *wĕhattorā ʾāmĕrā*, and see LXX for a similar understanding of *bāʾādām* [see n. 12, above]; in both cases, *ʾādām* is understood to refer to the victim, rather than to the murderer or the one who will slay the murderer, as in the interpretations cited in Chapter 2, nn. 41–42.) Gen. 9:6, then, is presented as the mandate for a social, nonjudicial response to the would-be murderer. But note that it is this same source that provides the basis of the formal *hatrāʾā* for murder, to be punished in a court, as discussed above. Essentially, then, murder is an act that demands the response of society's members, whether to prevent its commission or to punish its committer. Anyone can kill the murderer in any way, whether to keep him from killing or to respond to his having killed. Formalized for the judiciary, this translates into the court imposing the *mitā* of *hereg* for murder. But the laws of *bĕkhol ʾādām* and *bĕkhol mitā* emphasize that the original mandate to human society to respond to murder is not superseded; it is merely implemented through the court, when that is possible. See below for *hereg* as the court's implementation of human society's response to murder.

32. Or Num. 35:21, if the word *huʾ* is not present after the words *goʾēl haddām*. In both verses, the words that are quoted in the continuation of this passage follow the words just quoted.

33. bSan 45b; compare Sifre beMidbar 160 (219), where the rule that someone else kills the intentional murderer if there is no *goʾēl haddām* is derived from the redundancy of Num. 35:21 with Num. 35:19. The Sifre passage, though, does not talk about the court appointing a surrogate *goʾēl haddām*.

34. See Num. 35:26–27. The second of these verses allows for different constructions, depending on how the verse is parsed. The traditional parsing lends itself to a reading that suggests that the *goʾēl haddām* is expected to kill the unintentional murderer: "If the murderer leaves the border of his city of refuge to which he has fled, and the *goʾēl haddām* finds him outside of the border of his city of refuge, *then* the *goʾēl haddām* shall murder the murderer; he has no bloodguilt." An alternative reading emerges if the main break in the second verse appears before the final clause, instead of where the word "then" appears in the rendering that I just offered. This parsing locates the *goʾēl haddām*'s killing of the murderer with the apodosis of the sentence, suggesting that the killing of the unintentional murderer by the *goʾēl haddām* is merely allowed: "If the murderer leaves the border of his city of refuge to which he has fled, and the *goʾēl haddām* finds him outside of the border of his city of refuge, *and* the *goʾēl haddām* murders the murderer, *then* he has no bloodguilt." See mMak 2:7 and the dispute that appears in bMak 12a as to whether the *goʾēl haddām* is expected or merely allowed to kill the unintentional murderer and whether other people are allowed to do so. For the latter issue, compare Sifre beMidbar 160 (220).

35. bSan 45, s.v. *wĕgoʾēl haddām*.

36. An additional problem with this interpretation lies in the difficulty of reconciling this passage, if interpreted this way, with the *baraita* in bMak 12a that discusses whether Num. 35:27 commands or permits the *goʾēl haddām* to kill the unintentional murderer and whether individuals other than the *goʾēl haddām* are permitted or forbidden to kill this person.

37. See n. 34, above, for two different readings of this verse.

38. This verse is quoted in a *baraita* in bMak 10b in the context of the procedure for bringing murderers to trial after their initial flight to the city of refuge; for this procedure, see also mMak 2:6 and Sifre beMidbar 220. In Sifre Devarim 186–87 (226), the rule that anyone can kill the murderer if he does not die at the hands of the *goʾēl haddām* is derived from this verse.

39. This understanding is adopted by the Yad Rama (89) and the author of Chidushei haRan, though they do not make reference to the Deuteronomy passage. The latter, though, foregrounds another role of the *goʾēl haddām* or his surrogate: to prosecute the murderer in court. (See bSan 33b and n. 16, above. See also Num. 35:24–25, where the community is charged with judging between the murderer and the *goʾēl haddām*; these verses are understood in rabbinic texts to refer to a formal judicial process. In fact, these verses are offered as the source for the constitution of the court in which capital offenses are tried [mSan 1:6, tSan 3:7, Sifre beMidbar 160 (220)].) Nachmanides (on *Sefer haMitzvot*, in his

mitzvat ase 13) also highlights the *goʾēl haddām*'s role in the judicial process, but somewhat differently: it is the *goʾēl haddām*'s job to seek vengeance by pursuing the murderer and bringing him to justice; but it is only if the court is unable to execute the murderer that the *goʾēl haddām* does so. The *goʾēl haddām*, then, stands behind the judicial process but does not actually participate in it. Maimonides' position is difficult to pin down. In *Hilkhot Rotzeach* 1:2, he says that the *goʾēl haddām* kills the convicted murderer; if he doesn't want to or is unable to, or if there is no *goʾēl haddām*, then the court executes the murderer by sword. (Note that Maimonides does not describe this as the court appointing a surrogate *goʾēl*, and note also the repetition here of "by sword" when this was already stated as the designated mode of execution for murder in 1:1. Does this imply that Maimonides thinks that the *goʾēl haddām*, if willing and able to kill the murderer, does so in any way he sees fit—that is, that the *goʾēl haddām* does not perform a judicial execution, but rather has the murderer handed over to him by the court—and that there is a judicial execution only in the absence of a *goʾēl haddām*? On the other hand, see *Hilkhot Sanhedrin* 13:1 and 14:8; the first explicitly mentions the witnesses as executing the murderer. (Perhaps, though, we ought to take this in the context of the suggestion in the parenthetical comment above: Maimonides sees the murderer as either handed over to the *goʾēl haddām* to be killed or executed formally by the court; in the latter case, Maimonides takes the execution to be carried out by the witnesses, as he holds all judicial executions to be; see Chapter 1, n. 41. If this is so, then Maimonides' position is different from, say, that of the Yad Rama or Chidushei haRan: they have the *goʾēl haddām* executing the convicted murderer with a surrogate *goʾēl haddām* appointed by the court in his absence, while Maimonides has either the *goʾēl haddām* killing the convicted murderer outside of standard capital procedure or the court executing him under standard procedure for the execution of criminals.) Each of these interpretations, it should be emphasized, affords a role for the *goʾēl haddām* that is absolutely unique within sinaitic criminal law.

40. It is interesting in this regard that mSan discusses irregular punishments at the end of the chapter that talks about murder. See especially mSan 9:6, which talks of crimes that evoke a communal response.

41. In bBava Metzia 31b, the only other crime punishable by *hereg* is also said to have the dispensation of killing in any way possible. Based on a midrashic reading of Deut. 13:16, the Gemara says that the inhabitants of *ʿir hanniddaḥat*, for whom the Torah mandates death by sword, can be killed in any way available if it is not possible to kill them by sword. (Tannaitic sources mention other crimes for which, if you cannot impose the designated mode of capital punishment, you impose an alternative mode of execution. See *Mekhilta deRashbi* on Exod. 21:15–17 (172–73) [for one who strikes father or mother, for one who steals and sells a person, and for one who curses father or mother], and Sifre Devarim 94 (155), for the law of *ʿir hanniddaḥat*. These sources, though, seem to suggest only that the court can impose one of the other forms of *mitat bēt din*, not that the criminals in these cases can be killed in any way at all, which is what bSan 45b and bBava Metzia 31b say for the cases of murder and *ʿir hanniddaḥat*. See Shemesh, "*ʾĒlu hēn hannehĕrāgin*," and see Tosafot on bMak 2a, s.v. *kol hazzomĕmin maqdimin lĕʾotah mitā*.) See Chapter 1, n. 15, on the killing of the inhabitants of *ʿir hanniddaḥat* in the Torah as a social, rather than judicial, response to their apostasy. While rabbinic texts see the killing of these people in a judicial context, perhaps we should see *ʿir hanniddaḥat* as well as murder as cases where rabbinic sources regulate the social response through judicial procedure, but as

retaining in rabbinic sources the underlying notion of a social response—first, in that the designated *mitat bēt din* is *hereg* and, second, in the fact that formal execution is not the only way in which the violator can be killed.

42. mSan 7:3.

43. Both tSan 9:10 and ySan 7:1/24b comment, in relation to the four modes of judicial execution (mSan 7:1), on the more limited mandate to the government (generally taken to refer to the Jewish king, as opposed to the non-Jewish monarch of mSan 7:3) to execute only by sword; this comment does not appear in the Bavli. See Gerald Blidstein, "On Political Structures: Four Medieval Comments," *Jewish Journal of Sociology* 22 (1980), 47–58, for some medieval discussions of the power of the king; and see Chapter 1, n. 6.

44. See the comment of the *Or Sameach* on Maimonides, *Hilkhot Melakhim* 3:10 (the power of the king to execute a murderer based on the testimony of one witness); he sees both the power of the king and the mandate of the *go'ēl haddām* as deriving from the same need for social order (*tiqqun hammĕdinā*) that underlies noachide law. Note that Maimonides includes noachide law in *Hilkhot Melakhim*. See Nachum Rakover, "Jewish Law and the Noachide Obligation to Preserve Social Order," *Cardozo Law Review* 12 (1991), 1073–1136, for the notion that *din melekh* is a form of the noachide law/natural law obligation to preserve justice; and see Arnold Enker, "Aspects of Interaction Between the Torah Law, the King's Law, and the Noachide Law in Jewish Criminal Law," *Cardozo Law Review* 12 (1991), 1137–56, on the relationship between the supplementary powers of the court and king to preserve social welfare and the noachide obligation of *dinin* (note, however, that the supplementary powers of the court are not, in fact, limited to crimes relating to social welfare; see bSan 46a). The notion that *dinin* has its proper place within society (see, for example, the *Mishne Tora* passage discussed in Chapter 2, n. 33), though it specifically mandates the institution of courts to regulate and formalize the social response to criminal behavior, is parallel to the notion that murder is properly responded to by the *go'ēl haddām* or other members of human society (see n. 31, above), though the court is empowered to regulate and implement the social response to murder.

45. Two other indications that murder, unlike other crimes within the sinaitic system, is seen as retaining a natural law character merit consideration. First, the murderer who was unaware of the illegality of his act (*'omēr muttār*) is not considered to have acted *bĕšogēg*; he is in the category of *qārov lĕmēzid* (bMak 7b). See Chapter 2, n. 49, on the idea that ignorance of the law is not an excuse for violations of noachide law. While the murderer who acts in ignorance of the law is not punishable in *bēt din*, the fact that his act is not treated as *šogēg* suggests that knowledge of the prohibition is not the fundamental ingredient in rendering an act of murder criminal. And, by being excluded from obtaining sanctuary in the city of refuge, this murderer is vulnerable to being killed by the *go'ēl haddām* (see Maimonides, *Hilkhot Rotzeach* 6:4 and 10).

Second, in its discussion of which crimes one ought to give up one's life rather than violate (bSan 74a), the Bavli bases its inclusion in this category of murder on *sevara*—reason—rather than on biblical texts, from which the other laws in this category are derived. (In fact, sexual offenses are derived from a biblical text that juxtaposes adultery and murder [Deut. 22:26], though the derivation of murder itself is not scriptural.) The implication is that, even in the hard case of "one should be killed and not transgress," we can conclude the wrongness of murder based on reason; a biblical text is not necessary to teach this law. (I am indebted to David Silber for pointing out the relevance of this passage to the argument presented here on the nature of murder. See also J. D. Bleich, "Judaism and Natural Law," *Jewish Law Annual* 7 (1988), 6–42.

It is noteworthy, though, that Rashi's understanding of this passage locates the *sevara* squarely within a positivist framework. Rashi understands the question "who is to say that your blood is redder than his [i.e., that the blood of the person who is told to kill or be killed is redder than the blood of the proposed victim]" as canceling out the consideration of *wĕḥay bāhem* (Lev. 18:5)—understood as the injunction to preserve life even if means violating a commandment, rather than relinquish life to avoid violating a commandment. That is, for Rashi, we analyze the prohibition of murder no differently from any other prohibition: fundamentally, we must not disobey "the word of the king," but the principle of *wĕḥay bāhem* tells us that, generally, God prefers that we preserve life even if it means violating a commandment. In the case of murder, though, life would not be preserved if the commandment is violated; there is loss of life whether the person transgresses or does not transgress, and who is to say that the life of the person who must decide whether or not to kill is more valuable to God than the other person's life? Since we cannot apply the consideration of *wĕḥay bāhem* to allow transgression of God's command, we are left bound by that command not to kill. While the Gemara seems to see this choice as based on reason, Rashi sees it as deriving from a clear-cut prohibition; the *sevara*, according to Rashi, only serves to show why we cannot, in this case, apply the usually overriding divine imperative of *wĕḥay bāhem*. See the discussion of Tanna deve Menashe's prohibition of crossbreeding in Chapter 2, n. 40, for another example of Rashi interpreting from a positivist perspective a statement that I have suggested reflects a natural law conception.

46. Though see n. 29, above.

47. See Peter Brooks's discussion of the imposition of the requirement of confession by the Church in the thirteenth century in relation to "the emergence of the modern sense of selfhood and the individual's responsibility for his or her own actions, intentions, thoughts," in *Troubling Confessions: Speaking Guilt in Law and Literature* (Chicago: University of Chicago Press, 2000), 5. In comparing acceptance of the *hatrā'ā* to confession (in either the religious or legal context), it should be noted that acceptance of the *hatrā'ā* takes place at a different point from confession; in fact, according to rabbinic texts, after-the-fact admission to having violated the law has no role in judicial proceedings (see tSan 9:4, and see bSan 9b and parallels and the passages discussed in Aaron Kirschenbaum, *The Criminal Confession in Jewish Law* [Hebrew] [Jerusalem: Magnes, 2005], 129–57. It should be noted, though, that rabbinic texts also discuss confession before execution [see mSan 6:2 and tSan 9:5], but this is a general confession for sins and its stated goal is atonement; the court's ability to execute the convicted person is not dependent on this confession). Nevertheless, like the kinds of confession that Brooks discusses, acceptance of the *hatrā'ā* lays bare the deliberateness of the person's action, and it is the revealing of this internal state that allows for conviction for the crime that is committed.

48. While the comparison between acceptance of the *hatrā'ā* and confession is only partial (see preceding note), it is worth considering what Brooks says about the role of confession in contemporary criminal investigations and judicial procedure (*Troubling Confessions*, 4–5): "To do its job—to pass judgment—the law needs to insist upon traditional notions of responsibility. . . . Yet . . . where confession is concerned, the law needs to recognize that its conception of human motivation and volition are particularly flawed, even perhaps some-

thing of a fiction." If, similarly, the conception of human action expressed by the acceptance of the *hatrā'ā* is "something of a fiction," then the question that I am seeking to address is: What is the meaning or purpose of the fiction that is created by the rabbinic texts that describe criminal procedure?

49. Note that the idea that one can escape the consequence of one's actions because of lack of full awareness and, thus, responsibility for one's actions makes sense only within a framework of command and punishment. In the real world, the consequences of one's actions come whether one acted in full awareness or not. (See Steinmetz, "Vineyard," for a discussion of this point in relation to the stories of Adam, Cain, and Noah.) Thus, in a natural law framework (such as noachide law), the consequences of actions are unrelated to knowledge or intention, while in a positive law framework, consequences come only with knowledge and intention. See the discussion in Chapter 6. My argument (see below and next note) is that the Rabbis' construction of law combines an assertion of human responsibility with the acknowledgment that human beings are often less than fully responsible.

50. An illustration of the idea that an extreme construction of free and knowing agency creates room for recognizing that behavior is most often less than fully purposive is the Kol Nidre service, which inaugurates Yom Kippur. The service begins with *hattārat nĕdārim*, the annulment of vows, a procedure that is based on the notion that people make vows with less than full awareness of the circumstances and consequences of their actions. Had the person known all the circumstances and consequences, we claim, the person would never have taken the vow, and so the vow, we declare, was no vow at all. But of course, the very idea that vows that are made with less than full awareness are not vows is generated by a vision of the ideal vow that is taken with full knowledge of the circumstances and consequences.

Immediately after *hattārat nĕdārim* follows a recitation of Num. 15:26: "And it shall be forgiven for all of the congregation of the children of Israel and for the stranger that sojourns in their midst, because for all of the people it is in error [*bišgāgā*]." The parallel to *hattārat nĕdārim* is clear. The Numbers verse appears in the passage that goes on to talk about purposeful violation of God's commandments; purposeful violation results in *kārēt* (see the discussion of this passage in Chapter 5). Just as the Kol Nidre service begins with a statement that vows were taken in error—that is, with less than full knowledge of the circumstances and consequences—it continues with the statement that the sins that were committed by the congregation were committed in error. Just as a vow that was taken in ignorance is no vow, a sin that was committed in ignorance is to be forgiven. The claim with which we begin the day, then, is that human mischoice is to be forgiven because, at its core, it was based in error.

But, of course, we can only make that claim once we have a vision of intentional action, action that is based on full knowledge and is thus fully responsible. Just as the possibility of annulling vows can only emerge from an extreme construction of a binding vow as one that is based on full knowledge of circumstances and consequences, the declaration that sin is unintentional and to be forgiven emerges from an extreme construction of intentional sin as action that is based on full knowledge of circumstances and consequences. It is this kind of action that is portrayed in the image of the person who is about to sin accepting upon himself the *hatrā'ā*: "I know, and I do it on that condition."

Thus, it is the extreme affirmation of human freedom and moral agency that makes room for human frailty. The day on which we assert our responsibility as moral agents, on which we repeat over and over again the confession of sins, begins with an assertion of less than full moral agency, of human ignorance and frailty. We demand forgiveness for actions that we have done, based on the claim that we just did not know better, and we simultaneously assert that we have the power to change ourselves and to act as full moral agents. (In fact, the word "demand" may be too mild a characterization of what we are doing in this part of the service. The word *wĕnislaḥ*, which in its biblical context means "and it shall be forgiven," can also mean "and we will forgive." It is possible that the liturgical use of this verse plays on this meaning—that is, just as the community has just declared vows to be annulled, it now declares sins to have been forgiven. For the community—or court—taking action to enable atonement for sin, see the discussion of *malqut* in Chapter 5. Note that the notion that a vow is not unequivocally binding, that it can be annulled by a court, is a rabbinic invention, parallel to the rabbinic denial of the inevitability of *kārēt* as a consequence of sin and the court's imposition of *malqut* to trump *kārēt*. See also the discussion in Chapter 5 of the talmudic passage that shows God agreeing to the determinations of the human court; compare the recitation of the passage that concludes "And God said: I have forgiven in accordance with your words" (Num. 14:19–20) that follows the recitation of Num. 15:26 in the Kol Nidre service. Note in relation to these observations the custom of two people flanking the leader of the Kol Nidre service, symbolizing a court of three.) (I am indebted to David Silber for some of these thoughts about the Kol Nidre service.)

This is the very same pair of moves that I am locating in the Rabbis' radical assertion of human freedom that is expressed in rabbinic texts about criminal procedure and punishment. The emphasis on full moral agency leaves the whole range of less than fully responsible action, and we seek to excuse ourselves for our errors at the same time that we assert responsibility for our actions and the power to transform ourselves. Thus, the construction of an imagined world of criminal law that so constrains the arena of liability both sets out a vision of what it means to be fully free and responsible and acknowledges a world of activity in which we are to be at least partially excused.

Chapter 5

1. The word *ʾĕmunā* in the Habakkuk verse is often translated as "faith," but *ʾĕmunā* in biblical texts means "trust" or "trustworthiness/faithfulness." For a review of biblical occurrences of the word and its meaning in each occurrence, see Yoel Bin-Nun, "*ʾĔmunā ʾel mul hăfākhehā*," in M. Halbertal, D. Kurzweil, and A. Sagi, eds., *ʿAl hāʾĕmunā* (Jerusalem: Keter, 2005), 190–99. As Bin-Nun notes (196–97), the other biblical verses adduced in the homily make it clear that the word is being understood here as connoting the moral quality of "trustworthiness/faithfulness." The rendering "faith(fulness)" in the translation is meant to retain the biblical meaning of the word while reflecting later interpretations, such as Paul's, which read in this verse the idea of faith. See n. 52, below, for references to scholarly discussions of Paul's rendering of the verse; and n. 68 for the distinction between faith and faithfulness. It should be noted that the understanding of *ʾĕmunā* that is reflected in the homily in bMakkot is most probably "faithfulness" or "trustworthiness," given the emphasis in the preceding sections of the homily on qualities of justice and righteousness.

2. See also Matt. 22:39, Mark 12:31, and Luke 10:27. These passages have

been discussed also in relation to the teaching of Rabbi Akiva in Sifra on Lev. 19:18.

3. Sanhedrin and Makkot originally constituted a single tractate. See Saul Lieberman, *Hilkhot hayyĕrušalmi lĕrabbēnu Moše ben Maymon z"l* (New York: Jewish Theological Seminary, 1947), appendix 1 (67 n. 8), for Makkot as the final three chapters of Sanhedrin in the Yerushalmi, an arrangement that is reflected, as well, in the Parma and Kaufman manuscripts of mMakkot. While the Bavli knows Makkot as a separate tractate (see bShev 2b and cf. bMak 2a), it is not clear at what point in time Sanhedrin-Makkot came to be seen as separate tractates. It is possible that, at early stages of the Bavli's development, Makkot and Sanhedrin were still seen as a single tractate. But, even if the two tractates became separated in Babylonian tradition early on, it is still appropriate to see the final *sugya* of Makkot as the coda of Sanhedrin-Makkot, since the two tractates are clearly continuous both thematically and stylistically. See Tamás Turán, "Talmud Bavli, Tractate Makkoth, Chapter Three (*Elu Hen Ha-Loqin*): A Critical Edition and a Critical Commentary" (Ph.D. diss., Jewish Theological Seminary, 2004), 31–32, for references to passages from geonim and rishonim that reflect a view of some or all of bMakkot as part of bSanhedrin.

It is worth noting that seeing bSanhedrin and bMakkot as some kind of literary unit allows for the interesting observation that there is a reflection on the number of *mitzvot* at both the middle and end of this unit: the discussion of 613 sinaitic *mitzvot* reduced to one *mitzva* in the final *sugya* of bMakkot and the discussion of seven noachide laws in the middle of bSanhedrin.

4. I am referring to the final mishna according to the mishna division in the Bavli; this corresponds to the final two mishnayot in texts of the Mishna: mMak 3:15–16. For the purposes of the discussion here, I will consistently refer to this passage as the final mishna of Makkot.

5. Yaakov Nachum Epstein, *Māvō' lĕnusaḥ hammišnā* (Jerusalem: Magnes, 2000), 2:977–78, writes that Chanania ben Aqashia's teaching appears to be a later addition to the mishna, and the view that this teaching is an aggadic addition to the end of mMakkot has become commonplace. Epstein brings no evidence in support of this conjecture, however; he bases it solely on the fact that this teaching is added to the end of the sixth (extra-mishnaic) chapter of Avot (and, in liturgical practice, to the end of each chapter of Avot) as well as on the addition of a teaching of Chanania ben Aqashia to the end of mQinim. As Epstein notes, however, the teaching appears and is discussed in a Geniza fragment of yMakkot (the text can be found in Lieberman, *Hilkhot hayyĕrušalmi*, 67); working with the assumption that the teaching is not integral to the mishna, Epstein suggests that it is, in fact, a *baraita* that the Yerushalmi brings in relation to the mishna. Absent any evidence to support the contention that the teaching is a late addition to the mishna (and especially given that the Geniza fragment can well be taken as evidence to the contrary); given that the mishnaic context is already aggadic and, even without Chanania ben Aqashia's teaching, would end the tractate on a positive note (and thus the idea that Chanania ben Aqashia's teaching was added to the mishna in order to end on a positive note is less compelling than similar arguments about other such endings); and noting (as will be discussed below) that Rabbi Simlai's teaching about 613 *mitzvot* can well be seen as appearing in the *sugya* in relation to Chanania ben Aqashia's teaching about the plurality of *mitzvot*, I will be working on the assumption that this teaching was part of the mishna as it appeared before the redactor of the Bavli *sugya* (which does not mean, of course, that it could not have been added at some point later than the original redaction of the Mishna).

6. Text and translation follow the Vilna edition; significant variants are discussed in the notes.

7. See the parallel in bSan 81a and the discussion of these two passages below.

8. This formulation suggests that *kārēt* is a sanction that is imposed on the person, which does not necessarily correspond to the biblical concept of a person being cut off from his people; see below about the variety of understandings of this biblical idea. I am using this formulation here as an approximation of the term *ḥayyĕvē kārēt*, a term that assimilates *kārēt* to a system of punishments for which one may be liable or from which one may be exempt.

9. See Rashi, s.v. *ʾēlu hēn halloqin*, and Tosafot, s.v. *wĕʾēlu hēn halloqin habbāʾ ʿal ʾăḥoto*, for attempts to account for the list of violations in this mishna and for the point that the mishna includes violations subject to *kārēt* in order to teach that those subject to *kārēt* receive *malqut*. See Aharon Shemesh, *ʿOnĕšim wĕḥaṭṭāʾim: Min hammiqrāʾ lĕsifrut ḥazal* (Jerusalem: Magnes, 2003), 178–204, for a detailed discussion of the components of the list in mMakkot 3. Note that the first crime listed in the mishna is brother-sister intercourse, the biblical verses about which are discussed above in Chapter 3 as the locus of principles of law within rabbinic texts; one of the principles mentioned there appears in the Gemara's presentation of a three-way tannaitic dispute in relation to this mishna.

10. See the discussion of Rabbi Chanania ben Gamliel's position on bMak 23b and the comments of Rabbi Zerachia Halevi, Nachmanides, and the Ritva. For a brief discussion about the relationship between Rabbi Akiva's and Rabbi Chanania ben Gamliel's teachings and for summaries of some classical and contemporary approaches to this question, see Shemesh, *ʿOnĕšim wĕḥaṭṭāʾim*, 89 and n. 97.

11. This is the element of Rabbi Akiva's argument on which the Gemara focuses in its discussion of the *baraita* (bMak 13b–14a). The focus of the Gemara's discussion is on understanding the rationales behind the three different positions in the *baraita*. It takes Rabbi Akiva's teaching, which follows in the *baraita* the position of Rabbi Yishmael that a person subject to judicial execution incurs the penalty of *malqut*, to be articulating not only why the person subject to *kārēt* does receive *malqut* but also why the person subject to judicial execution does *not* receive *malqut*. Even if this understanding of Rabbi Akiva's teaching is accepted, it does not rule out a further explanation of why the person subject to *kārēt* should receive *malqut*. That is, this aspect of Rabbi Akiva's teaching explains only why it is not a violation of the rules of judicial punishment for a person subject to *kārēt* to receive *malqut*, but it does not explain why the person *should* receive *malqut*. There is more than one possible answer to this question; one possibility not discussed here is that Rabbi Akiva believes that it is essential for a human court to impose punishment on the violator of law. Such a position could be based in the notion that it is essential for the community to enact its condemnation of the person who violates law (see Chapter 1, nn. 41 and 43), or it could be related to a general view of the centrality of human action, rather than leaving things for God to take care of (see the discussion of human action later in this chapter and in Chapter 6).

12. That is, the first reading sees Rabbi Akiva's teaching as explaining only why the court *may* inflict *malqut* on the person subject to *kārēt* but as silent as to why the court *should* do so. The second reading takes Rabbi Akiva's teaching to speak to why the court not only *may* but *should* inflict *malqut* on the person who is subject to *kārēt*.

13. See Shemesh's discussion of Rabbi Akiva's position in relation to Sifre beMidbar 112 (121), in *ʿOnĕšim wĕḥaṭṭāʾim*, 88–89.

14. And so might well maintain that exemption from *kārēt* can occur even without *malqut*, if the person repents on his own, though it is possible that he sees *malqut* as essential, as well. See Shemesh, *ʿOnĕšim wĕḥaṭṭāʾim*, 89.

15. See n. 10, above. Note that the question of whether *malqut* itself brings atonement or whether it is an opportunity for repentance, and it is repentance that brings atonement, is reflected in halakhic literature on the custom of flagellation before Yom Kippur. See Tur, *Orach chayim* 607 and Beit Yosef (though the issue there is complicated by the fact that the flagellation that was practiced did not fulfill the legal requirements of *malqut*, a concern that was a factor in the *sĕmikhā* controversy in which R. Yosef Karo was involved; see Jacob Katz, "*Maḥloqet hassĕmikhā bēn rabbi yaʿăqov bĕrāv wĕharalbaḥ*," *Ṣiyyon* 16 [1951], 28–45). See Shemesh, *ʿOnĕšim wĕḥaṭṭāʾim*, 97–98. For descriptions of the custom, see Daniel Sperber, *Minhāgē yiśrāʾēl: Mĕqorot wĕtolĕdot* (Jerusalem: Mossad Harav Kook, 2003), 7:252–97.

16. Shemesh, *ʿOnĕšim wĕḥaṭṭāʾim*, 98 n. 110, notes that the mention of the recitation of *wĕhuʾ raḥum* in mMak 3:4 is a late addition to the mishna, probably influenced by the Yom Kippur eve tradition that is reflected in Rema's comment in *Darkhe Moshe* 4 on Tur, *Orach chayim* 607.

17. Compare the discussion in mYoma 8:8 and bYoma 85b–86a about the interplay of repentance and other means (such as sacrifices, Yom Kippur, and suffering and death) in the attainment of atonement.

18. Shemesh, *ʿOnĕšim wĕḥaṭṭāʾim*, 90–91, 96–97.

19. For a brief overview of the range of traditional and contemporary opinions, see Jacob Milgrom, *The JPS Torah Commentary: Numbers* (Philadelphia: Jewish Publication Society, 1990), 405–8. See also William Horbury, "Extirpation and Excommunication," *Vetus Testamentum* 35 (1985), 13–38.

20. The verb nearly always occurs in passive forms (*wĕnikhrĕtā*, *wĕnikhrāt*, *wĕnikhrĕtu*, and *hikkārēt tikkārēt*, the last appearing only in Num. 15:31), although active forms with God as the subject appear in Lev. 17:10 and 20:3, 5, and 6. See also the active form of the verb in a command addressed to Moses and Aaron: "Do not cut off" (Num. 4:17, in reference to the Qehatites), followed by "But thus do to them, that they may live and not die" (4:18).

21. See Shemesh, *ʿOnĕšim wĕḥaṭṭāʾim*, 58–59; and see Milgrom, *Numbers*, 405–6. Milgrom argues that *kārēt* is a divinely imposed sanction, which is also the classical rabbinic view.

22. Even one for which the Torah specifies a different sanction, as in Exod. 31:14, concerning Shabbat. Note that the passage immediately following the passage about *kārēt* in Num. 15:30–31 is the story of the person who gathers wood on Shabbat (Num. 15:32–36). He is executed by the people, but the juxtaposition of this story with the rules concerning unintentional and intentional violation of law, the latter of which results in *kārēt*, suggests that the wood gatherer's violation of Shabbat is an illustration of intentional sin that results in *kārēt*. Thus, this passage is consistent with the assignment of both execution and *kārēt* to Shabbat violation in Exod. 31:14, supporting the possibility that *kārēt* might well be the consequence of any intentional sin. For a discussion of the wood-gatherer passage in relation to the *kārēt* passage, see Milgrom, *Numbers*, 408–10. Milgrom (407–8) sees the passage about Shabbat as well as the passage about *molekh* in Lev. 20:2–3 as support of the idea that *kārēt* is a divine punishment that can be conjoined with human punishment. Classical rabbinic interpretation, though,

sees the Torah's mandate of *kārēt* for sins for which there is judicial execution as applying only if the court is unable to execute the sinner. But see the passage about the wood gatherer in Tanchuma Buber *beMidbar* 28, on Num. 4:17 (on this verse, see n. 20, above; see Shemesh's brief reference to the Tanchuma passage in *ʿOnĕšim wĕḥaṭṭāʾim*, 90 n. 98). This passage juxtaposes *kārēt* and execution and also suggests the possibility that violation of any command leads to *kārēt*.

23. Shemesh, *ʿOnĕšim wĕḥaṭṭāʾim*, 60, 80, 91–96.

24. Ibid., 59, 91–92.

25. See mKar 1:1.

26. But see below, n. 34.

27. See, for example, the contrasting terms *bĕhikkārēt* and *biydē ʾādām* in bMak 23b.

28. Whether *kārēt* implies death or/and some form of being cut off from the people, either in life or after death—or both in life and after death, as in Sifre beMidbar 112 (121) and bSan 90b.

29. Modern psychology research supports the idea that people's judgments of a person's morality are asymmetrical with respect to good and bad deeds. See Glenn D. Reeder, "Trait-Behavior Relations and Dispositional Inference," *Personality and Social Psychology Bulletin* 19 (1993), 586–93.

30. Such as the covenantal blessings and curses of Deuteronomy 27–29; see especially 29:17–20.

31. The life-giving quality of the *mitzvot* is a common theme in Deuteronomy in particular; see, for example, 30:15–20.

32. It should be noted that the standard sanction in the Dead Sea texts is exclusion from the community. Depending on the nature of the violation and on whether the violation was done intentionally, exclusion could be temporary or permanent. Shemesh sees the biblical sanction of *kārēt* and the biblical linkage of covenant and exile as two different models on which the sect built its penal code, the former generating the idea of permanent exile from the sect (Shemesh notes, in particular, the term *bĕyād rāmā*, which occurs in the biblical passage about *kārēt*—Num. 15:30—and in sectarian passages about exile from the sect—for example, 1QS 8:22–9:2) and the latter generating the idea of temporary exclusion; see *ʿOnĕšim wĕḥaṭṭāʾim*, 60–82. Whether or not *kārēt* and covenant/exile serve as distinct models for the Dead Sea sect, though, I am treating the range of biblical ideas about the consequences of sin—*karet*, exclusion from the covenantal community, and not meriting life—as a single cluster, any element of which evokes the whole idea of the sinner being cut off from life within God's community.

33. Note the parallel to this passage in bSan 81a, where Rabban Gamliel is responding to a passage from Ezekiel, which is working with Lev. 18:5—*wāḥay bāhem*. Here Rabban Gamliel says: "It is only the person who does *all of these* who will live!" See n. 61, below. I will return below to Rabbi Akiva's response in the bMakkot and bSanhedrin passages, as well as to a closer look at the verses that prompt Rabban Gamliel's despair in each of these passages.

34. Though Shemesh, *ʿOnĕšim wĕḥaṭṭāʾim*, 92–96, argues that rabbinic texts retain the idea that *kārēt* is applicable to any purposeful violation of God's law, and he suggests that Rabbi Chanania ben Gamliel's teaching about *malqut* and *kārēt* reflects this position, since Rabbi Chanania ben Gamliel's second teaching in the mishna talks about *any* transgression. According to Shemesh, the list of violations in mKar 1:1 is not meant to limit the applicability of *kārēt* but rather to indicate for what nondeliberate violations of law one must bring a *ḥaṭṭāʾt* sac-

rifice. The subject of mKar is really the *ḥaṭṭāʾt*, while the subject of mMakkot 3 is *kārēt*, Shemesh suggests, for mMakkot 3 is the final chapter of a tractate (Sanhedrin-Makkot) that discusses sanctions in order of increasing severity.

35. Many other theorists write about the distinction between shame and guilt from within a variety of disciplines. The psychological and anthropological literature on the subject is reviewed briefly in June Price Tangney and Ronda L. Dearing, *Shame and Guilt* (New York: Guilford, 2004), 12–24. As the subtitle of Morris's book (*On Guilt and Innocence: Essays in Legal Philosophy and Moral Psychology* [Berkeley: University of California Press, 1976]) indicates, Morris writes about shame and guilt from the perspective of legal philosophy and moral psychology. His paradigms of shame and guilt are theoretical constructs, and I am using these constructs here as a lens through which to look at questions about punishment and moral responsibility, without making assumptions about the empirical validity of these paradigms in relation to the social sciences. It is worth noting, though, that there are strong correlations between elements of Morris's paradigms and the results of the psychological research reported by Tangney and Dearing; see especially 18–25. For a philosophical discussion that is largely congruent with Morris's paradigms, see John Rawls, *A Theory of Justice* (Cambridge, Mass.: Harvard University Press, 1999), 390–91 and 422–24.

36. Morris, *On Guilt and Innocence*, 62.

37. See bSan 90b and the parallel in Sifre beMidbar 112 (121), where *teshuva* serves this same function; through an exegesis of Num. 15:31—"that soul shall surely be cut off; its iniquity is in it"—the Rabbis determine that the soul is only permanently cut off if its iniquity is still in it—that is, if the person has not repented. See also the discussion above of Rabbi Akiva's teaching in the *baraita* at the beginning of the third chapter of bMakkot, which says that repentance exempts one from *kārēt* and which can be understood as suggesting that *malqut* is an opportunity for repentance.

38. See Shemesh's discussion in *ʿOnĕšim wĕḥaṭṭāʾim*, 96–97, and his reference to bShev 21a, where the very final "for the Lord will not cleanse" (Exod. 20:7) is interpreted thus: "*God* will not cleanse, but the court below flagellates him and cleanses him."

39. Shemesh, *ʿOnĕšim wĕḥaṭṭāʾim*, 90–91.

40. In fact, this final section is more complex. The Gemara's initial discussion of Rabbi Elazar's teaching elaborates his point about the appearance of the holy spirit by demonstrating through exegesis of biblical verses that God indeed spoke up during cases "tried" by Judah, Samuel, and Solomon; yet the purpose of the heavenly voice in these three cases is to support a determination that would otherwise be impossible for the human judge to make with certainty. Rava, though, challenges this by arguing that heavenly support was not necessary in these cases in order for the human judge to have been certain about his decision and that, in fact, it is not clear from the verses that a heavenly voice appeared. The passage concludes, finally, with the assertion that the teaching about the appearance of the holy spirit in these three cases is a traditional teaching, not one that is generated by exegesis. Note, then, that in the initial discussion, which attempts to derive the appearance of the heavenly voice in the human court, the derivation is based on the inadequacy of human reason or human power to establish the truth. Rava rejects this assertion of human inadequacy and, in the process, the derivation through exegesis of God's support of human determination. Ultimately, though, the Gemara suggests that the appearance of the divine voice can go hand in hand with the notion of human reason

as adequate to determine and establish the truth; God's voice, then, is not needed by human beings, but it comes, presumably, to confirm what they have already correctly established as true. Interestingly, though, this final point leaves the fact of the appearance of God's voice as a tradition, rather than as something that we can determine through *derasha*, the starting point introduced by Abaye. Thus, there is a complex interplay in this final section between human determination and divine input, an interplay that merits further analysis.

In relation to Rava's stance in this passage, compare the statement of Rava in bMak 22b: "How foolish are the other people who stand before a Torah scroll but do not stand before a great man, for in the Torah scroll it says 'forty' [lashes] and the Rabbis came and reduced them by one." Note that here, too, a ruling about *malqut* is the occasion for an observation about the relative weight of God's word and the interpretation of the Rabbis.

41. It is noteworthy that the parallel to the Rabban Gamliel/Rabbi Akiva anecdote in Midrash Tehillim 15 conflates that story with elements that appear in the two stories about Rabbi Akiva at the end of this *sugya*. In Midrash Tehillim, Rabban Gamliel is crying but Rabbi Akiva laughs, as in the stories about Rabbi Akiva and the sages at the end of bMakkot, and the passage ends with Rabban Gamliel saying, "You have comforted us, Akiva, you have comforted us," as the sages say at the end of this *sugya*. The passage in Midrash Tehillim seems clearly to be dependent on the Bavli, especially because it mentions Rabban Gamliel crying both in relation to Psalm 15, as in bMak 24a, and in relation to Ezekiel 18, as in bSan 81a, and it would seem that the composer of this passage noted the connection between the story of Rabbi Akiva's response to Rabban Gamliel's despair and the stories at the end of the *sugya* of Rabbi Akiva's responses to the despairing sages. Yaakov Gartner, "*ʿIbbud bavli šel dĕrāšat rabbi śimlay ʿal taryag miṣwot*," *Sinay* 96 (1985), 236–49, notes links between the Rabbi Simlai passage, including the anecdote about Rabbi Akiva and Rabban Gamliel, and the last two sections of the *sugya*. Note, too, the similarity between Rabbi Akiva's argument in the first of the two stories at the end of the *sugya*: "If to those who violate his will it is thus—how much more so to those who do his will"; and Rabbi Chanania ben Gamliel's second teaching in the mishna: "If one who transgresses a single transgression loses his life on account of it, one who does a single commandment—how much more so that his life will be given to him."

42. To Rabbi Akiva's response and to Rabbi Chanania ben Gamliel's teaching, compare tQid 1:13: "Whoever does a single *mitzva* . . . and whoever transgresses a single transgression. . . ." The formulation in mQid 1:10 is less clear and potentially less paradoxical: "Whoever does a single *mitzva* . . . and whoever does not do a single *mitzva*. . . ." The mishna may be saying the same thing as the passage in the Tosefta (see Shamma Friedman, "The Primacy of Tosefta to Mishnah in Synoptic Parallels," in Harry Fox and Tirzah Meacham, eds., *Introducing Tosefta: Textual, Intratextual, and Intertextual Studies* [New York: Ktav, 1999], 120–21), or it may be saying something different: the antithesis in the mishna may be between someone who does even a single *mitzva* and someone who does not do even one *mitzva*. If one accepts the latter reading, the mishna avoids the paradox generated by the Tosefta's formulation (how can the teaching apply to someone who does some *mitzvot* but who also sins—that is, everyone?) and offers a teaching consistent with Rabbi Akiva's message—that doing even a single *mitzva* grants life (even if the person also sins). See the conflicting *derashot* of ben Azai and Rabbi Akiva in yQid 1:10/61d, and note that both the Yerushalmi and bQid 39b–40b discuss the mishna in Qidushin in relation to the mishna in Mak-

kot (note that both Talmudim interpret the teaching about a single *mitzva* in relation to the *balance* of *mitzvot* and transgressions, a single *mitzva* able to tip the balance in a person's favor; see also tQid 1:14). See the discussion in E. P. Sanders, *Paul and Palestinian Judaism* (Philadelphia: Fortress, 1977), 128–39 (henceforth referred to as Sanders, *PPJ*).

43. Note that, in Sifre beMidbar 112 (121), R. Yishmael derives the idea of a person's freedom from the iniquity of his ancestors from Num. 15:31: "that soul shall surely be cut off; its iniquity is in it," the verse from which the preceding opinion derived the idea that a person is freed from his own iniquity after repenting (see n. 37, above).

44. Moshe Greenberg notes the "black-and-white terms" of Ezekiel's description of the righteous and wicked person and discusses the lists of righteous deeds here and in other biblical passages in relation to New Testament and rabbinic texts, including the Rabbi Simlai passage, in *Ezekiel, 1–20*, The Anchor Bible, vol. 22 (Garden City, N.Y.: Doubleday, 1983), 340–47.

45. And similar teachings elsewhere about the power of repentance, such as the one in bSan 90b, discussed in n. 37, above. See also the inventory of means of atonement in bYoma 86a, mentioned in n. 17, above.

46. The essay was reprinted along with three additional brief essays under the title "Persons and Punishments," in Morris, *On Guilt and Innocence*, 31–88. My discussion focuses on the main essay along with the first addendum, entitled "Guilt and Shame."

47. Morris, *On Guilt and Innocence*, 62.

48. Ibid., 45.

49. See n. 52, below.

50. E. P. Sanders, *Paul, the Law, and the Jewish People* (Philadelphia: Fortress, 1983), 13–14 n. 18 (henceforth referred to as Sanders, *Law*), discusses the problem of how to translate words with the root *dik-* in such a way that neither obscures Paul's argument by translating different uses of the root differently nor prejudices a reading of Paul by using a translation that favors one over another interpretation of Paul. Sanders prefers "be made righteous" over "be justified" because the latter tends to connote to "be declared or found innocent," while Sanders thinks that "the question is precisely whether or not Paul has shifted the meaning beyond that of the law court"; see n. 52, below. In the translations that I offer here, I translate words with the root *dik-* consistently as "just, justice, be justified," in order to preserve the connection between all the words with the root *dik-*. In discussion, however, I use forms of "just" and "righteous" interchangeably.

51. Note that 3:24 can also be seen as working off Gen. 15:16, as does 3:8. But Paul is identifying the teaching of the Genesis verse and the Habakkuk verse in relation to justification, so it makes the most sense to see him as referring in 3:24 to both the Genesis verse and the Habakkuk verse, rather than as referring to one or the other. I am stressing the echo of Habakkuk here to highlight the structure of 3:21–24 in relation to 3:10–13.

52. There is significant scholarly discussion about Paul's presentation of Hab. 2:4 here and in Rom. 1:17 in relation to the MT and LXX versions of this verse as well as about how to construe the syntax of the verse as Paul presents it. See, for example, James D. G. Dunn, *Romans 1–8*, Word Biblical Commentary 38A (Dallas: Word Books, 1988), 44–46; Richard N. Longenecker, *Galatians*, Word Biblical Commentary 41 (Nashville, Tenn.: Thomas Nelson, 1990), 118–19; Sanders, *PPJ*, 484 n. 38; Sanders, *Law*, 53 n. 23; Richard B. Hays, *Echoes of Scripture*

in the Letters of Paul (New Haven, Conn.: Yale University Press, 1989), 202 n. 14. The two possible ways of construing the syntax of *ek pisteos* generate the following possible translations: "The one who is righteous by faith shall live" and "The righteous one shall live by faith." If, however, one sees righteousness/justification in Paul as essentially coterminous with gaining life, the issue of deciding between these constructions is much less significant. (For a similar argument, see Richard B. Hays, *The Faith of Jesus Christ: An Investigation of the Narrative Substructure of Galatians 3:1–4:11* [Chico, Calif.: Scholars Press, 1983], 150–51. Contrast Sanders, who rejects the judicial meaning of *dik-* in Paul and who thus can accept the idea of being justified through something without that thing granting life. Thus, Sanders can understand Rom. 10:5 as saying "that the Jews might have righteousness by doing the law, but that one does not 'live' thereby" [*Law*, 63 n. 132].) Daniel Boyarin, *A Radical Jew: Paul and the Politics of Identity* (Berkeley: University of California Press, 1994), 117, argues that justification should be understood in terms of the Hebrew *yiṣdaq*, "which means both to be just or righteous and to be *declared* or *recognized* as just or righteous." The term "justification" "refers to the situation of the believer at her last judgment (whether eschatological or merely after death is irrelevant here), where the question is: Will I be acquitted by the divine court? Justification means acquittal." From this perspective, being justified is equivalent to living before God, and thus I have used the terms interchangeably throughout my discussion.

53. Sanders, *Law*, 21, argues that Paul was compelled to cite Deut. 27:26 because he needed a verse that connects the law with a curse, in order to set up the contrast with the blessing that is promised to Abraham through faith. (See Heikki Räisänen, *Paul and the Law* [Philadelphia: Fortress, 1986], 95 n. 13; and Boyarin, *A Radical Jew*, 139.) Thus, Sanders argues that other terms of Paul's rendering of Deut. 27:26 are incidental to the main thrust of Paul's use of the verse, and therefore that significance should not be attributed to the word "all"; see next note.

54. This point is much discussed and much contested in the scholarly literature. See, for an example of an opposing argument, James D. G. Dunn, *Jesus, Paul, and the Law: Studies in Mark and Galatians* (Louisville, Ky.: Westminster/John Knox, 1990), 226 (and see the secondary literature cited on 234 n. 41); and, for an example of a supporting argument, Räisänen, *Paul and the Law*, 95 (and see the secondary literature cited on 94 n. 2). Räisänen, like others, cites Gal. 5:3 as confirmation of the idea that Paul is pointing to the problematic nature of the need to obey *all* of the law; interpretation of this verse is, like interpretation of 3:10, a point of scholarly disagreement. See, further, the secondary literature cited in Longenecker, *Galatians*, 118; and Sanders, *Law*, 52–53 n. 22. And see n. 62, below.

For a parallel to the understanding of Gal. 3:10 that is suggested here, see James 2:10: "And whoever keeps the whole law, but stumbles in one thing, has become guilty of all." While James's overall argument about law is radically different from Paul's, his articulation of the idea that imperfect obedience to the law makes one "a transgressor of the law" (2:11) suggests that this idea may well have been commonplace. See below on Paul's exegesis of Eccles. 7:20 in Romans 3.

55. Shlomo Naeh, "Why Did Rabban Gamliel Cry? Some Aspects of the Last Mishna of Makkot and Its *Sugya* in the Bavli," presented at a conference in tribute to Professor David Weiss-Halivni (New York, May 30, 2005), notes that the word "all" appears in LXX for Lev. 18:5: "And you shall keep all of my statutes

and all of my judgment and do them, which a person shall do and live by them," as it does in MT in similar verses, such as Lev. 19:37.

56. In relation to Paul's emphasis on *doing* the law, see the discussion of Rom. 10:5, below.

57. See n. 5, above.

58. Though whether the thrust of the bMakkot passage is as radically different as the analysis presented to this point would suggest is reevaluated in the final section of this chapter.

59. Naeh, "Why Did Rabban Gamliel Cry?," argues that originally the mishna ended with Rabbi Shimon's citation of this verse.

60. See the comment of the Ritva, s.v. *bāʾ ḥabbāquq wĕheʿĕmidān ʿal ʾaḥat,* which understands the Habakkuk citation in relation to Lev. 18:5, though it is not clear that the Ritva is drawing this connection in relation to the mishna's citation of the Leviticus verse.

61. Naeh, "Why Did Rabban Gamliel Cry?," points out that ms Munich has this version of Rabban Gamliel's statement in bMakkot. Naeh argues that the original story was told in relation neither to the Ezekiel verse, as in bSanhedrin, nor to the Psalms verse, as in bMakkot, but in relation to Lev. 18:5: "which a person shall do and live by them." (And, as noted above, n. 55, the LXX of 18:5 includes the word "all," exactly the reading that Rabban Gamliel assumes and that Rabbi Akiva argues against.) Whether or not one accepts Naeh's reconstruction, it is noteworthy that his source-critical argument leads to the same idea that I am arguing here from a literary/theological perspective: that Rabban Gamliel despairs in relation to the Torah's promise that one gains life through obedience to God's commandments. Nevertheless, the two approaches have different implications for whether one seeks to interpret the place of this story with the larger *sugya*; see nn. 117 and 122, below.

62. It is noteworthy that the word "all" *does* appear in Deut. 28:58; this and the following verse are read, according to mMak 3:14, while the person who is liable for *malqut* is flogged. See Longenecker, *Galatians,* 117, who cites these verses in relation to Paul's quotation of Deut. 27:26 in Gal 3:10. Hays, *Echoes of Scripture,* 43, sees Gal. 3:10 as conflating Deut. 27:26 with Deut. 28:58; he also notes Deut. 28:15, a verse that introduces the curses that will come upon the one who does not do "all" of the commandments.

63. These recastings are noted and discussed by Dunn, *Jesus, Paul, and the Law,* 199, and *Romans 1–8,* 153–55. My discussion diverges from Dunn's interpretation of these elements, which rests heavily on his understanding of Paul as criticizing observances that mark Jews "as distinctively God's people," an understanding that, in turn, rests on Sanders's work on Paul and the law (see *Romans 1–8,* lxiv–lxxii). See also Boyarin's discussion of "flesh" in Paul's writings in *A Radical Jew,* especially 130–35, where Boyarin argues that there is a connection between the connotation of "flesh" as "sinning through the flesh," the meaning discussed here, and as "commitment to the literal, outward doing of the law." See also Boyarin's discussion on 139–42 of "doing," as opposed to "fulfilling," the law and his understanding of Paul's interpretation of "to *do* them" (Deut. 27:26) in Gal. 3:10 in relation to "he that *does* these things shall live by them" (based on Lev. 18:5) in Gal. 3:12. Boyarin's interpretation of "flesh" makes sense of both of the ways in which Paul recasts Ps. 143:2, his substitution of "flesh" for "one living" and his addition of "by the works of the law."

64. It is a commonplace that Paul is working with Ps. 143:2 here, but the preceding verse is not usually discussed in this context (one exception is Boyarin, *A*

Radical Jew, 118–19). I present the Masoretic parsing of 143:1, which takes *beʾĕmunātĕkhā* as connected with *ʿănēni bĕṣidqātekhā*; taking *beʾĕmunātĕkhā*, alternatively, as concluding the preceding clause does not affect the suggestion that Paul is reading in this verse the idea of justification through the faith of Christ, since in such a construction of the verse the words *beʾĕmunātĕkhā* and *bĕṣidqātekhā* are parallel. Dunn, *Romans 1–8*, 133 (on God as "true" in Rom. 3:4), points out that *ʾĕmunā* in Psalms is generally translated as *alētheia* in LXX, as opposed to as *pistis* when it occurs elsewhere; nevertheless, he suggests that "there is a Hebraic connection of thought" between these two words as used by Paul. See Hays, *Echoes of Scripture*, 202 n. 8, for Paul's use of *alētheia* with "covenantal connotations." My interpretation of Gal. 2:16 as working with Ps. 143:1 as well as with the following verse rests on the assumption that Paul is understanding *ʾĕmunā* here as suggesting "faith." See n. 66, below, on Paul's use of "truth" in the opening chapters of Romans.

65. See Dunn, *Romans 1–8*, 46: "To expound his theme with Hab. 2:4 understood thus is the task he sets himself in this letter."

66. See n. 64, above, on *ʾĕmunā* as *alētheia* as well as *pistis*. The use of "truth" in Romans 1 is probably a working out of the meanings of *ʾĕmunā*; thus, Paul is probably juxtaposing Hab. 2:4 with Ps. 143:1–2 already in Rom. 1:17–18, where God's justice (Ps. 143:1) and human *in*justice (Ps. 143:2) are juxtaposed, as are faith (*ʾĕmunā* in Hab. 2:4) and truth (*ʾĕmunā* in Ps. 143:1). See n. 72, below, for references to Ps. 143:1–2 earlier in Romans 3.

67. The reference to "flesh" is particularly apt here, given the preceding catena composed of verses that describe sinfulness largely in reference to body parts: throat, tongues, lips, mouth, feet, and eyes (Rom. 3:13–18). See further below on body parts as sinning or as doing good.

68. See Dunn, *Romans 1–8*, 166–67, and Longenecker, *Galatians*, 87–88, on whether the genitive in this frequently appearing phrase should be construed as Christ's faith(fulness) or as faith in Christ. See also the argument for the former reading in Hays, *The Faith of Jesus Christ*, 157–76; and the argument for the latter reading in Stephen Westerholm, *Israel's Law and the Church's Faith: Paul and His Recent Interpreters* (Grand Rapids, Mich.: Eerdmans, 1988), 111–12 n. 12; and see Boyarin, *A Radical Jew*, 119 and 294–95 n. 27.

69. Compare Phil. 3:9: "not having a justice of my own, which is of the law, but that which is through the faith of Jesus Christ, the justice from God, based on faith." See n. 87, below.

70. It is instructive to contrast Paul's use of this verse with the occurrence of this verse in a story about Rabbi Akiva in bSan 101a. Rabbi Akiva and his colleagues go to visit their teacher, Rabbi Eliezer, who is ill. As in the stories at the end of bMakkot, the other disciples cry while Rabbi Akiva laughs. Rabbi Akiva explains that he is happy because Rabbi Eliezer's pain demonstrates that his merit has not been exhausted—that is, he is being punished in this world but will merit eternal life. In response to Rabbi Akiva's interpretation of his suffering, Rabbi Eliezer argues that he has not neglected any of the Torah. Rabbi Akiva responds by quoting Eccles. 7:20 as a teaching of Rabbi Eliezer himself.

As in the bMakkot stories, Rabbi Akiva is able to see something different in the reality that confronts him from what is apparent to his colleagues. But here, in addition, Rabbi Akiva cites his teacher's teaching to teach his teacher something that his teacher has not understood. While in the mouth of Rabbi Eliezer, the verse from Ecclesiastes might have been a pessimistic teaching (see Hans Joachim Schoeps, *Paul*, trans. H. Knight [Philadelphia: Westminster, 1961],

185), Rabbi Akiva employs it to teach a salvific message. In fact, the teaching is very much in line with the teaching about *malqut* and *kārēt* in relation to Rabbi Akiva's reply to Rabban Gamliel in bMakkot. The fact that there is no one who does not sin does not mean that life is unattainable through human action; at the same time, the fact of sin requires means of atonement, so that people can merit life through (even incomplete) fulfillment of *mitzvot.* Rabbi Eliezer's suffering, much like *malqut,* is an essential component of a view that asserts that life can be merited through *mitzvot* but that takes human imperfection seriously. (The difference, of course, is that Rabbi Eliezer's suffering is attributed to God, while *malqut* is imposed by the human court; as discussed above, the power of human action and human self-determination is central to the bMakkot *sugya.*) Thus, while Paul sees Eccles. 7:20 as denying the possibility of justification through deeds, Rabbi Akiva uses it to explain the necessity of human suffering in such a way that affirms the capacity of human beings to merit life through fulfillment of *mitzvot.*

It is noteworthy that the story in bSanhedrin is paired with a similar story in which Rabbi Akiva celebrates suffering as a catalyst for repentance. See the discussion above on whether *malqut* brings atonement in and of itself or whether it brings atonement by spurring the sinner to repent.

71. Ps. 143:1–2 is juxtaposed with Eccles. 7:20 also in Midrash Tehillim 143. The midrash illustrates the impossibility of a human being being vindicated (*z-k-h/ṣ-d-q*) in judgment before God since all human beings sin, citing 1 Kings 8:46 ("When they sin before you—for there is no person who does not sin") and Eccles. 7:20. The midrash is probably taking the word *ṣaddiq* in the latter verse as connoting "one who is declared just/who is vindicated" in the judicial sense (see n. 50, above), as it takes *yiṣdaq* in Ps. 143:2 as meaning "is declared just/is vindicated" in judgment.

72. The interweaving is more complex than this summary indicates, given the subtle references to Ps. 143:1–2 throughout this chapter. The central section, which establishes universal sinfulness (3:9–23), comes after a passage that is knit together by "the faith of God," "the justice of God," and "the truth of God" (3:2–7) (see Dunn, *Romans 1–8,* 136; and see nn. 64 and 66, above, on *ʾĕmunā* as both "faith" and "truth"), the first two of which recur in the verses that immediately follow this section (3:24–26). Thus, overt or more subtle references to Ps. 143:1–2 are truly interwoven with the demonstration of universal sinfulness, supporting the idea that the latter is essential for Paul's argument that justification can only come through faith.

73. This is how, for example, Ibn Ezra understands the verse: " 'who does good' always 'and does not sin' ever."

74. This is how Rabbi Akiva understands the verse in the story discussed in n. 70, above.

75. For sin as a power in Romans, see Dunn, *Romans 1–8,* 148–49; and B. Roberts Gaventa, "The Cosmic Power of Sin in Paul's Letter to the Romans: Toward a Widescreen Edition," *Interpretation* 58 (2004), 229–40.

76. Thus, chap. 5 begins with the assumption that justification by faith has been established. Chap. 5 serves as the conclusion of chaps. 1–4 and as the introduction to chaps. 6–11 (for a discussion of views of the structure of the letter and the place of chap. 5 within this structure, see Dunn, *Romans 1–8,* 242–44).

77. Paul, in fact, sets the stage for the explicit introduction of this verse in chap. 4 in 3:28: "For we account a man to be justified by faith, without the works of the law." Paul here introduces the notion of accounting, *ḥ-š-v,* which he works out in the following chapter in relation to Gen. 15:6.

78. Sanders, *PPJ*, 484, understands Paul's use of Gen. 15:6 in Galatians in this way: "Righteousness *cannot* be by law, *since it is by faith*." For Sanders, the antithesis is alone enough to prove that righteousness cannot be by law, since, if it could be, then Christ died in vain. Paul's view of the law, according to Sanders, is prompted by Paul's conviction of the necessity of the Christ event; see, for example, *PPJ*, 482. Sanders sums up this understanding in his famous statement that Paul worked backward, "from solution to plight" (see, for example, *Law*, 68; and see the discussion below).

79. Dunn, *Romans 1–8*, 301–2.

80. The relationship between law and the accounting of sin in 5:13 resonates with the idea of reckoning in chap. 4.

81. Paul describes the relationship of the person of faith to the death of Christ in a variety of ways, including the idea that Christ's death is an atoning sacrifice (for example, Rom. 3:25) and the idea that one dies with Christ (for example, Gal. 2:19).

82. Dunn, *Romans 1–8*, 302, notes that the word *pistis* does not occur in chaps. 6 through 8 of Romans.

83. The passage in Deuteronomy uses the word *mitzva* in the singular. While the word can be taken to connote the commandments in general, Nachmanides offers an alternative interpretation: that the word refers specifically to the commandment of repentance, taking *wĕhašēvotā* and *wĕšavtā* earlier in the chapter (Deut. 30:1–2) as commands (rather than as indicative of what will happen in the future). (I am indebted to David Silber for calling this interpretation to my attention in relation to this discussion of the Romans passage.) The possibility of reading Deut. 30:11 in relation to repentance raises the intriguing possibility that Paul's reinterpretation of the passage not only suggests that doing the commandments is an unattainable goal (as I discuss shortly) but that repentance for those who fail to fulfill the commandments is also unattainable (on the almost complete absence of repentance in Paul's writings, see below). It should be noted that the link between 30:11–14 and repentance likely would have been salient for Paul whether or not he understood the word *mitzva* in 30:11 to refer to repentance, since the entire preceding section (30:1–10) talks about repentance and since the biblical passage juxtaposes the idea of repentance with the idea of the commandments beings accessible/fulfillable. The biblical passage emphasizes the capability of the person to fulfill the *mitzvot* as well as to repent of failure to fulfill the commandments; Paul denies both.

84. My discussion of this passage until this point is heavily indebted to Hays, *Echoes of Scripture*, 78–82. Hays comments that Paul's choice of this biblical passage "is daring and perhaps deliberately provocative. It would not be easy to find another text in the Old Testament that looks less promising for Paul's purposes." On the other hand, Paul needs to address this passage, since it explicitly responds to the concern that the commandments are unfulfillable. See below on the force of Paul's erasure of Deuteronomy's answer to the problem of the commandments' inaccessibility.

85. Rom. 2:13—"For not the hearers of the law are just before God, but the doers of the law shall be justified"—supports the idea that Paul is focusing on the problem of *doing* the law. Law requires doing, while faith requires merely hearing. (See also Gal. 3:2 and 5.) Thus, in Romans 10, faith is attainable (it speaks and need merely be *heard*), while the law is out of reach (as it must be *done*).

That the focus in Rom. 10:5 and in Gal. 3:10, 12 is on *doing* the law (and on what the implication of such a focus might be) is much disputed; see, for example, James D. G. Dunn, *Romans 9–16*, Word Biblical Commentary 38B (Nashville, Tenn.: Thomas Nelson, 1988), 601. See also the reference to Boyarin's discussion of "doing" the law in n. 63, above. For Sanders's view, see *PPJ*, 483 n. 37, and *Law*, 54 n. 30. Sanders rejects the idea that Paul addresses the problem of unfillability, the impossibility of *doing* the law. For Sanders, Paul rejects the very premise of Lev. 18:5, that law could (at least in principle) bring life, since, for Paul, justification can be achieved only through faith. For the alternative view advanced here, that law could bring life were people able to fulfill the law, see, for example, Brendan Byrne, *Sons of God, Seed of Abraham* (Rome: Biblical Institute Press, 1979), 152 and 231, and idem, *Romans*, Sacra Pagina Series, vol. 6 (Collegeville, Minn.: Liturgical Press, 1996), 317 and 321.

86. For *telos* in 10:4 as connoting both "goal/fulfillment" and "end," see Dunn, *Romans 9–16*, 589–91. Westerholm, *Israel's Law*, 130, argues for the meaning "end," working with the understanding adopted here that Paul accepts the potential life-giving capacity of the law along with the actual inability of law to grant life because people cannot fulfill the law. Thus, Westerholm sees this passage as saying that now, with the possibility of justification through faith in Christ, there is no further need for law. See also Räisänen, *Paul and the Law*, 53–56.

87. The implication of "their own" has been a point of great scholarly dispute. For summaries of and responses to the Lutheran view, see, for example, Dunn, *Jesus, Paul, and the Law*, 223; Sanders, *Law*, 38; and Boyarin, *A Radical Jew*, 293–94 n. 23. The interpretation offered here coincides with that of Westerholm, *Israel's Law*, 130 and 172.

88. See the discussion of Romans 3, above, and especially nn. 66 and 69.

89. As in Gal. 3:11–12 and the ensuing argument.

90. See n. 5, above.

91. Compare the parallels in Shemot Rabba 9:1; Vayiqra Rabba 31:8; BeMidbar Rabba 14:10, 15:2, and 17:5; Tanchuma *Vayeira* 8 and *Tazria* 9; Tanchuma (Buber) *Va'eira* 11, *Beha'alotekha* 2, and *Shelach* 28; and Pesiqta Rabbati 40. These parallels make it clear that *lĕzakkot* is interchangeable with *lĕhaṣdiq*, both referring to vindication in judgment and to granting life. See Herbert W. Basser, *Studies in Exegesis: Christian Critiques of Jewish Law and Rabbinic Responses 70–300 C.E.* (Leiden: Brill, 2000), 123–24.

92. The connection between Isa. 42:21 and the idea of 613 *mitzvot* is made explicitly in Shemot Rabba 14:10. Alternatively, one could see Rabbi Simlai's homily as included here in relation to the mishna's teaching about doing even one *mitzva* (Shlomo Naeh, oral communication); the focus, according to such a reading, is not on the great number of *mitzvot* with which the homily begins but rather on the idea of the *mitzvot* being reduced to one. See below on Rabbi Akiva's response to Rabban Gamliel echoing both the mishna's teaching about doing one *mitzva* and the culmination of Rabbi Simlai's homily about the reduction of the *mitzvot* to one. It is noteworthy that both Rabbi Simlai's homily and the mishna talk of both many *mitzvot* and a single *mitzva*, the mishna moving from the idea of one to the idea of many and the homily moving from many to one.

93. Compare the catalog of sinning body parts in Rom. 3:13–18.

94. For a recent summary of the main points of the New Perspective, as well as a critique of some of those points, see Brendan Byrne, "Interpreting Romans: The New Perspective and Beyond," *Interpretation* 58 (2004), 240–52.

95. See, for example, Sanders, *PPJ*, 474, and *Law*, 27.

96. See Sanders, *PPJ*, 482, and the formulation in *PPJ*, 552: "In short, *this is what Paul finds wrong in Judaism: it is not Christianity*."

97. Sanders, *Law*, 47.

98. See especially Sanders, *PPJ*, 75 and 236.

99. See, for example, Sanders, *Law*, 6–10.

100. The latter position is that of Bultmann; for a summary of Bultmann's view, see Westerholm, *Israel's Law*, 71–75.

101. See Sanders, *Law*, 27–28; and Boyarin, *A Radical Jew*, 138. Sanders writes (28): "All the rabbis whose views are known to us took the position that all the law must be accepted. . . . No rabbi took the position that obedience must be perfect. Pharisees and rabbis of all schools and all periods strongly believed in repentance and other means of atonement in the case of transgression." But this seems to confuse the fact that the Rabbis emphasize a solution with the idea that they do not perceive a problem; see below.

102. Though this is certainly possible.

103. As opposed to Sanders's idea that Paul simply reasons that, if justification is by faith, it cannot be by law; see n. 78, above.

104. Westerholm, *Israel's Law*; Byrne, "Interpreting Romans." See also Byrne's review of *PPJ* in his *Sons of God*, especially 229–31.

105. Note that rabbinic texts assert that even those who are condemned to execution are not permanently cut off; see mSan 6:2, on the purpose of confession before execution (compare bYoma 86 on suffering and on death effecting atonement even for the most egregious sins).

106. Morris, *On Guilt and Innocence*, 41; see also 47–48. See the argument about acceptance of the *hatrā'ā* in Chapter 1. The language of choice in relation to punishment is not unproblematic. For one perspective on using this language in relation to the punishment that is imposed—rather than in relation to the act that was done—in an *educational* setting, see Alfie Kohn, *Punished by Rewards: The Trouble with Gold Stars, Incentive Plans, A's, Praise, and Other Bribes* (Boston and New York: Houghton Mifflin, 1993), 238–39.

107. Morris, *On Guilt and Innocence*, 42.

108. Ibid., 60–62.

109. Thus, as noted above, the citation in this *sugya* of a verse from Ezekiel 18 not only rejects the notion of children dying for the parents' sins (the explicit reason for the verse's citation) but also affirms the idea that each person determines his own nature and has the power to change it at any time (the fundamental theme of this chapter of Ezekiel).

110. See Schoeps, *Paul*, 187–88; George Foot Moore, *Judaism in the First Centuries of the Christian Era: The Age of the Tannaim* (Cambridge, Mass.: Harvard University Press, 1959), 3:150–51; and Sanders, *PPJ*, 499–501. Repentance is mentioned only one time in all of Galatians and Romans, in Rom. 2:4. (The word appears as well in 2 Cor. 7:9–10 and 12:21.) Both Byrne (*Romans*, 85) and Dunn (*Romans 1–8*, 82) explain the occurrence of this word in Rom. 2:4 in relation to Paul's rhetorical use of traditional Jewish language in this passage.

111. See the discussion of Gal. 3:20–22 and of Rom. 10:3, above, and nn. 69 and 87.

112. With corresponding different assumptions about the nature of law—Paul perhaps reflecting a natural law conception in contrast with the Rabbis' positivist conception of law. (The issue of Paul and natural law is too complex to be addressed here; for a brief review, see Michael B. Crowe, *The Changing*

Profile of the Natural Law [The Hague: Martinus Nijhoff, 1977], 52–57.) On a natural law conception as having natural consequences that do not admit to mitigation based on repentance or excuses, see Devora Steinmetz, "Vineyard, Farm, and Garden: The Drunkenness of Noah in the Context of Primeval History," *Journal of Biblical Literature* 113 (1994), 193–207, as well as Chapter 4, n. 49, and Chapter 6.

113. It should be noted that, within Dead Sea texts, the standard sanction of expulsion from the community correlates with a deterministic view of human nature as well; see Shemesh, *'Ōnĕšim wĕḥaṭṭā'im*, 3 and 61–62. See n. 32, above, for the idea that expulsion is a realization of *kārēt*; thus, the sanction of expulsion represents the antithesis of the mishna's teaching about *malqut* reincorporating into the community the one who would be "cut off." See further Chapter 6, n. 16.

For recent discussions of Paul's "anthropology" that emphasize Paul's deterministic view of human nature, see Timo Laato, *Paul and Judaism: An Anthropological Approach* (Atlanta: Scholars Press, 1995); and Timo Eskola, *Theodicy and Predestination in Pauline Soteriology* (Tübingen: Mohr Siebeck, 1998).

114. It should be noted that Morris raises the question of in what settings and under what conditions a guilt or a shame model might be more appropriate (*On Guilt and Innocence*, 62–63):

> A clue here is that guilt finds a natural role within the law. . . . The law is concerned primarily with maintaining a certain balanced distribution of freedom and does this by ordering relationships among individuals through rules that set up a system of reciprocal rights and duties. There are a number of implications to such arrangements that provide useful leads in answering the question I have raised. . . . First, in law our major concern is the maintenance of a minimum level. Second, the concern is that conduct, relating to values sought to be protected, reach a minimum. Third, relatively precise guides and rules are seen as assuring maintenance of the distribution of value in the community. Fourth, there is a recognition that strong inclinations operate against compliance and there is the need for incentives. Fifth, there is an absence of concern for motives, with purity of heart, grandeur of soul. Diminishing harm to others is the predominant goal. Sixth, there is incentive put forward for restoring relationships. Finally, the relations are between individuals who do not ordinarily have close ties that would, apart from obligations or a sense of obligation, provide strong motives for satisfying the interests of others. It is, I think, whenever interests of this kind predominate that one is pulled to responses that generate the conception of guilt. It will be, for example, when we view as pre-eminently important a certain balanced distribution of freedom that we shall think in terms of rights and duties and move to concepts of wrongdoing and guilt. Shame will arise when our concern is achieving more than a minimum, when our concern is that individuals realize to the fullest what they have within them, when what one is takes priority over a nice balance in relations with others with respect to particular types of conduct.

Morris notes that the models of guilt and shame fit with different goals as well as with different kinds of social relationships (or different assumptions about what relationships ought to be fostered) within different settings. Thus, for example, even if one were to embrace a guilt model for a legal system, one might gravitate toward a shame model for an educational setting such as school or family. But it is important to point out that, while we talk about "law" in Judaism, the role and nature of law within a religious system is not identical to that within a secular, political framework. Thus, even if we accept Morris's correlation of a guilt model with law, the question of whether a guilt model adequately describes a system of *mitzvot* needs to be addressed.

115. Compare Fuller's distinction between "the morality of duty" and "the morality of aspiration," in Lon Fuller, *The Morality of Law* (New Haven, Conn.: Yale University Press, 1964), 5–9.

116. Note Paul's contrast in Gal. 5:19–23 between the (negative) "works of the flesh" and the (positive) "fruit of the Spirit." The latter list consists entirely of virtues, that is, qualities that may inform behavior but that are not, in themselves, behaviors. The former, as Paul's category "works" implies, includes behaviors as well as qualities. (Some of the items in the list of "works of the flesh" are not simple to categorize as behaviors or qualities. See Longenecker, *Galatians*, 253, for this first list as including both singular and plural nouns and for the tendency of many scribes to recast the singular nouns in this list as plurals. Longenecker notes: "Greek abstract nouns are often, though not always, used in the plural to signify manifestations or demonstrations of the quality denoted in the singular, and thus to mean 'displays of' or 'actions expressing' that quality.")

117. It bears emphasizing that the readings of the *sugya* that I will offer approach the *sugya* synchronically, that is, as an integrated literary unit in which the interplay of the parts may be read as generating significance independent of the textual histories of those parts. From such a perspective, we can speak of Rabban Gamliel's despair in relation to the Gemara's elaboration of the Psalms passage quoted in the Rabbi Simlai homily, whether or not the anecdote about Rabban Gamliel originated in relation to the passage from Psalms (see n. 61, above) and granting, of course, that the Gemara's elaboration of this passage postdates Rabban Gamliel by hundreds of years. That is, I am asking neither (the historical question) "Why did Rabban Gamliel cry?" nor (the source-critical question) "In relation to what biblical passage did the original version of the story portray Rabban Gamliel crying?" but rather, "What is the meaning of Rabban Gamliel's despair and Rabbi Akiva's response within the context of the Bavli *sugya* on the final mishna of Makkot?"

118. See n. 122, below.

119. The *sugya*'s linking of several of these characteristics to mythically righteous figures of the biblical and rabbinic pasts, such as Abraham and Abba Chilqiya, enhances the sense of the unachievability of the righteousness portrayed in the psalm: One would need to have the outstanding characteristics of Abraham *plus* of Abba Chilqiya and of other such figures in order to fulfill the vision of the psalm!

120. See Rivan, s.v. *wĕheʿĕmidān ʿal ʾaḥat ʿeśrē.*

121. This interpretation might well be based on the idea that one cannot be righteous simply by desisting from doing the (particularly egregious) sins listed in this verse (see next note). In addition, the Ezekiel passage soon goes on to list positive behaviors that could well be seen as markers of a righteous person—such as clothing the naked and doing true justice (18:7–8)—so perhaps the interpretation is partially motivated by a quest to see these first elements in the passage as similarly describing positive behaviors that define a person as righteous.

122. Naeh ("Why Did Rabban Gamliel Cry?") notes the difficulty of seeing Rabban Gamliel as despairing in relation to this biblical passage. In fact, Naeh notes, in a parallel to the final mishna of Makkot in Sifre Devarim 286 (304–5), Rabbi cites the Ezekiel passage and comments on it—"But what did he do?!" (that is, he merely desisted from sinning)—leading to the conclusion that one who desists from sinning is rewarded as if he had fulfilled a *mitzva.* Rabbi's read-

ing of the passage fits well with Ezekiel's list of ways in which one desists from sin and highlights the lack of fit between Rabban Gamliel's despair and the Ezekiel passage, according to the passage's plain meaning. Thus, Naeh argues that the anecdote about Rabban Gamliel crying could not originally have been told in relation to the Ezekiel passage (he makes a similar argument in relation to the Psalms passage, which also appears in the Sifre parallel); see n. 61, above. As noted in n. 117, above, my goal here is not to reconstruct the original anecdote about Rabban Gamliel crying in relation to a biblical passage but rather to understand the anecdote as it appears within the Bavli *sugya*.

Chapter 6

1. The situation might be different when the violation is essentially a violation of a relationship, that is, when what one has done wrong is to go against the wishes of another. In such a case, the absence of knowledge or intent might have implications for the consequences of one's action. (Think of the standard apology: "I'm really sorry that I hurt you. I didn't realize such-and-such.") But this underscores the point that I am making, because violation of a command is similar to this; it is, in a sense, the violation of a relationship rather than the commission of an act that is wrong per se. (Note that, within the extended passage distinguishing between a shame morality and a guilt morality, parts of which are quoted in Chapter 5, at n. 108, Morris characterizes a guilt morality as valuing "a relationship with others" and as based on "a conceptual scheme of obligations and entitlements.") If, on the other hand, the violation is the doing of something that is wrong per se, rather than wrong in the sense of violating someone's will or a command, then the act is wrong whether or not one meant to do wrong, and the consequences come independently of intent or knowledge. See the following note, about violation of law in ignorance of the prohibitedness of the act.

2. See bMak 9b, discussed in Chapter 2, n. 49. In contrast, in the rabbinic view of sinaitic law, ignorance of the law not only generates exemption from punishment; it might even generate exemption from the need to atone for the act. See the discussion in bShab 68a–69a about what kind of awareness of a prohibition obligates the inadvertent violator of law to bring a *ḥaṭṭāʾt* sacrifice. According to one opinion, only if the person had at one time been aware of the prohibition is he obligated to bring a sacrifice if he violated the law in current ignorance of the prohibition. In other words, according to this opinion, it is not the act that obligates one to seek atonement; even for inadvertent violation, the focus is on whether one can be construed to have violated a command—if one had no way of knowing that the act was prohibited, then there is no violation that needs to be atoned for. (To extend the comparison to violations of a relationship between people in the preceding note: whether the person who has hurt another needs to make amends might well depend on whether the person *could* have known and thus *should* have known that what he did would hurt the other person. We can well imagine the person to whom he is apologizing saying, "Well, but you *should* have known" and continuing to bear a grudge until somehow amends have been made. But if the person who did the act had no way of knowing that the act was against the other's wishes, then it is most likely that the other will forgive him rather than continuing to feel that he has been wronged.)

3. This is not to say that noachide law does not include judicial punishment,

especially in the version of the Sages, but this is constructed more as the consequences of one's act than as the imposition of a judicial sanction for violating law; see the discussion in Chapter 2 of the nature of the punishments in the two versions of noachide law.

4. For the lack of inevitability, note both the superseding of *malqut* discussed in Chapter 5 and texts such as mMak 1:7 that discuss the de facto restriction or elimination of capital punishment.

5. Weinreb notes: "from Homer until the transmission of Greek culture to Rome, the belief that the course of events fulfilled an inherent normative order affected Greek thought profoundly and pervasively" (Lloyd L. Weinreb, *Natural Law and Justice* [Cambridge, Mass.: Harvard University Press, 1987], 15). Weinreb traces the belief in a normative natural order from early Greek writings through the Stoic philosophers, Cicero, and the Roman jurists on 15–46.

6. One notable exception is the practice of not eating the *gid hannāše* (Gen. 32:33). Note Maimonides' denial with respect to this practice that its observance nowadays is based in anything other than God's command to Moses (commentary on mChul 7:6). Maimonides takes all of the *mitzvot* to be based in command and sees even *mitzvot* that were commanded before Sinai (such as the commandment of circumcision) to derive their current authority from God's command to Moses. See the following note, and see the discussion of circumcision, below.

7. Rabbinic midrashim occasionally describe the patriarchs as observing the *mitzvot* (see Chapter 1, n. 74), and some texts describe the Torah as preexisting the world. But neither of these ideas is the same as seeing law as embedded in the world as it is. For whether the Rabbis believe that law can be derived from the narratives of the patriarchs, see Moshe Potolsky, "*Hakkĕlal ʾēn lĕmēdin miqqodem mattān torā*," *Dinē yiśrāʾēl* 6 (1975), 195–230. But even if law *can* be so derived, that does not mean that the source of its authority for those commanded at Sinai is based in something other than command. See bSan 59a about laws that appear before Sinai and are rearticulated at Sinai.

8. This and the following quotations from Jubilees are from the translation by O. S. Wintermute, in James H. Charlesworth, *The Old Testament Pseudepigrapha* (Garden City, N.Y.: Doubleday, 1985), vol. 2. (Note that the word "eightieth" in the second sentence of the second paragraph in this passage appears in the Charlesworth edition as "eighth.")

9. Cana Werman explains the *tora* and the *tĕʿuda*, translated here as "the law and the testimony," as "the historical sequence of events from beginning to end." ("The *Torah* and the *Teʿudah* Engraved on the Tablets," *Dead Sea Discoveries* 9 [2002], 75–103.) The *tĕʿudā* is "the preordained march of history," while the *torā* is "the laws and commandments inserted in the *teʿudah*." Werman notes that sometimes Jubilees seems to suggest that an action is taken in accordance with a law that is already in place and that sometimes it seems to suggest that the law becomes formulated in accordance with an action that has been taken (as in this passage); she suggests that these two portrayals are equivalent and that the latter is drawn when the event is caused by God. Werman also notes the similar meaning of *tĕʿudā* in Qumran texts; there, the term connotes "something destined or preordained to take place, a law or action imposed upon all creatures by divine decree." See the discussion of determinism below.

10. In fact, I would suggest that the fact that the law is observed and the fact that the law is written on the heavenly tablets are, essentially, one and the same thing—or, minimally, that these two facts come along with each other. That is, law is a real thing; it cannot exist without being observed—observance of the

law, then, is the same thing as existence of the law. Law does not exist simply as will expressed in words; it exists as that which is done in the world. This, of course, is closely related to the conception of law as embedded in the way the world is.

11. See n. 17, below.

12. Not to obscure the chronological distance between rabbinic texts and the non-rabbinic texts discussed here.

13. See Weinreb, *Natural Law*, 37–38. See also Corrado Martone, "Qumran and Stoicism: An Analysis of Some Common Traits," in L. Schiffman, E. Tov, and J. C. VanderKam, eds., *The Dead Sea Scrolls: Fifty Years after Their Discovery* (Jerusalem: Israel Exploration Society, 2000).

14. See, for example, Jubilees 10:7–9; 11:4–5.

15. As well as about the calendar; see 1QS 10:1–8, and see Jacob Licht's introduction to this passage, *Mĕgillat hassĕrākhim* (Jerusalem: Bialik, 1965), 204–8. It is worth quoting a passage from 1Enoch that Licht mentions in relation to the worldview that is reflected in this passage: "Observe ye every thing that takes place in the heaven, how they do not change their orbits, [and] the luminaries which are in the heaven, how they all rise and set in order each in its season, and transgress not against their appointed order. . . . But ye—ye have not been steadfast, nor done the commandments of the Lord, but ye have turned away and spoken proud and hard words with your impure mouths against His greatness" (2:1; 5:4; trans. R. H. Charles, *The Book of Enoch* [Oxford, 1912], 8–11). See n. 9, above, about the meaning of the term *tĕʿudā* in Jubilees and Qumran texts.

16. The most famous passage in this regard is 1QS 3:13–4:26. Note that, within Qumran texts such as Serekh Hayachad and the Damascus Document, the main form of punishment is exclusion from the community. See Chapter 5, nn. 32 and 113. This, of course, is a corollary of the deterministic viewpoint reflected in these texts, since misdeeds demonstrate the person to be one of the sons of darkness. Unlike in rabbinic texts, in which—to return to Morris's categories—sin is a violation of law that demands paying the price, here sin is a demonstration of the person's essential unworthiness: the sinner is not "your brother," and hence the sinner must be excised from the community.

17. For a brief discussion of commonalities and differences between Qumran texts and Stoicism, see Martone, "Qumran and Stoicism." See also Magen Broshi, "Predestination in the Bible and the Dead Sea Scrolls," in idem, *Bread, Wine, Walls, and Scrolls* (Sheffield: Sheffield Academic Press, 2001), 238–51. Broshi discusses predestination in central Qumran texts in relation to Josephus's description of the Essenes and in relation to Paul's writings. See also Daniel Schwartz, "Law and Truth: On Qumran-Sadducean and Rabbinic Views of Law," in D. Dimant and U. Rappaport, eds., *The Dead Sea Scrolls: Forty Years of Research* (Leiden: Brill, 1992), 229–40, who sees the issue of determinism versus free will and the question of the possibility of repentance as corollaries of what he portrays as the different approaches of the Qumran sect and the Rabbis in relation to what he terms "realism" and "nominalism."

It is worth noting that both Martone and Broshi discuss the interest in astrology in relation to determinism (Martone discusses this issue in regard to both Qumran and Stoic writings). Should we see the intense interest in the calendar in relation to this issue? Certainly, in rabbinic writings, the determination of the calendar is presented as a, or perhaps *the*, paradigmatic example of human decision making—decision making that shapes reality in relative disregard of the facts of the natural world. (And it should be noted that rabbinic texts describe the monthly setting of the calendar as a *judicial* act. Thus, the setting of the calendar is not just parallel to an idea opposing natural law; it is actually an instance of judicial decision making. I am indebted to David Silber for this point.) The calendar of Jubilees and Qumran, in contrast, is presented as that which is fixed in nature and must not be violated by human beings. Astrology takes this one step further: not only are we bound to follow the calendar that is fixed by the heavenly bodies; we are bound in the same determined course as the heavenly bodies follow. (In Martone's formulation in relation to Stoicism: "fate . . . governs both cosmic order and individual life.")

The Rabbis' rejection of astrology is strongly linked to their assertion of human freedom from the constraints of nature and of the human being's capacity for self-transformation. For a striking example of this connection, see the midrashic interpretation of God's response to Abraham's complaint about his lack of a child: "And he took him outside, and he said: Count the stars. . . ." (Gen. 15:5), in Bereshit Rabba 44:10 and 12 and bNed 32a. The midrash portrays Abraham as bound to a belief in a fate that can be discerned by means of astrology; God demands that he relinquish this belief and understand that he is not bound by the course of nature. (Note that, in Bereshit Rabba 44:10, the rejection of astrological fate is tied to the idea of human transformation; God says: "It is indeed as you say: Abram and Sarai cannot give birth—Abraham and Sarah will give birth." See n. 26, below.) It is interesting that Martone hypothesizes a Babylonian origin for the determinism and interest in astrology of both Qumran texts and Stoicism. Certainly, it is the Babylonian conception of fate from which the Rabbis are seeing God as freeing Abraham in this story, which goes on to have God identify himself as having taken Abraham out of Ur Kasdim (Gen. 15:7).

18. Aquinas, for example, offered an understanding of natural law that affirms human freedom (see Weinreb, *Natural Law*, 56–59), and various versions of compatibilism assert that determinism and free will are not incompatible.

19. Note that Deut. 14:1–2 emphasizes Israelite distinctiveness in relation to practices that mark them as different from the surrounding culture.

20. See parallels in Bereshit Rabba 11 (a *philosof* questions R. Hoshaia), Bereshit Rabba 46 (Abraham questions God; see below, n. 22), Pesiqta Rabbati 23 (a *philosof* questions Rabbi), and Tanchuma *Tazria* 5.

21. Marc Hirshman analyzes Bereshit Rabba 11, in which conversations about both circumcision and Shabbat appear, and discusses this passage and parallels, in comparison to Justin's *Dialogue with Trypho*, in relation to the connection between nature and the commandments. See Hirshman, *A Rivalry of Genius: Jewish and Christian Biblical Interpretation in Late Antiquity* (Albany: State University of New York Press, 1996), 31–54.

22. A third conversation between R. Akiva and Turnusrufus about law is worth mentioning, though the parallels are too complex to allow for discussion here. (See Hirshman's analysis of one of the parallels, cited in the preceding note.)

> And this question too the evil Turnusrufus asked Rabbi Akiva—he said to him: "How is this day [i.e., Shabbat] different from other days?"
> He said to him: "And how is this man different from other men?"
> He said to him: "Because my master so desires."
> "Shabbat also, because my master so desires."
>
> (bSan 65b)

Shabbat is perhaps the one *mitzva* that has ready to hand a Jubilees-like explanation: we rest from work on Shabbat because God ceased God's creative labor on Shabbat. Shabbat, like law in general for Jubilees, is embedded in the way the world was created. And yet this is not the answer that R. Akiva gives to Turnusrufus. To the question "How is this day different?" he simply invokes God's will. Law is based in God's will as expressed in command, not in the way the world came to be or in the natural order.

23. See Bereshit Rabba 11 and 46 and Pesiqta Rabbati 23. Some commentators see this as the same as the question "Why are men not born circumcised?," but I think that it is raising a different, though related, issue. The question "Why was circumcision not commanded to Adam?" is based on two assumptions about law: that it is universal and that it cannot come into being at a given point in time. Both these assumptions derive from a view of law as embedded in nature, the same view that generates the question in our text: "Since he desires circumcision, why does the person not come out of his mother's womb circumcised?"

In Bereshit Rabba 46, it is Abraham who asks this question of God. Is the midrash portraying Abraham as reflecting a pagan perspective (see n. 17, above), or is it that this question makes sense, even from a rabbinic perspective, in the special case of Abraham? After all, since the requirement of circumcision precedes Sinai, it cannot have its source in sinaitic command; why, then, should it not have been required from the beginning?

24. See Arthur Marmorstein, *Studies in Jewish Theology* (London: Oxford University Press, 1950), 213; and Marcel Simon, *Verus Israel* (New York: Oxford University Press, 1986), 165. Note that the same question appears in Christian sources in relation to Shabbat: see Marmorstein, *Studies,* 212; and Simon, *Verus Israel,* 323. Simon points out that Chrysostom argues not only that, if Shabbat observance were required, it would have been prescribed from the beginning of human history but that it would have been prescribed also for all of creation, both animate and inanimate.

See also the arguments against law in Christian sources based on the fact that laws contradict each other; for example, the requirement of circumcision supersedes Shabbat (Hirshman, *Rivalry of Genius,* 40; Simon, *Verus Israel,* 166 and 463 n. 79). The conflict of rules, though, only constitutes a contradiction from a natural law perspective; from such a perspective, if Shabbat demands desisting from labor, then that demand remains in place no matter what else one might need to do on that day. From a positive law perspective, though, law can include second-order rules about cases in which rules conflict (see the discussion of conflicts between laws in Joseph Raz, "Legal Principles and the Limits of Law," *Yale Law Journal* 81 (1972), 829–34); thus, from the rabbinic perspective, if circumcision is mandatory on Shabbat, then doing that act does not constitute a violation of Shabbat.

25. There is an irony to this argument, because the very point of the human being being a part of the natural world, which, as we have seen, correlates with a limited view of human freedom, is here being used to emphasize human freedom and the potential for self-transformation through action, since all of nature (including the human being) requires transformation and can be transformed. The next step of the argument, though, focuses on the distinctiveness of human beings as transforming and self-transforming actors.

26. The example of circumcision, then, is paradigmatic of law's transformative and self-transformative quality. Note the complete verse that is cited in this passage as the source for the refining quality of *mitzvot*: "God—his way is perfect;

the saying of God is refined; it is a shield for all who trust in him" (Ps. 18:30). The midrashic connection to the commandment of circumcision is probably based on links between the first and last parts of this verse and the two passages of the Abraham narrative in which God promises Abraham a child. "God—his way is perfect" recalls "walk before me and be perfect" (Gen. 17:1), the verse that introduces the covenant of circumcision, Abram's and Sarai's transformation to Abraham and Sarah, and the announcement of the birth of Isaac. "It is a shield for all who trust in him" recalls "I am your shield" (Gen. 15:1) and "And he believed in [i.e., trusted—see Chapter 5, n. 1] God" (Gen. 15:6), the verses that envelop God's promise of a child to Abraham. For the midrashic connection between this promise, the transformation of Abraham, and freedom from the determined course of nature, see n. 17, above.

Bibliography

Albeck, Chanokh. *Sēder nĕziqin.* Jerusalem: Dvir, 1953.

Anderson, Gary A. "The Status of the Torah Before Sinai." *Dead Sea Discoveries* 1 (1994), 1–30.

———. "The Status of the Torah in the Pre-Sinaitic Period: St. Paul's Epistle to the Romans." In *Biblical Perspectives: Early Use and Interpretation of the Bible in Light of the Dead Sea Scrolls,* ed. M. Stone and E. Chazon. Leiden: Brill, 1998.

Aptowitzer, Victor. "Observations of the Criminal Law of the Jews." *Jewish Quarterly Review,* n.s., 15 (1924–25), 55–118.

Basser, Herbert W. *Studies in Exegesis: Christian Critiques of Jewish Law and Rabbinic Responses 70–300 C.E.* Leiden: Brill, 2000.

Baumgarten, Joseph. "Does TLH in the Temple Scroll Refer to Crucifixion?" *Journal of Biblical Literature* 91 (1972), 472–81.

Bin-Nun, Yoel. "*ʾĔmunāʾel mul hăfākhehā.*" In *ʿAl hāʾĕmunā,* ed. M. Halbertal, D. Kurzweil, and A. Sagi. Jerusalem: Keter, 2005, 190–242.

Bleich, J. David. "Capital Punishment in the Noachide Code." In *Contemporary Halakhic Problems.* New York: Ktav, 1982, 2:341–67.

———. "Judaism and Natural Law." *Jewish Law Annual* 7 (1988), 6–42.

Blidstein, Gerald. "Capital Punishment—The Classic Jewish Discussion." *Judaism* 14 (1965), 159–71.

———. "On Political Structures—Four Medieval Comments." *Jewish Journal of Sociology* 22 (1980), 47–58.

Boyarin, Daniel. "On the Status of the Tannaitic Midrashim." *Journal of the American Oriental Society* 112 (1992), 455–65.

———. *A Radical Jew: Paul and the Politics of Identity.* Berkeley: University of California Press, 1994.

Brooks, Peter. *Troubling Confessions: Speaking Guilt in Law and Literature.* Chicago: University of Chicago Press, 2000.

Broshi, Magen. "Predestination in the Bible and the Dead Sea Scrolls." In *Bread, Wine, Walls, and Scrolls.* Sheffield: Sheffield Academic Press, 2001, 238–51.

Brüll, Nechemia. "Miscellaneous Notes" (Hebrew). *Bēt talmud* 4 (1885), 7–11.

Byrne, Brendan J. "Interpreting Romans: The New Perspective and Beyond." *Interpretation* 58 (2004), 240–52.

———. *Romans.* Sacra Pagina Series, vol. 6. Collegeville, Minn.: Liturgical Press, 1996.

———. *Sons of God, Seed of Abraham: A Study of the Idea of the Sonship of God of All Christians in Paul against the Jewish Background.* Rome: Biblical Institute Press, 1979.

Charles, R. H. *The Book of Enoch.* Oxford: Clarendon, 1912.

Charlesworth, James H. *The Old Testament Pseudepigrapha.* Vols. 1 and 2. Garden City, N.Y.: Doubleday, 1983 and 1985.

Cohn, Haim H. "The Penology of the Talmud." *Israel Law Review* 5 (1970), 53–74.

Crowe, Michael B. *The Changing Profile of the Natural Law.* The Hague: Martinus Nijhoff, 1977.

Davis, Michael. "Punishment Theory: Making Sense of What We Know About Punishment." *NYSBA Law Studies* 22 (1998), 3–10.

Dienstag, Jacob. "Natural Law in Maimonidean Thought and Scholarship (On *Mishneh Torah, Kings* VIII.11)." *Jewish Law Annual* 6 (1987), 64–77.

Dunn, James D. G. *Jesus, Paul, and the Law: Studies in Mark and Galatians.* Louisville, Ky.: Westminster / John Knox, 1990.

———. *Romans 1–8.* Word Biblical Commentary 38A. Dallas: Word Books, 1988.

———. *Romans 9–16.* Word Biblical Commentary 38B. Nashville, Tenn.: Thomas Nelson, 1988.

Enker, Arnold. "Aspects of Interaction Between the Torah Law, the King's Law, and the Noachide Law in Jewish Criminal Law." *Cardozo Law Review* 12 (1991), 1137–56.

———. "*Yĕsodot bĕmišpāṭ happĕlili hāʿivri.*" *Mišpāṭim* 24 (1994), 177–206.

Epstein, Yaakov Nachum. *Māvoʾ lĕnusaḥ hammišnā.* Vol. 2. Jerusalem: Magnes, 2000.

Eskola, Timo. *Theodicy and Predestination in Pauline Soteriology.* Tübingen: Mohr Siebeck, 1998.

Finkelstein, Louis. *Pharisaism in the Making.* New York: Ktav, 1972.

Fitzgerald, P. J. *Salmond on Jurisprudence,* 12th ed. London: Sweet and Maxwell, 1966.

Foucault, Michel. *Discipline and Punish: The Birth of the Prison.* Trans. Alan Sheridan. New York: Knopf, 1995.

Fox, Marvin. "Maimonides and Aquinas on Natural Law." *Dinē yiśrāʾēl* 3 (1972), v–xxxvi.

Friedman, Shamma. "The Primacy of Tosefta to Mishnah in Synoptic Parallels." In *Introducing Tosefta: Textual, Intratextual, and Intertextual Studies,* ed. Harry Fox and Tirzah Meacham. New York: Ktav, 1999.

Frymer-Kensky, Tikva. "The Atrahasis Epic and Its Significance for Our Understanding of Genesis 1–9." *Biblical Archaeologist* 40 (1977), 147–55.

Fuller, Lon. *The Morality of Law.* New Haven, Conn.: Yale University Press, 1964.

Gartner, Yaakov. "*ʿIbbud bavli šel dĕrāšat rabbi śimlay ʿal taryag miṣwot.*" *Sinay* 96 (1985), 236–49.

Gaventa, B. Roberts. "The Cosmic Power of Sin in Paul's Letter to the Romans: Toward a Widescreen Edition." *Interpretation* 58 (2004), 229–40.

Geertz, Clifford. *The Interpretation of Cultures.* New York: Basic Books, 1973.

Goldberg, Avraham. "*Haddĕrāšot hakkĕfulot bimĕkhiltā dĕmiluʾim.*" *Sinay* 89 (1981), 115–18.

Greenberg, Moshe. "The Biblical Concept of Asylum." *Journal of Biblical Literature* 78 (1959), 125–32.

———. *Ezekiel, 1–20.* The Anchor Bible, vol. 22. Garden City, N.Y.: Doubleday, 1983.

———. "More Reflections on Biblical Criminal Law." In *Studies in Bible,* ed. Sara Japhet Jerusalem: Magnes, 1986 (*Scripta Hierosolymitana* 31), 1–17.

Halbertal, Moshe. *Interpretive Revolutions in the Making* (Hebrew). Jerusalem: Magnes, 1997.

Halperin, David. "Crucifixion, the Nahum Pesher, and the Rabbinic Penalty of Strangulation." *Journal of Jewish Studies* 32 (1981), 32–46.

Hart, H. L. A. *The Concept of Law.* New York: Oxford University Press, 1997.

———. "Positivism and the Separation of Law and Morals." *Harvard Law Review* 71 (1958), 593–629.

———. *Punishment and Responsibility: Essays in the Philosophy of Law.* New York: Oxford University Press, 1968.

Harvey, Warren Zev. "Liberal Democratic Themes in Nissim of Gerona." In *Studies in Medieval Jewish History and Literature,* ed. Isidore Twersky and Jay Harris. Cambridge, Mass.: Harvard University Press, 2000, 3:197–211.

Hayes, Christine. *Between the Babylonian and Palestinian Talmuds: Accounting for Halakhic Difference in Selected Sugyot from Tractate Avodah Zarah.* New York: Oxford University Press, 1997.

Hays, Richard B. *Echoes of Scripture in the Letters of Paul.* New Haven, Conn.: Yale University Press, 1989.

———. *The Faith of Jesus Christ: An Investigation of the Narrative Substructure of Galatians 3:1–4:11.* Chico, Calif.: Scholars Press, 1983.

Heinemann, Joseph. "Early Halakha in the Palestinian Targum." *Journal of Jewish Studies* 24 (1974), 114–22.

Hirshman, Marc. *A Rivalry of Genius: Jewish and Christian Biblical Interpretation in Late Antiquity.* Albany: State University of New York Press, 1996.

Horbury, William. "Extirpation and Excommunication." *Vetus Testamentum* 35 (1985), 13–38.

Ish-Shalom, Meir. "Essay on the Issue of *ʿĒdim Zomĕmim* and the Issue of *Hatrāʾā*" (Hebrew), part 2. *Bēt talmud* 5 (1886), 259–61.

Jackson, Bernard S. *Essays in Jewish and Comparative Legal History.* Leiden: Brill, 1975.

———. "Secular Jurisprudence and the Philosophy of Jewish Law: A Commentary on Some Recent Literature." *Jewish Law Annual* 6 (1987), 3–44.

Katz, Jacob. "*Maḥloqet hassĕmikhā bēn rabbi yaʿăqov bĕrav wĕhāralbaḥ.*" *Ṣiyyon* 16 (1951), 28–45.

Kirschenbaum, Aaron. *The Criminal Confession in Jewish Law* (Hebrew). Jerusalem: Magnes, 2005.

Kohn, Alfie. *Punished by Rewards: The Trouble with Gold Stars, Incentive Plans, A's, Praise, and Other Bribes.* Boston and New York: Houghton Mifflin, 1993.

Kosman, Adiel. "Kissing the Dead—Transformation of a Custom" (Hebrew). *Tarbiṣ* 65 (1996), 483–508.

Kraus, Samuel. "*Pereq biysurē hagguf.*" *Dĕvir* 1 (1923), 88–112.

Laato, Timo. *Paul and Judaism: An Anthropological Approach.* Atlanta: Scholars Press, 1995.

Lauterbach, Jacob Z. *Rabbinic Essays.* Cincinnati: Hebrew Union College Press, 1951.

Leaman, Oliver. "Maimonides and Natural Law." *Jewish Law Annual* 6 (1987), 78–93.

Licht, Jacob. *Mĕgillat hassĕrākhim.* Jerusalem: Bialik, 1965.

Lichtenstein, Aharon. "Does Jewish Tradition Recognize an Ethic Independent of Halakha?" In *Modern Jewish Ethics: Theory and Practice,* ed. Marvin Fox. Columbus: Ohio State University Press, 1975, 62–88.

Lieberman, Saul. *Greek in Jewish Palestine.* New York: Jewish Theological Seminary, 1942.

———. *Hilkhot hayyĕrušalmi lĕrabbēnu Moše ben Maymon z"l.* New York: Jewish Theological Seminary, 1948.

Longenecker, Richard N. *Galatians.* Word Biblical Commentary 41. Nashville, Tenn.: Thomas Nelson, 1990.

Lorberbaum, Yair. "Blood and the Image of God: The Punishment of Beheading in Early Rabbinical Literature" (Hebrew). *Meḥqĕrē mišpāṭ* 15 (2000), 429–56.

———. *Ṣelem ʾĕlohim.* Tel Aviv: Schocken, 2004.

Marmorstein, Arthur. *Studies in Jewish Theology.* London: Oxford University Press, 1950.

Martone, Corrado. "Qumran and Stoicism: An Analysis of Some Common Traits." In *The Dead Sea Scrolls Fifty Years after Their Discovery*, ed. L. Schiffman, E. Tov, and J. C. VanderKam. Jerusalem: Israel Exploration Society, 2000.

Milgrom, Jacob. *The JPS Torah Commentary: Numbers.* Philadelphia: Jewish Publication Society, 1990.

Moore, George Foot. *Judaism in the First Centuries of the Christian Era: The Age of the Tannaim.* Vol. 3. Cambridge, Mass.: Harvard University Press, 1959.

Morris, Herbert. *On Guilt and Innocence: Essays in Legal Philosophy and Moral Psychology.* Berkeley: University of California Press, 1976.

Murphy, Jeffrie G. *Punishment and Rehabilitation.* 3rd ed. Belmont, Calif.: Wadsworth, 1995.

Murphy, Jeffrie G., and Jules L. Coleman. *Philosophy of Law: An Introduction to Jurisprudence.* Boulder, Colo.: Westview, 1990.

Naeh, Shlomo. "Why Did Rabban Gamliel Cry? Some Aspects of the Last Mishna of Makkot and Its Sugya in the Bavli." Presented at a conference in tribute to Professor David Weiss-Halivni, New York, May 30, 2005.

Novak, David. *The Image of the Non-Jew in Judaism.* New York: Edwin Mellen, 1983.

———. "Natural Law, *Halakhah*, and the Covenant." *Jewish Law Annual* 7 (1988), 43–67.

Potolsky, Moshe. "*Hakkĕlal ʾēn lĕmēdin miqqodem mattān torā.*" *Dinē yisrāʾēl* 6 (1975), 195–230.

Prejean, Helen. *Dead Man Walking: An Eyewitness Account of the Death Penalty in the United States.* New York: Vintage, 1994.

Räisänen, Heikki. *Paul and the Law.* Philadelphia: Fortress, 1986.

Rakover, Nachum. "Jewish Law and the Noachide Obligation to Preserve Social Order." *Cardozo Law Review* 12 (1991), 1073–1136.

Rawls, John. *A Theory of Justice.* Cambridge, Mass.: Harvard University Press, 1999.

Raz, Joseph. "Legal Principles and the Limits of Law." *Yale Law Journal* 81 (1972), 823–54.

Reeder, Glenn D. "Trait-Behavior Relations and Dispositional Inference." *Personality and Social Psychology Bulletin* 19 (1993), 586–93.

Rofe, Alexander. "On the Origins of the Cities of Refuge in Biblical Law" (Hebrew). *Bēt miqrāʾ* 31 (1985–86), 110–33.

Rubenstein, Jeffrey. "Nominalism and Realism in Qumranic and Rabbinic Law: A Reassessment." *Dead Sea Discoveries* 6 (1999), 157–83.

Sanders, E. P. *Paul, the Law, and the Jewish People.* Philadelphia: Fortress, 1983.

———. *Paul and Palestinian Judaism.* Philadelphia: Fortress, 1977.

Schoeps, Hans Joachim. *Paul.* Trans. H. Knight. Philadelphia: Westminster, 1961.

Schwartz, Daniel. "Law and Truth: On Qumran-Sadducean and Rabbinic Views of Law." In *The Dead Sea Scrolls: Forty Years of Research*, ed. D. Dimant and U. Rappaport. Leiden: Brill, 1992, 229–40.

Schwarzschild, Steven S. "Do Noachites Have to Believe in Revelation?" *Jewish Quarterly Review* 52 (1961–62), 297–308, continued in vol. 53 (1962–63), 30–65.

Segal, Peretz. "*Ḥiyyuv biydē šāmayim": Ḥiyyuvē mitot bēt din wĕhiyyuvē mitā lĕšāmayim.*" Ph.D. diss., Hebrew University, 1986.

———. "Postbiblical Jewish Criminal Law and Theology." *Jewish Law Annual* 9 (1991), 107–21.

Shemesh, Aharon. "*ʾĒlu hēn hanneherāgin: ʿIyyun bĕfereq mittorat hāʿonĕšim šel ḥazal.*" *Šĕnāton hammišpāṭ hāʿivri* 21 (1998–2000), 267–90.

———. "*Kāmā mitot nimsĕru lĕvēt din wĕlāmā himṣiʾu hazal ʾet mitat ḥeneq.*" *Meḥqĕrē mišpāṭ* 17 (2002), 509–29.

———. *ʿOnĕšim weḥaṭṭāʾim: Min hammiqrāʾ lĕsifrut ḥazal.* Jerusalem: Magnes, 2003.

———. "4Q271.3: A Key to Sectarian Matrimonial Law." *Journal of Jewish Studies* 49 (1998), 244–63.

Silman, Yochanan. "Halakhic Determinations of a Nominalistic and Realistic Nature: Legal and Philosophical Considerations" (Hebrew). *Dinē yisrāʾēl* 12 (1984–85), 251–66.

Simon, Marcel. *Verus Israel.* New York: Oxford University Press, 1986.

Sperber, Daniel. *Minhāgē yisrāʾēl: Mĕqorot wĕtolĕdot.* Vol. 7. Jerusalem: Mossad Harav Kook, 2003.

Steinmetz, Devora. "Vineyard, Farm, and Garden: The Drunkenness of Noah in the Context of Primeval History." *Journal of Biblical Literature* 113 (1994), 193–207.

Stern, Sacha. *Jewish Identity in Early Rabbinic Writings.* Leiden: Brill, 1994.

Stone, Suzanne. "Sinaitic and Noahide Law: Legal Pluralism in Jewish Law." *Cardozo Law Review* 12 (1991), 1157–1214.

Tangney, June Price, and Ronda L. Dearing. *Shame and Guilt.* New York: Guilford, 2004.

Turán, Tamás. "Talmud Bavli, Tractate Makkoth, Chapter Three (*Elu Hen Ha-Loqin*): A Critical Edition and a Critical Commentary." Ph.D. diss., Jewish Theological Seminary, 2004.

Urbach, Ephraim E. "Courts of Twenty-Three and Laws of Judicial Execution" (Hebrew). In *Hahalākhā: Mĕqorotehā wĕhitpatḥutah.* Jerusalem: Yad Latalmud, 1984, 47–53.

Walfish, Avraham. "Creative Redaction and the Power of Desire: A Study of the Redaction of Tractate Qidushin: Mishna, Tosefta, and Babylonian Talmud" (Hebrew). Forthcoming in *Jewish Studies, an Internet Journal* (*JSIJ*).

Weinfeld, Moshe. *Deuteronomy and the Deuteronomic School.* Oxford: Oxford University Press, 1972.

Weinreb, Lloyd L. *Natural Law and Justice.* Cambridge, Mass.: Harvard University Press, 1987.

Westerholm, Stephen. *Israel's Law and the Church's Faith: Paul and His Recent Interpreters.* Grand Rapids, Mich.: Eerdmans, 1988.

Werman, Cana. "The Law of Covering Blood and Eating It in Priestly Halakha and the Halakha of the Sages" (Hebrew). *Tarbiṣ* 63 (1994), 173–83.

———. "The *Torah* and the *Teʿuda* Engraved on the Tablets." *Dead Sea Discoveries* 9 (2002), 75–103.

Yadin, Azzan. *Scripture as Logos: Rabbi Ishmael and the Origins of Midrash.* Philadelphia: University of Pennsylvania Press, 2004.

Yadin, Yigal. *Mĕgillat hammiqdāš.* Vol. 1. Jerusalem: Israel Exploration Society, 1977.

Zohar, Noam. "Ancient Rituals Transmitted by R. Judah: Evidence of a Transformed Understanding of 'Blood Is Life'" (Hebrew). *Tarbiṣ* 58 (1989), 525–30.

Index of Primary Sources

Index of Subjects

Acknowledgments

I am happy to acknowledge the help of the following individuals in various stages of the research, thinking, and writing that generated this book: Ruth Fagen, Dudi Goshen, Arthur Jacobson, Richard Kalmin, Yair Lorberbaum, Shlomo Naeh, David Shatz, Aharon Shemesh, Suzanne Stone, Avraham Walfish, and, most especially, my husband, David Silber, who has listened to and critiqued my ideas and read through each part of the manuscript, in some cases several times.

I am grateful to the Shalom Hartman Institute and to its founder and director, David Hartman, for giving me a place in the Institute for Advanced Study during the sabbatical year in which I began the research for this project. My thanks, too, to the Jewish Theological Seminary and its former provost, Jack Wertheimer, for granting me a semester's leave to work on the finishing stages of the manuscript. I also appreciate the support of Eliezer Diamond and Joel Roth during their tenures as chair of the Department of Talmud and Rabbinics at the Seminary.

I would like to express my gratitude to the Lucius N. Littauer Foundation for a grant to help bring this book to publication. I appreciate the help of Adam Parker in preparing the transliteration and indexes.

I have benefited from the comments of the anonymous reviewers as well as from the suggestions of Daniel Boyarin, editor of the Divinations series of the University of Pennsylvania Press. It has been a pleasure to work with Jerry Singerman, Humanities Editor of the Press, and with Erica Ginsburg, Associate Managing Editor. My thanks to Janice Meyerson for her care in copyediting the manuscript.

Chapters 1 through 4 are an expanded presentation of ideas that were developed in a pair of articles that appeared in the *Journal of Jewish Studies*: "Crimes and Punishment, Part I: *Mitot Beit Din* as a Reflection of Rabbinic Jurisprudence," *JJS* 55 (spring 2004), 81–101; and "Crimes and Punishment, Part II: Noachide Law, Brother-Sister Intercourse, and the Case of Murder," *JJS* 55 (fall 2004), 278–305. Chapter 5 is a revised version of an article that appeared in *Hebrew Union College Annual*: "Justification by Deed: The Conclusion of Sanhedrin-Makkot and Paul's Rejection of Law," *HUCA* 76 (2005), 133–87. My thanks to the editors of these two publications for permission to use this material here.

My family has been privileged over the past several years to come to know people who have extended themselves to us in extraordinary acts of *ḥesed.* While these individuals will remain unnamed, I want to acknowledge their kindness by offering a *derasha* on the words of Habakkuk, *wĕṣaddiq beʾĕmunāto yiḥye: ʾAl tiqrē yiḥye ʾellā yĕḥayye.* Your steadfastness has sustained us. We are boundlessly grateful.